THE GREEN SEAGULL

DAVID PARTRIDGE

MINERVA PRESS
MONTREUX LONDON WASHINGTON

THE GREEN SEAGULL
Copyright © David Partridge 1995

All Rights Reserved

ISBN 1 85863 572 1

First Published 1995 by
MINERVA PRESS
1 Cromwell Place
London SW7 2JE

Printed in Great Britain by
B.W.D. Ltd., Northolt, Middlesex.

THE GREEN SEAGULL

For all who find themselves square pegs in round holes
or round pegs in square ones.

Front cover illustration by Edward Partridge
Drawings by Francesca Ross

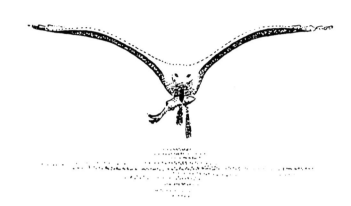

January

February

CONTENTS

gloom of Chernobyl as it brings on a pessimist's
nightmare.

THE GREEN SEAGULL

A lot of what follows is a personal account of one late twentieth century pilgrimage: the story of a struggle to find a path through our truculent times. And yet I trust it's not just one person's story.

To begin at the beginning. One day about fifteen or so years ago I remember staring out of the window and seeing a green seagull. 'Someone's escaped parrot', I naturally assumed. But then I recalled that there had been other eye-witness accounts of similar sightings in the local press, following word-of-mouth rumours. To put the matter beyond all doubt, eventually the press published a colour photo of the same phenomenon on its front page.

Much speculation followed. How did the seagull acquire its greenness? Did it fall into a pot of paint or dye? Was it the victim of some industrial waste? Had the local lads or lasses - or even some very late-developing adults - been up to their tricks again? Or could a heavy dousing in pond algae better explain its colour?

The letter columns, like my own school assemblies, positively bristled with inquisitive interest, before, like everything else newsworthy, she or he of the green hue vanished from the pages of the press and our local skies, never to be seen or heard of again.

For me at least, part of the fascination of that strange little ornithological episode is that there remained at least the philosophical possibility that here was indeed a hitherto unknown variant of the Laridae family. Down over the flatlands where I move, live and have my being, representatives of the gull family are never far from our shores or skies. Could this indeed have been some intrepid immigrant from afar, even rarer than the black swan which occasionally brazens it out amongst the otherwise white community on our millpond?

Well, of course, saner, more worldly-wise explanations of the green one's phenomenal appearance eventually won the day. The more biologically minded children from the middle to back rows of the school assembly had no doubts at all on the subject. What is he blathering on about? Pond algae were responsible for the seagull's colour change, end of story.

But for me the story didn't end there and never will. This is not, I trust, because of any more than occasional hankering after fairies at the bottom of the garden - although to rule out that possibility entirely, like children's make-belief, would make my own world a much duller one. Much rather, I think, it is because of some instinctive drive in me, like day following night, to go on searching. That's the only way to describe it really. I know this is in me. I believe it's in other people. I know it's in children, even the pond algae aware ones.

I'm not an ornithologist. Botany and a love of wild flowers: that was my Pilgrim's Creek, my baptism into wonder, as well as searching. But, long after the wild flowers made their mark on me, the search goes on. I hope it always will do. And I find I identify enormously with other searchers: whether it's the explorer studying butterflies in the Amazon jungle or the naturalist looking for the snow leopard in Nepal, or the French philosopher Simone Weil refusing to be baptised into the Church because the Church had failed to answer her questions, or Bertrand Russell, aged ninety-six, sitting in protest about nuclear weapons in Trafalgar Square. These explorers, searchers all, with or without names, have always been my leading lights and mentors.

But I move on from the green one seen in our local skies. Part of her or his fascination for me has always been because of the questions this phenomenon raised and still raises for me. If the pond algae explanation really suffices, then can nature and reason account for everything that is? Are there no areas of mystery left? If all life can be explained, then why, for goodness' sake, religion or superstition? Why do we go on about miracles, long after the pond algae experts, young or old, have proved their point?

Just how young the experts can be these days came home to me a few years back when one of our local youngsters, not otherwise known for exemplary behaviour, passed me near my back garden bonfire. With an almost contemptuous nod he floored me with his ever so knowledgeable observation. 'Burning another hole in the ozone layer are we, Vicar?' Standing near the same area, he or his brother had once commented on the state of my strawberry patch. 'Johnny is accusing me of stealing your strawberries. That's not fair, is it?' 'Of course not, Craig,' I responded. 'Besides,' he said, 'your strawberries aren't quite ready yet, are they?'

Two things I remember most about the green seagull that day: firstly, that she or he looked and felt very alone. Sundry imaginings about her or his excommunication from the species, her or his possible persecution, even cruel death, at the beaks of former colleagues, were certainly fuelled further by the eventual picture in the local press. No seagull ever sat on an old packaging box or whatever it was - and it could have been some primitive altar table, come to think of it - looking more lonesome. You'll never fly alone: except when the rest of the species chooses to ignore or reject you. That was the experience of Joseph, Jeremiah, Jesus, and has been of countless other 'green seagulls' since. And sometimes that lonesomeness comes even from inside a crowd of supporting friendship. In the poignant cry of the psalm writer, 'But it was even thou, mine own familiar friend, who didst betray me.' The other thing which struck me on reflection was that no way could the gull of different hue have been personally, solely and ultimately responsible for its greenness. Its colourful condition came from an outside agency: it was an accident. The green seagull acquired its colour through no choice of its own. Or, rather perhaps, we should say that from all our knowledge of nature, no gull in its senses looks for different coloured plumage. That's not the way of gullery or snakery or beetlery, or whatever. The green one acquired its distinguishing mark by dint of circumstances beyond its control.

The experience of falling into a pot of paint or diving into a quagmire of industrial waste we might describe as rash or stupid, except that our behavioural judgement would tend towards a human rather than ornithological one. Through another set of spectacles - cleanliness being next to godliness, for most of us, naturally - we could comment on the possibility that here was a rather remiss gull who had failed to look after its personal hygiene and clean itself up following a longish session in amongst the green algae. And, if by outside chance, the green one really was the victim of some human prank, young or old, the responsibility factor falls even further away. In fact, the paint hypothesis to explain the green one's condition - whether accidentally or prankishly applied - falls away, too, once the aerodynamics of the case are considered. Birds plastered with paint tend to be fairly earth-bound.

But two other matters need to be addressed here. The first, to do with the question of credibility. How does the sighter of a flying green seagull actually convince anyone that she or he is telling the truth and not either lying or under the influence of alcohol or affected by some hallucinating drug? How do we distinguish truth from falsehood, reality from hoax? The question of credibility presses whether it's the religious questions to do with a reported virginal birth and resurrection appearance; or whether it's testing the guilt or innocence of the suspected murderer and terrorist; or, indeed, the evidence of the prosecuting police. However better and more developed our technological proofs of evidence become, as painful recent experiences remind us, still the ultimate questions of truth or falsehood, reality or hoax, remain.

And, secondly, there is the vexed matter of personal responsibility. All through the pages that follow, something like a subliminal question is never far away: how far were the people and situations described responsible for their condition? Were they to be blamed at all; partially to blame; ultimately to blame, after all extenuating circumstances have been taken into account; solely to blame?

Reading along that spectrum from left (not to be blamed at all) to right (solely to blame), I'm very aware of where the green seagull of my experience would normally stand. Was she or he pushed, or did she or he jump? No question, m'lord. The green seagull was in the grip of extenuating circumstances beyond all gullery's control.

I know that this touches one of the deepest debates of the age. And those of us who would opt for lifting all personal responsibility from the gulls of different hue in our experience have a tough case to argue in the present climate.

But before I try to develop the human aspects of the green seagull story, it's worth quoting the ornithologically aware comments of a friend at that time. I described to him the press picture.

'This seagull was just sitting there on a rubbish dump, looking utterly forlorn and cut off.' It reminded me a bit of that rubbish-dump outside Jerusalem, the famous Green Hill Far Away.

'Utterly forlorn and cut off?' my ornithological friend replied, with all his pond algae wisdom to the fore. 'Well, yes, but a lot depends on whether birds can make colour distinctions. If they can't, your theory about rejection and excommunication from the flock rather falls away. Another thing, remember, rubbish dumps are paradise for the gull population, there's no other place a gull would rather be.'

The possibility that I might have got hold of the wrong end of the stick altogether here stared me in the face. Here was no rejected excommunicate about to be crucified outside the city walls, my friend was suggesting with his assured pond algae-type diagnosis. Here was the Queen of Hearts herself in person, the King of the Dump himself!

The Green Seagull thesis wobbled on its legs as if struck by a fairly blunt instrument. Except that, as I eventually reflected, the rubbish dump in question here clearly looked to be far more like a furniture tip than the Corporation's scrap-heap, which I readily agree would have been gullery paradise. No nice juicy morsels here, just old prams, fridges and car tyres; purgatory rather than paradise, in other words. But the point about whether birds can make colour distinctions I find an interesting one. If all birds are colour-blind, I want to respond, why the differently hued plumage? All the same, it's a pity the question about colour-blindness couldn't be answered in a different way when it comes to the species Homo Sapiens.

Some time after the sighting of this phenomenon I wrote a piece for our local paper about 'Percy' which seemed to ring bells for some readers anyway. And I hasten to add that I wrote this in the pre-gender inclusiveness days of the late seventies. In other words, for Percy now read Penny - or some neutral-sounding character in between.

Looking back over the last few years I can see how much of my inclination and energy has been spent responding to Percy's and Penny's human counterparts, in myself as much as others, and finding there some kind of Easter hope.

In my mind, at the time of writing, was a conviction which has grown apace over the years that most people I seem to bump into start from a position of feeling minus twenty-five; for whatever reason they believe they can't make it or they don't fit. Which, incidentally, puts heavy question-marks round the Church's traditional stress on repentance before the Christian gospel can be received. If you're crawling around in inadequacy or non-confidence already, to be told that you need to crawl still further, through the broken glass of sin and guilt, hardly comes as liberating Easter news.

Hello, my name is Percy and I'm a seagull. You may have read about me in the letters near this column a few weeks ago. One Saturday I even made the front page in full colour - and higher than that you cannot fly.

That's right. I'm the GREEN seagull. I must say it was very interesting reading all the theories about my colour (I'm a regular News reader, as you see). Very amusing, too. The funny thing, you see, is that I really am a green seagull. Pond algae, green dye? Forget it. I'm green all the way through; as green as the Great Seagull above made me.

Mind you, my parents didn't come from these parts originally. They migrated here some years ago from down under, decided to set up nest and home - and then came me. Spitting image of my Dad, they all said. And he was as green as they come, too.

I had quite a happy childhood really - lovely school down there on the shore, plenty of fresh air and sea breezes and lots of understanding from all the kid seagulls around me. A few minor troubles, but nothing to upset too much. 'Greenie' they called me and mostly in fun.

The real trouble started when I left school and flew out into the big wide world. It's very hard for you sensible humans to appreciate the point, but seagulls can be very unpleasant to members of the species they think are different from themselves, like me in my greenness.

'Go back to where you came from!' they squawk at me. 'You're not a gull, you're a gog!' 'Clear off, Greenie! We've met your sort before!' And so on.

Perhaps you sensible humans can help me out. On a lot of things, you see, my brother and sister gulls can be perfectly reasonable. But as soon as the likes of me appears on the scene - wham! they go wild. Even to the point of pecking me to bits and trying to pull my feathers out.

I tell you what, I get the feeling sometimes that they've got to take their frustrations out on someone - and so muggins is the scapegull.

The thing I simply can't get them to appreciate is that there is nowhere else I can go. This is my home. There's no question of flying off to where I came from, because there is no such place. I'm a British gull from the tip of my beak to the end of my tail feathers.

The other thing I can't make much headway on is that I can't help being green. For some reason the Great Seagull above made me that way. He made some gulls white, some a brownie colour - and me (and my Dad and Mum) green.

Don't fly away with the impression, though, that I'm making myself out to be a martyr. I'm not in that league for a start - and martyrs are difficult to live with anyway.

———————

LABORATORIES OF LOVE

There remain at least three other heffalump traps before I try to explore the human implications of the seagull story. One danger is that greenery, in the pond algaed or for whatever reason differently coloured sense as already described, doesn't *necessarily* refer to something ecologically acceptable, part and parcel of today's conventional wisdom. It could do, certainly in terms of the historical evolution of the Green Movement, most of whose early pioneers knew the Penny and Percy experience in earnest, and still do where the full coming of ecologically aware civilisation has yet to dawn.

Another danger is that I appear to be using the green category here to describe oddness rather than today's commendable or fashionable coloration. The green seagull was a freak, full-stop. Here was the exception proving the normal rule for all seagullhood. Its human equivalent might be the woman who lives to the incredibly ripe old age of 120 years or the man who walks out of some jungle existence 7'5" in height. As with alleged Loch Ness Monster or Abominable Snowpeople sightings, these human phenomena have a Guinness Book of Records interest. But neither the long-living woman nor the giantlike man tells us anything useful about human life, if only because we can't identify with their condition. We simply don't see life either from the vantage point, more likely agony and frustration level, of that number of years or through the eyes of that height.

The green seagull story certainly runs the danger of failing to connect with the normal human condition. Just as, heffalump trap number three, there could be the hidden agenda kind of interpretation. Well, of course, as any psychologist would tell us, the greenery at issue here refers to some third sex or unicorned kind of creature and betokens a profound state of inhibited insecurity in the image's user: that kind of interpretation is certainly possible. A longish session in Dr Anthony Clare's psychiatric chair might throw some light on the matter.

Dave Allen had a sketch of a wedding group posing for a photo with the Vicar standing in the back row. Photographer: 'Can you move to the right just a bit, Vicar? It looks as if a tree is growing out of your head.' As the Vicar moves to the right, the tree moves with him.

I'm sure that the greenery at issue here will always have a positive clutter of question-marks around it. Part of my thesis is that it should have. In Sydney Carter's phrase, nothing is 'fixed or final'. But in the last resort I don't want to talk about green seagulls as odd-bods, because all the people and causes I'm trying to describe are for me intensely human, they are the most real 'phenomena' I have known. The category of freakiness, like much talk of miracles, is wide of the mark.

And I suppose a lot of my loyalty to the green seagull stems from the experience of her or his famous cousin, Jonathan Livingstone, who was doing the rounds of the school assemblies and youth weekends as Penny or Percy appeared briefly in our local skies. I've no wish to be rude to this legendary flyer but he did rather sum up the entrepreneurial, highly individualistic, 'achieve or bust' decade whose people and causes I shall be describing most. JL bursting through the record flight barriers, athletic, intelligent, the only downwardly mobile one ever to score rapidly, upwardly mobile respect and position with the rest of the flock: I read him to the children like every other commender of life stories, but now I look back on it with some shame. How could I have been so dense not to see that the exploits of the great Jonathan Livingstone Seagull, like Scott to the Pole, Hilary and Tensing on Mt Everest, or his middle namesake as well (all of whose stories I also have often commended in my time), were far out of reach for us lesser gulls? In the last resort, like the life-style implied in the advertisements for the very best Grouse Whisky in the rundown bus-stops of our poorest housing estates, don't all these beacons of excellence appear tantalisingly, cruelly distant from the members of the flock being addressed?

So if this seagull story comes out as the opposite side of Jonathan Livingstone's coin I don't mind at all; the protest against the hidden assumptions of all the high-achieving world we have been asked to belong to, willy-nilly, still needs to be made. JL's poor relations, that's it and all: let them have their turn in the skies.

The makings of greenery began for me with the minus-twenty-five situations I met during work in Bolton and London.

My mind speeds back to a baptism of fire when as a young Northern curate I found myself trying to stage Ernest Marvin's passion play, 'A Man Dies'. The local youth group provided the entire cast, but from the first chaotic rehearsal right through to the even more chaotic dress rehearsal it remained a very open question whether the play would ever actually be performed. Not least because of a maverick character called Mel whose predictability about anything was hard to gauge. His reputation for violence, daring, police-dodging, fast driving, hard drinking, and many other esteemed graces, was legendary. He also happened to play the piano; very much to his own particular style, though. Time and time again he would arrive late. And since 'A Man Dies' relies rather heavily on its musical accompaniment, Mel's lateness only served to underline his total indispensability to the whole production. But then the whole cast had to wait still further while the piano was stripped piecemeal of every item of woodwork it possessed in order to provide maximum volume, or so we were informed, until, with said piano looking suitably skeletal and bare-boned, and with Sir himself at what remained of the keyboard, we were ready to begin; always allowing extra time for the maestro to strip off several layers of his own clothing, too.

The star of the whole production, though, turned out to be someone other than Big Mel, no doubt much to Big Mel's initial chagrin. Ian, who played Christ, was a rather gangly youth, well over six foot of him, with a curly haystack on top and spongy 'brothel-creepers' down below. From the word go it was obvious to all present that he had to be the Man; quite simply because no-one else could mime in the way he did. When he staggered down through the hall miming the carrying of the cross, the crowd actually shrank back, so struck by his conviction were we all.

But the moment when the Holy really came home - only a very insensitive gull would have missed it altogether - was when this curly-topped, spongy-shoed youth mimed the taking and the breaking of the bread at the Last Supper table. I still find myself thinking of those hands and fingers; an angel must have passed as he got those fingers together in just the way he did, without opening his mouth.

Even Big Mel perhaps was happy to give pride of place, for once. The last time I heard of him he had taken a girl to wife in a caravan near Manchester and produced a happy family life. But, to my constant amazement since, Big Mel actually made the performance night and on time, too. As he stripped off the woodwork as well as his own dirty boots perhaps something of the Holy had struck him.

And I think of Maggie. I found her one day early on in my time as a curate, living at the top end of a cobbled street, with a damp outer wall which peeled all the inside papers, a 'draughty' corner if ever there was one (and I can still hear her saying the word with a shudder). There was always a fire in her grate, morning, noon and night, winter and summer; always her ironing over the rails above. Her sister died and then she had nothing; no relations, no visitors, the barest of larders, few funds for her old age.

No 73 Darwin Street. I'm sure the Great Man himself would have allowed for the possibility of a chance meeting, such as ours was initially, evolving into a lifetime's inspiration. She had nothing and in her quiet struggle to cope with the rest of her earthly life, she gave me all.

St Martin-in-the-Fields, London, provides a sanctuary for many green seagulls. The OAP from round the corner on the third floor of the Peabody Estate who spends her days sitting in the churchyard or hanging round the church's skirts, a few words with the Vicar as her daily support, the Darby and Joan outing or a major service at festival times as her occasional treat; the gentleman of the road who comes into the warm church for a sleep in one of the hen-coops, sometimes with the further intention of a laundry visit in the loo downstairs; the young migrant from a childhood polio disease and subsequent rejected family life in Africa who tramps daily to the church's Social Unit asking for a sweeping job; the Canadian refugee dressed from head to toe in white who is convinced that she is the subject of a massive conspiracy involving virtually the rest of the world; the ageing transvestite whose female self-identity is traumatically mangled by her occasional appearance at Bow Street Magistrates' Court under the gender role preferred by the powers that be: all these seagulls of greenish hue find their way into St Martin's skies.

The legendary story of Dick Sheppard's removal of a smoking visitor during one of the church's early broadcast services, with the gentle rebuke, 'I hope you will understand, Mr. Smith, but we do find it gets rather stuffy in there,' has found an echoing response in the many forms of St Martin's social work since. 'Is this where the wartime people sleep?' visitors to the crypt still occasionally ask.

'That's the church where all the film-stars go.' I remember sitting behind an American as she made this comment on the top of a proverbial bus. One of the great debates during my 'flying' time at St Martin's concerned the relationship between upstairs and downstairs on a Sunday morning: how did the very international congregation in the church upstairs relate with the soup-kitchen congregation in the crypt? By about the third hymn of the Sunday morning service the smell of lentil soup used to creep up the staircases into divine worship as a somewhat less than universally acceptable sweet-smelling offering. How could 'the church of the film stars', not to mention the Admiralty's traditional place of worship and the royal parish church, the church as concert hall and the church as the host for the world's pilgrim visitors, relate and respond to the needs of the gulls dropping out of London's very demanding, winner-takes-all skies?

For me the twilight world between the acceptable and unacceptable faces of our present British society were forever summed up in a short dialogue involving an elderly member of St Martin's congregation. The redoubtable Amelia won through to a wholly creditable measure of self-respect from crippled early childhood. She remembered William Gladstone - 'Mr Gladstone', always said with great stress on his title - preaching at the non-conformist chapel behind St Martin's Lane; and on other occasions she recounted standing and looking through the bars on the church portico steps at all the 'lords and ladies' - again said with great relish - arriving for Sunday morning worship. Standing outside the vestry door one day, this very respectable and wholly admirable old lady found herself on the receiving end of a lorry-load of abusive observations from one of St Martin's many colourfully-tongued gulls. She is said to have replied: 'Dear me, Mr. Jones, I'm sure the Vicar would not like to hear you talking like that!'

Many of my own responses to the greenish-hued gull, in another superficially respectable parochial situation, were schooled by the extraordinary laboratory of love which was especially St M's.

Which brings me to our present patch here, where I've been for close on 25 years, and two situations which left a big impression on me.

I hadn't seen the caller at the door for a long time. The same goes for a lot of his colleagues of the road, as well. Time was when the pilgrims' path round the country's network of hostels ('spikes') brought many weary travellers to the door, sometimes whilst their travelling companions waited for the news of the call's outcome in the neighbouring churchyard. But then they closed a lot of the hostels and the pilgrims' map of Britain changed. Old friends still turn up but not so regularly.

His carrier bag tells almost all. Last time he called we had a fair time together working out what its contents should include; before, issue by issue, the matter of the contents of my wallet was eventually raised.

'You haven't seen me because I've been inside for the last two years for forging cheques.' He talks fast, with his eyes coming to rest throughout on a point in the background of the front porch roughly behind my right shoulder. 'You must appreciate I'm no fool. This is my way of life and I'll be absolutely straight with you. All I need to see me through... If you can possibly... I swear to God I won't bother you again... As sure as I stand here, if you find me here again, then you have my permission to call the police.'

The eyes bothered me. At some point when they were young, very young possibly, someone said through her eyes, possibly his, 'I do not want thee, thou hast no place or rhyme for living on Planet Earth. Out of our lives, a wanderer thou shalt be.'

The immediate issue was, as always, where do we go from here? Even to think of money is fatal in the eyes of many of my colleagues. Aren't you compounding their sickness, aren't you egging them on, aren't you tinkering around with the problem rather than going to its roots, aren't you paying to get rid of them? The journey round to the station to ensure 'he' actually makes the train and isn't deflected from his path by the call of a local hostelry is certainly one option. I know most of the arguments against the money bargaining discussion. ('And with a cheque-forger? You must be out of your mind!') It is just that the alternative is not always obvious, or, admit it, would be too costly in time and effort.

'... Inside for the last two years'; and I guessed there weren't many waiting at the prison gates to welcome him back rapturously to the next chapter of his life and saga.

He called again; late at night this time. The anger in me boiled over and I came down heavily, lest it ever be said I'm a soft touch. He'd heard the lines before, though; his eyes, still over my right shoulder, waited patiently until the end of my speech - before his argument quietly resumed from the point where he left off. 'I can appreciate your anger,' he said at one point. A telling blow, that one. In an ideal world, I readily grant, we just wouldn't be standing there shouting the odds at each other late on a Sunday night. Except that I did the shouting and he stayed clam. But in an ideal world wasn't where we happened to be.

Some words of Shirley Williams in a recently read article came to mind: '... the third thing, which I've inherited from my mother, is a very strong feeling - I don't know what to do with it sometimes - of obligation when people turn to me for help. I feel that I am lucky and I'm quite well off and I have a nice job and my child and lots of friends, and here is some poor miserable character in trouble and I feel I have to do something.'

Echo, echo, as the caller at the door and I arrived eventually at yet another compromise solution.

And the second local memory, involving a very obvious gull of green hue.

It was Whitsunday, Pentecost. I had just returned from an open-air Festival celebration on a nearby hill-top when the doorbell rang. A rather flustered former confirmation candidate of years back stood there with a concerned look on her face. 'I've got a family here. Met them at the station looking very lost and so brought them round to you. I couldn't think of anywhere else to go. Can you do something, please?'

The relief on her face when I said I'd try was obvious. And so off she went, while I refocused my eyes on the 'family' at the gate. There are times and times, and this wasn't exactly the best. It had been a heavy morning, three stretching services, plus the open-air event. Sunday lunch was on the go fairly soon and there was a big Guides' Jamboree in the early afternoon.

Her eyes told me almost all without the need for a single question. She was finished, with no distance or further mileage in her at all. The cry of utter dereliction spread out quietly, without any shouting or anger, from her whole being. Not a step further could she go. And now, as if cemented to the ground already, there she stood surrounded by a sea of cases, carrier bags and children, one in her arms ('He hasn't eaten since Friday'), one inside her ('Due in September'), two round her sides like limpets clutching at the very last bit of available rock.

Once inside, with toys and drinks and baby-food in support, out the story gradually came. They had left Dublin the previous night, with her mother's full knowledge and financial support, in desperate flight from a household which had become intolerably violent. ('We were just madly in love when we married. I never suspected this side of his character.') She had £20 left on her (honestly admitted, I thought). She had tried to contact the step-sister-in-law on whom she had planned to land but over the phone had been firmly rebuffed. ('She would have taken me on my own, it was the children she didn't want to know about.'). She had nowhere else to go.

Some parts of the body politic, in inner-city areas especially, must be more used to this kind of visitation from another planet, but for us it is a comparative rarity. Time was when the re-focusing mechanism in me operated more swiftly; there was a routine procedure to be followed regarding bolts from the blue like this. 'Will you wait in the room next door, please, while I make a phone call or two to arrange for your overnight accommodation?' Charity has become business-like, efficient, matter-of-fact.

But Sunday afternoons in this particular stretch of the body politic are not our most business-like, efficient, matter-of-fact time of life. Offices tend to be closed, phones ring pointlessly into empty, echoing rooms; all the official, statutory and voluntary, sons and daughters of mercy tend to be hard if not impossible to raise. As I was gradually discovering amidst the chaos of bags, cups, toys and nappies: and as she must have been only too painfully aware, as well. Was her cry of dereliction compounded by the sound of her condition being spelled out over the phone ('I have a family here who have just arrived from Dublin...'), for all the world as if they were as disposable as the nappies for which she needed another plastic bag? Or was her cry of dereliction in some small way finding an echo in the sound of my flounderings?

Out of the blue, again, an angel of mercy eventually came on the line. A tragedy involving two members of his family in the Irish Sea some years ago has left him sensitive and open to human agonies; he has worked through the bitterness and resentment with an impressive dedication to all the suffering bits he happens to touch. I've noticed the expression of shared pain on his face many times before. Sometimes he turns up at a special service in church (his is in no way a Sunday religion). He would never spell out these words, but I often think he sits there wondering, 'But how does all that affect me in practice?'

'You have a problem, David?' Seldom have I been more glad to hear such a human voice travelling along the wires. It might have been the 'came over from Ireland last night' part of the story which produced from his depths such an instant response. Without a moment's hesitation he added, 'Well, I'm sure we can fix this. If it's OK with you, let's meet at the Refuge in fifteen minutes' time.'

And there he was, with his smiling welcome, the human voice sensitively incarnate at the appointed place and time, as we staggered to the front doorway with all the bags and cases and push-chairs. Cups of tea were whistled up, the children befriended immediately by the other 'battered' families present. And through all the dereliction and exhaustion of the last forty-eight hours she still managed a smile as she sank back in the settee, assured of her haven and refuge.

Other angels of mercy helped in the next few days. When I called later Kevin, the eldest boy of nine, had even been to school, such was the speed and efficiency of the statutory and voluntary network on Monday morning; Kevin, who looked so distrustful of men ('His father had no time for him at all'), with no appetite for anything. It may well take a lifetime...

Much shooting of bolts and undoing of locks as I called. And they didn't recognise me! Could I have been part of their common background of dreaded violence? I suddenly realised I was in my gardening clothes, dressed in unrecognisable garb.

But at the end of the day *you* came out of a thick Irish mist on this Pentecost Sunday and saved the day... Is this where the Church is for a lot of the time today: holding the hard-graft charity fort when all the other offices are closed? 'Streets of London' last thing at night on the radio that day sounded, for once, distinctly sloppy.

The point I'm endeavouring to come on to is that others have brought home to me the nature of green seagull-hood. I haven't gone out with my binoculars looking for the category. More often than not it has landed on my doorstep. Sometimes the experience has felt like a solo or a duet, at other times like a massive chorus. In the years when I used to go to the Notting Hill Carnival with members of the family and their friends, it always struck me how here of all places was ample witness to the enormous number of unemployed, quietly protesting gulls of great dignity - for all the press and media reports about their behaviour to the contrary - who find themselves on the margins of the still massive Anglo-Saxon assumptions of our present society. In the flatlands these 'Carib' gulls are only occasionally sighted. The inner-city world wherever attracts far more vivid examples of gulls with green plumage than the rural outbacks and suburban striplands. But they, too, know the green seagull, even behind the lace curtains where gin may come in with the weekly grocery order or a bed of cancer leaves an empty space.

I used to think that people looked on the priest as a society parasite, with hostility and aggression. I remember passing a building-site once during the impressionable curacy years in Bolton, and hearing the spit collect in a man's throat and land on the pavement behind, with guffaws of laughter from his mates to follow. Transport cafés used to be threatening, much more than pubs for some reason. Discos are hardest and most threatening of all, perhaps. All those lads and lasses I've known from tots, and here they are in party costumes - dancing and prancing about, whilst I sit huddled with one or two familiar faces amongst the senior citizens. I find it hard to let my hair completely down in a dance or disco situation. Memories of one such occasion a few years ago, but it was miles and miles away from home, with a crowd of *au pair* gulls as our company. That felt different, somehow.

Along with many others, no doubt, I feel like a rubbish collector, a dustbin for unwanted emotional and psychological refuse, most of it from the deeply buried past of other people's childhood days which so often echoes my own. Occasionally I feel like a lightning conductor, finding myself playing a protective role against huge destructive forces. I don't like to think of myself as a laughing-stock. But if I am then it doesn't greatly bother because, in terms of today's circumstances, who is to have the last laugh?

The green seagull stands on the foreshore amongst the drift-wood, flotsam and jetsam, pottering around, floundering about, amongst the agonies - occasionally the ecstasies - of her or his contemporaries.

What my longish apprenticeship in meeting so many gulls of different hue seemed to do was to reach parts of my personhood I didn't know existed. In one way or other they helped me to flesh out an understanding of Christ's gospel; their stories became my parables in a continuing laboratory of love.

Before leaving this theme I need to refer to some experiences which served to shape my own green seagullhood. On several occasions I found myself well and truly caught out at St Martin's. Once I foolishly signed a document from a Scottish jewellers. 'I brought this ring for my fiancée,' said a young Scotsman who came out of the blue to the door. 'Would you kindly act as my guarantor until I pay the full amount in two weeks time?'

'Sure, sure.' Four weeks later I found myself faced by a bill for £75 from the said Scottish jewellers. The green curacy days, indeed. On another occasion I married a 'Charles' and 'Betty' in their Westminster flat because 'Charles' was too sick to come to the altar. A few days later the powers that be rang up to point out in no uncertain terms that the marriage was invalid. Since 'Charles' was a person of some substance he had made out a will for the benefit of Betty, his new wife. I found myself praying pretty hard in the week or so before the legal occasion which had to be rearranged somewhat hastily at the altar. Fortunately, 'Charles' recovered from his sickness to get to the church on time and didn't have to be carried there on a stretcher.

So the greening process continued: helped considerably by the likes of Old Moore, nicknamed Moses because of his enormous 'WG' beard, who used to walk up and down Oxford Street under an advertising sandwich-board. Moses's working day would often begin with an appearance - more like an apparition - at the early Communion service in St Martin's. About a quarter-way through the service at the side altar the celebrant would suddenly become aware of this Mosaic figure heaving himself down the main aisle, to spread himself over one of the side pews after a rousing 'G'morning' to all and sundry. From this semi-prone vantage-point he proceeded to scratch the upper half of his personage under the invariable mackintosh which did duty for a shirt as well. Come Communion time he would rouse himself sufficiently to make the altar rail, where very frequently he knelt next door to an impeccably dressed department manager from Moss Bros round the corner in Covent Garden. Moses and Moss Bros together at the altar rail: John Betjeman country, for sure, and for me a key influence for the future.

Having learnt my lesson over 'Charles's' ailing marital status, I found myself more on the alert when the Flower People who lived in the big public building next door, the former St Martin's School, requested through their leader, the legendary Sid Rawls, for a wedding in Hyde Park. Sid has kept up a remarkable consistency with his way of life. Not for him the abandonment of his Flower Power principles in favour of a City job, marriage and a semi-detached existence in Putney. From various articles I see periodically about him, almost thirty years on, I understand that he is still living in his tepee in mid-Wales, very much a Mosaic figure, surrounded by his commune and fairly extended family. But a marriage in the middle of Hyde Park, sacred ground for the green gull community as it is, was clearly not on, sadly.

There seems to be a direct line of descent between Moses, Sid, the Flower Power people and the travelling community in our own patch at the present tine; with 'John' and 'Sarah' and baby 'Bud' arriving from Leicestershire just in time for Christmas last year, for good measure. For us very settled gulls here the experience of these nomads in our midst has a strangely prophetic feel to it. My identification of 'John', 'Sarah' and 'Bud' with Joseph, Mary and baby Jesus, wasn't universally appreciated, I fear.

But now to two very personal experiences. It's hard not to describe either of these without giving the impression that the problem involved had no relationship to anything I've ever remotely known; that the two people I describe were 'sick' and I was and remain 'healthy' and 'normal'; that other people have problems relating to me, I have none relating to them. Some leading gulls in church and state regularly give vent to the view that our generation has become obsessed with sex; as frequently in their observations forgetting that there is much to be thankful for in today's openness and freedom. Many gulls of greenish hue have known the struggles and pains of sexual inhibitions and dilemmas. I found these in a single-sex school where homosexuality was rife even if talk and innuendo outran outright practice by far. The scars still remain. But for any gull who has ever felt the overwhelming sense of being the only member of the flock ever to face this or that fantasy or experience, today's greater honesty and sharing out loud can only come as balm and comfort. No green gull is as odd as she or he feels; and certainly not in sexual matters, praise be. But all the sex manuals and liberated literature in the world still don't alter the undoubted fact that many if not most members of the flock feel either inhibited or inadequate or unfulfilled sexually for much if not all of the time. 'I shall be a fugitive and wanderer on the earth,' cried Cain in the Bible. The green gull knows the privations, pains and pleasures of sex probably more than most, as a fugitive and wanderer on the earth.

The two experiences I briefly relate have a dreamlike quality to them. They were not life-determining in the same way as my mother's death when I was eight years old and my father's remarriage when I was thirteen years old. But these two mini-experiences affected my attitudes, as I've thought and dreamed many times since.

The first goes way back before St Martin's days to a walk with a male friend near Shrewsbury. I don't recall how we met, but, as we walked, it became very clear that he wished for a physical relationship between us. At no time did he use threats of violence against my refusals. Our walk ended, like our brief friendship. Homosexual leanings had been part of a schooldays' experience, but I knew that that chapter had now closed. Although, as I say, that snap from the past has a dreamlike quality about it now, years later, I have always since found in myself an empathy for males and females of homosexual persuasion.

The second mini-experience involved a meeting with a woman who came to St Martin's office near after-hours time when other members of the staff were not readily available. The interview room had three doors, I've always remembered that very clearly. As we talked, 'Joy' quickly and honestly confessed that she could only speak to any man by holding on to his testicles at the same time, whether the man in question were publican, priest or prime minister. Most of our unusual conversation is now lost in the mist. What was never lost was the discussion at the Staff meeting when I happened to mention the dilemma I found myself in the previous evening.

Staff breakfasts at St Martin's, round a lively table hosted by Daphne and Austen Williams, were always special. Sometimes the conversation could be very heady, helped by clerical luminaries amongst the part-timers with many contacts in their wider fields beyond. On one occasion we debated long on who would be the next Archbishop of Canterbury but two, aided by a member of the Abbey staff up the road who had an engaging habit of referring to James Gibbs's masterpiece, 'betwixt heaven and Charing Cross', as 'the tin tabernacle'. There was always politics but invariably with a goodly spicing of pastoral concerns as well. As the Curate on the ground, I guess I tended to be the member who raised the coal-face issues.

Nowhere more than in the business of personal morality are the churches liable to adopt idealistically respectable postures - like 'no sex outside of marriage' - which turn out to be light years away from where people happen to be living and having their beings.

'Would Jesus have allowed anyone to hold on to his testicles?' I bowled out to a bemused St Martin's staff the day after my meeting with Joy. It was one of the most engaged staff meetings I can remember, perhaps not very surprisingly. Almost from that moment on I knew that Jesus had his sexual struggles, too. Anyone who allows someone else to dollop expensive ointment over the topmost part of their being whilst at the same time having the bottommost part of the same dried with a highly provocative crop of hair just has to be in the business of human sexuality.

And so, via these and other laboratories of love, the greening had begun in earnest.

There's a story in the depths of the Old Testament part of the bible - almost just in amongst the small print - which I've always liked. It speaks to me of all who have found themselves at odds or out of sorts with their circumstances, proverbial pegs for wrong-shaped holes.

King David was a rotter, and very unappealing in the way he related to other members of the flock, not least the female members of the species. His one great virtue was that he knew a green seagull when he spotted one, and not just when she or he happened to be taking their bath in broad daylight on the top of next door's roof.

No more than the barest of brush-strokes indicates the relationship between David and Jonathan. The reader or hearer is left to guess and imagine. Close emotional encounters in the biblical record are seldom spelt out for the benefit of the prurient or inquisitive. The prophet Ezekiel, in similar fashion, is economic to a fault over a personal trauma when the Muse was upon him. In full prophetic flow to the people he records: 'Also the word of the Lord came to me: "Son of Man, behold, I am about to take the delight of your eyes away from you at a stroke; yet you shall not mourn or weep nor shall your tears run down".' And then with upper lip suitably stiffened he adds, almost as a throwaway: 'So I spoke to the people in the morning, and at evening my wife died. And on the next morning I did as I was commanded. And the people said to me, "Will you not tell us what these things mean for us, that you are acting thus?"' The prophetic gull at full stretch, with the intensely private dimensions of human existence mingling with a costly public role. No wonder Jesus later picked up the phrase 'Son of Man' to describe his own strange interface between the human and the representative: Immanuel, God-with-us, God-for-us.

Occasionally, though, the public veil is drawn aside and we see the human revealed: in the case of David's relationship with Bathsheba, with all its earthiness, but also with touching tenderness as in the story of Mephibosheth, son of Jonathan, grandson of Saul.

If ever there was a black sheep of the family it was Mephibosheth. Even his name suggested a half-baked, throwaway, runt of the litter status, the member of the flock for whom all the relations apologise; and yet, as frequently the case in family life, the one person who had the power to draw the otherwise warring relations together, if only because of his sheer uncompetitiveness. Mephibosheth? Why, everyone knows he's a loser! Didn't he spend most of his youth in the royal household with a 'D' for dunce on his head? Take him seriously? You must be joking. Which, of course, like the court jesters of old, was precisely why Mephibosheth could have such potential effect an close family affairs. Always the butt of everyone's jokes, and yet always the wild card with a wisdom on him no one could safely predict.

Whether or not it was because of David's own humble apprenticeship living out there amongst the sheep droppings - the member of the family treated as an afterthought - he certainly had a soft spot for Jonathan's funny lad. So often Mephibosheth had found himself used as a scapegoat by the family flock, it's understandable how he still came cringing into the royal presence during a time of massive tension, expecting to be given the 'D' treatment if not far worse. 'What is your servant,' he bleated, 'that you should look upon a dead dog such as I?'

Whatever the demerits of such a devastating inferiority complex display, the story ends with a glorious trumpet climax by way of balm for all dead dogs and green gulls on their bleakest days, as David the rotter looked into his soul-mirror and then threw down his own wild card by way of response to the cringing one before him: '"Mephibosheth shall always eat at my table"... So Mephibosheth dwelt in Jerusalem; for he ate always at the king's table. Now he was lame in both his feet.'

WASTELANDS OF THE SPIRIT

Our part of the country is flat. Travel inland a few miles and you come to the South Downs, the source of so much of our water supply over the centuries. The hillsides up there seem positively to spurt with spring water.

And it was up on the edge of these Downs years ago that I came on a wondrous find: some fossilised sea-urchins. Had some clever prankster scattered these about on top of the ploughed ground to confuse the likes of me? Scarcely so. Once the penny had dropped, my enthusiasm in subsequent school assemblies and family services knew no bounds. Down here, once upon a time, we were under perhaps hundreds of feet of water, on the bottom of the ocean's bed.

On top of those same Downs, too, the up-country pilgrim comes upon mysterious mounds surrounded by deep trenches, all of them high up with commanding views, and all of them still remarkably similar to the days when they were constructed; piles of stone and earth making their bold statements about the nature of human life to all the winds, almost defiant in their assurance to the spirits of those buried under them that for their last resting-place only the best view would do. Or maybe the view then was far more lowly, near the beachhead with the ocean only a few feet away rather than as a distant vista.

Echoes of that experience come to us now as we slowly appreciate that our particular stretch of coastline is one of the most vulnerable to sea changes in the country if not the world: worst case geologists in these parts assure us that over the next hundred years the level of the sea may well rise up to six feet.

I say, our part of the country is flat; once the ocean bed, once a port and a smuggler's haven, and now a 'computer-commuter' town through which most people seem to pass.

How can anyone tell of the spirit of those of us who stay and have our being here?

I've always tried to remember, for a start, that most people don't practise religion in public. The churches in this part of the world do relatively well in terms of attendance. Compared to Russia, say, or

America, the congregational numbers are nothing to write home about. But our churches 'do' relatively well all the same.

There are all sorts of dangerous assumptions in this doing-relatively-wellness: like thinking that the churches contain the sum total of godly belief about the nature of human life; or that anyone who chooses other paths for pilgrimage cannot possibly belong to the true faith; or, the easiest assumption of all, that our communication and presentation of spiritual matters is so limpidly clear, only the near brain-dead and emotionally unbalanced could possibly fail to connect with us. 'We've got the goods: if you don't want them or can't receive them, well, it's not our fault at all, that's your problem!'

I remember a sudden visit of my brother-in-law. He arrived looking and feeling decidedly groggy, having spent the night crossing the ocean ('Never been sicker in my life'). For the most part, he had been absolutely horizontal in a fo'c's'le cubbyhole.

I thought he would drop off completely once he sprawled himself out behind a lager beer. We talked about this and that, but, not for the first time, he caught me beautifully at one point.

I found myself talking somewhat slightingly about the maniac cyclists who tear down our main roads early Sunday mornings while there's reasonable quiet around, during their various club races and rallies. 'It makes you wonder, doesn't it?' I surmised. 'All hunched up like that, with your head fastened down on the tarmac, tearing your guts out - what's the point of it all?' He stayed his hand; the question didn't require an answer. Was he dropping off? More yawns. I tried again, this time leaning forward in more animated fashion. 'Sometimes I feel like stopping one of those middle-aged, greying-at-the-temples, characters roaring past and saying, "Are you sure you're seeing the fullness of life from that extraordinary position?"'

Whether at this point something fairly vital to his view of the universe surfaced in my brother-in-law's mind through the post-sea haze, I don't know; or whether it was because he has always been an Enthusiast himself and saw his species threatened by this apparent slighting of a perfectly harmless, rational Sunday morning occupation, I don't know. But up it came to take the game and rubber in a single trick.

'Yes, but don't you think religion can be like that, too?'

Except that religion at best always seems to be found in other places than the ones intended or expected. Consider, for instance, a visit to a Picasso exhibition which turns out to be a religious experience. Masses of fellow-pilgrims may be expected, but at this hour of the day there's only a fairly constant trickle. The temple dues paid, we make our may up a tunnelled ramp ('It feels as if we're being programmed,' you say), round a tunnelled corner and then, at the top of another ramp, he stands facing us: the Master himself, for all the world as if set in stained glass.

Inside the temple everyone speaks in whispers, lest the other worshippers have their concentration disturbed, while members of the temple staff stand guard at each corner like vergers lest any of the sacred relics be touched or molested. Overheard comments, even these assume a semi-religious form: 'It makes you think of a Book of Hours...', 'Completely amazing...', 'I'm lost for words.' Foreign words of worship, English words, old ones, young ones.

What are we worshipping? As many have remarked about our age, we go about the products of our artistic geniuses with all the relish and dedication that the medievals went about their pilgrimages to see saints' bones and finger-nails. I found myself for the greater part lost, wandering almost aimlessly in a world I could barely understand. The products of a cornucopic mind poured out before our wondering and blinkingly uncomprehending eyes. Recognisable themes were stated over and over again: beach scenes, breasts, brokenness (a very revealing Crucifixion series, showing figures composed from bits of bones pinned in a broken-down fashion to a helpless, hopeless situation); lots about loneliness and togetherness (the condition of aloneness for the owl and the goat as well, and the frantic, passionate attempt to escape from that condition). The words of the Preacher in Ecclesiastes, read recently, come hauntingly to mind: 'Two are better than one, because they have a good reward for their toil. For if they fall, one will lift up his fellow; but woe to him who is alone, when he falls and has not another to lift him up. Again, if two lie together, they are warm; but how can one be warm alone?' The artists and the religious look into the black holes of aloneness in ways the rest of us find too disturbing. As the Preacher implies, they are frantic and passionate - or horrendously disciplined - to find the warmth of their bearings again.

But what I find myself 'worshipping', with all the kindling of heart's cockles available to me, is the sources of creation. However little I understand of the cornucopia poured out before my eyes, this mind touches my own dreams and visions in the night.

Which is why I guess the coffee and bath bun served with delightful informality on the temple roof-top towards the end of the exhibition feel warmly like Holy Communion.

The Green Seagull hovers about on the margins of religion, frequently feeling lost, frequently stubbing the proverbial toe; above all perhaps, only too painfully aware of human limitations as she or he searches for creative truth amongst even the most apparently religionless or lost and loveless parts of our body politic.

Late-night pilgrims pass outside, by the sounds of it from one of the local hostelries, their colourful language leaving little to the imagination as it comes to me while I'm stooping over the milk bottles by the porch. Then, suddenly one of them spots me. A former church or state school lad? I can't see in the darkness. 'Shh...' he says, and the colourful language fades out. 'Good evening, Vicar.'

A strange place the Vicar occupies on the touchlines of society. Scotland may have beaten England at soccer, cups of consolation may have been drunk to the dregs in plenty, and yet, still, there are times when the language has to be cleaned up and made respectable. Unless the cups have taken over completely, swearing in front of the Vicar has to be apologised for, or 'shooed' out of sight. Residual respect or a harking back to the days of short trousers and memories of former selves may account for this. Times have changed considerably, the apologies now come far less. Spades are called spades. The Vicar's presence makes no ounce of difference.

But the lingering respect, if such it is, bothers me. It may spring from the same kind of source as the reaction to the suggestion of someone raping one's sister. But its wafer thin masquerading of real feelings gives naught for comfort.

'They will respect my son,' said God in one of the gospel parables. Well, they did, until the day came when their respect could stand the strain no longer, as it broke itself over the son's head in a crown of crucifying thorns.

Traditionally, the priest or shaman stands like Moses in the gap between the divine and human worlds; she or he is at the frontier, helping traffic through in both directions. What point any priesthood if it doesn't actively encourage ventures up to the frontier posts where the intimations of further reaches in the human spirit can be acknowledged and allowed expression? Secular or horizontal activism and commitment, like patriotism, is not enough, for some gulls anyway.

And yet here I become the Green Seagull completely, approaching all the intimations of 'green' around me with the trembles; aware of the Church's shabby track record (but not just the Church's); aware of the over-definitions and over-precisions that have been the pride and shame of so much so-called theology, even enlightened theology, hitherto; aware, too, of the shades of green which in no time can turn from freshness to mouldiness, from wide-eyed innocence to lynx-like envy. Not surprisingly, the frontier ministrations of others, for all their inadequacies and bumbledness, are far more easily perceived than one's own. A colleague's professional ministrations or struggling attempts to put her or his vertical experiences, the God intimations, into words, tell me far more of the wider vistas than any amount of personal soul analysis. Echo responds to echo, in another's knockings I hear my own; but it helps so much when she or he knocks first.

Members of my family, three of us, chat over the hallucination scene. 'Honestly! You ought to try it sometime! Every blade of grass suddenly assumes a new significance!' Their enthusiasm for the newfound territory is engaging. Their dizzy heights of spiritual ('cosmic') awareness make my own foothill trudges look very earthbound. All I know for sure is that the Green Seagull, if not so brilliant a traveller as his swifter-winged, exploring cousin, still flies at varying heights, picking up and helping to transmit the spiritual messages on the wind.

But because of all the politeness and relationship hang-ups, the real messages rarely get through.

A large man at the door, bursting with life - last time I saw him was when he was flat on his back, 'about to go down into the dungeons' for an op. 'Just to say thank you. I appreciated your coming to see me. Won't keep you a mo'.

We talk briefly and he tells me about his return of weight - at some length, to the point of my wondering whether it's really what he wants to say. We've talked before, but always there's a soulful look in his eye: as if we still haven't got anywhere near the real area.

The phone rings and... it's over. 'Thank you again.' But, still, as he goes there's the same searching look on him, away from me now down the street - with disappointment in his soul?

Something of this desire for ranging about, hovering spirituality has always driven me: what is not said being normally far more important than what is. At one time I used to write a regular column for the local press; in fact, for the very same paper which carried the GS story in the first place. 'Believers'' responses were always far hotter than 'non-believers''. It was always a hope, probably ill-founded for the most part, that if ever a piece got through the editorial sieve - and some didn't make it beyond the wastepaper basket or cutting floor - it might, even with the benefit or otherwise of the heavy red pen treatment, speak something vaguely meaningful to readers who found themselves, not necessarily in minus-25 spiritual situations, but of no fixed abode, perched as it were at some temporary resting-place of a none too easily locatable kind.

The largely unspoken assumption behind these 'non-assertive' articles was that most of those who read them would realise without much difficulty that God, if 'He' exists, could not possibly be like the picture I was describing. In other words, these little caricatures were intended to get people rolling up their own theological sleeves, substituting what they really believed for the light-hearted 'story' they were reading, whilst amending, or simply rejecting outrightly, the picture in front of them. Too often, I'm sure, we the 'preachers' put out our theological offerings in ready-made packages which require nothing in response other than boring acceptance.

Family life isn't like that. The cut-and-thrust of the daily work pattern isn't like that. Our involvement in a TV play, interview, talk-show isn't like that; so why on earth we should think our God-time should be altogether distinct from the way we tick and keep our adrenalin flowing in every other sphere just passes understanding.

At no other time must 'God' suffer more from our ready-made packages, with all their sickly, squirm-making messages attached, than at Christmas. The following was a little piece in the local paper series I mention, called 'The Happy Birthday':

All day long, all night long, God had been pacing round His big golden throne anxiously waiting for the news. The great plan to visit Planet Earth had swung into operation, following the announcement to a startled multitude of the angelic host.

Gabriel had been despatched with a letter under his wing with a very clear address on the envelope so as to make quite sure he didn't get it wrong (poor old Gabriel, awful job he had in charge of the heavenly postal service. Who would be a postie?).

And now all heaven was on tiptoe waiting. A thousand years in God's eyes normally seemed like a day, but today had certainly felt like a thousand years - and longer.

Suddenly the red scrambler phone beside the golden throne began to scramble. God rushed to pick it up and as soon as He put it to His ear the sound of trumpets and massed choirs of angels and archangels was deafening. So deafening that God thought He was going to faint. His knees began to buckle under Him. He sank back into His throne and let the news sweep over Him.

'Congratulations!' chanted the angelic choir. 'You're a Father! You're the Greatest!'

By the time the Good News had really sunk in and God had put the hot line back on its hook, great beads of sweat were standing out on His forehead. His legs felt like jelly. There had been some unexpected hitches down there on Planet Earth (an accommodation problem included) but the great thing was that He was a Father. A FATHER (the mere thought of it hit Him like a thunderbolt). And the Father of a great big bouncing Boy.

Gradually, a smile crept over God's face, and then a chuckle, and then a huge laugh, until He could contain Himself no longer. He leapt up from His throne and did a little jig while no-one else was looking, so happy was He.

Next morning all Heaven was a-flutter. The postal service went wild, letters and cards and telegrams arrived by the hassock-full (pity the poor posties). A cheeky card from the angel Josephine saying 'Hope Father is doing well'. Another from the angel Fred, equally cheeky, read 'Thought You'd never make it'. As for dear Hazel, she'd organised all the other angels in her office to write their names and wishes on a big Heavenly stork card. And there were dozens, nay myriads, more.

God was so pleased with His birthday mail He spent what seemed like ages and ages standing all the cards up on the mantelpiece behind the big golden throne, and then festooning them all round His sanctuary. The angels who saw Him thus said that He became like a little child all over again, hopping and skipping about and singing to Himself.

But suddenly the red scrambler phone went again. This time it was a prayer from the Boy's Mother on Planet Earth. The line wasn't very clear, but God could tell from Mother's voice that there were problems. Something about an eviction order and terrible violence, forcing the family - His family - to take to the roads. Crackle, crackle - and then the line went dead.

Very slowly God replaced the receiver. And from the depths of His Being something suddenly welled up that had been welling up for the whole of His eternal life. He could hold them back no longer and one by one the tears ran down His cheeks; happiness tears, thought the angels who saw Him. But God knew better about the life His Boy would have to live.

An amusing footnote to the tale. Some time after this offering appeared, for reasons I never quite grasped, I received a letter from the same local paper effectively firing me from the journalist's chair I had felt rather too comfortable in for rather too long. No explanations were given, other than a dark reference to a dawn coup involving 'a change of policy'. It was a shattering blow to the pride; but the blow was considerably eased with the discovery that one of my column colleagues had received the self-same letter. I was in good company, for the colleague in question was none other than the RC Bishop himself.

Rather more serious chapters were not far round the corner. Any seventies' pretensions I ever had of becoming a broadcaster or journalist gradually seeped away into the sand, as the issues of the eighties arrived in earnest; almost at the cost of humour, especially in terms of some of our internal parochial dialogues. So often what began as a mild little ripple on our millpond was quickly whipped into a raging storm by seemingly hurricane-force winds. There were sexuality issues, too.

Letters came once about homosexuality, with a meeting at home following an article. Steams various were generated, blood pressures raised, hidden nerves touched. 'Speaking as a biologist, let me give you the facts about it,' insisted one person present. The pure, undiluted facts? The more he talked about them, the more the defensiveness became apparent, one realised 'the facts' could not be quite so simple even when addressed by a biologist. I've always believed in a remark attributed to a wise old Northern priest. It seems apt here: 'The realisation of complexity is the beginning of wisdom.' 'It's not nearly so much of a problem for our age group,' said a young relation who happened to be present at the homosexuality meeting. Probably not.

But, in a way much more painfully, big divisions surfaced as we struggled over the nature of biblical truth. An apparently harmless discussion over a monthly Pastoral Lunch assumed huge proportions in consequence: a lively and fairly open-ended ecumenical life between our seven local traditions, coalescing for a time into a rather fragile Covenant, found itself eventually breaking apart. 'How these Christians love each other,' an outsider might have ruefully observed. 'Liberals' and 'literals' gathered into opposing camps, where we still glare at each other somewhat suspiciously behind our stockades of different conviction. The only consolation - hugely amplified in all the toing and froing which was to come over the ministry of women - was that what was happening in our community microcosm, both across the traditions and within our own denominations, was happening in large measure all over elsewhere.

In the light of the November, 1992 General Synod vote on the Ordination of Women, something I noted ten years or so ago has a green seagullish feel about it.

A real warmth and glow in me about the place of women debate. With no great prophetic insight, I now detect this is gathering apace. For many if not quite all Western institutions the debate was held many moons ago, the issue was settled once and for all time. Not so for the Church. Historical reasons manifold can be produced to account for this, but the root cause, I'm sure, is to do with male fear and defensiveness. The maleness of the Church is borne in on me daily.

The curious thing is that I don't feel like urging the feminists of my acquaintance to take up their cudgels with a view to storming the barricades. All I want to do with a great part of my being - complacency and lack of urgency charges notwithstanding - is to encourage, woo and generally waft into greater existence as convincing a case as possible for the feminine argument with the Church. We now have highly articulate women members on our staff and in our congregation; their contribution and potential are enormous for us. Male theology, male Church, male leadership, male everything: and now this warm, glowing opportunity on all sides to take the 'anima', the female spirit, into our life-heart as if for the first time; to explore the 'She's blackness' of God, the other side of the theological moon; but above all, for me at least, to let the female part of my own nature come to the fore at long last. In every man is there a woman longing to see the light of day? I can only speak for myself.

Many male green seagulls must know the feminine in them being addressed now as never before. But not all the other gulls in the flock agree with this kind of sentiment, as the sometimes red hot letters column of our parish mag amply illustrate.

Not that the freshness of the Good Friday procession, or Easter Sunrise, or Ascension Day Agape sharing or Pentecost Walk, has ever disappeared. Ecumenically we're much better out of doors than in. And what motley crowds we've sometimes been, with various courageous Green Gulls up front on Good Friday, sometimes costumed – for the first time this year the cross being carried by someone with a black face.

I don't know what the frustrated Bank Holiday drivers think of us year by year as we cross the Red Sea dividing our community, with the local police holding back the waves of traffic; nor what we look like really to the passers-by on the pavements and the watchers through the lace curtains. All I do know is that I frequently find myself walking arm-in-arm with a blind man and what seem like lots of young families with prams; also that half-way round the course we are usually joined by a spastic's family, wheel-chair and all. It has a pilgrim people feel about it. Not that we're really more than a handful compared with the 12,000 of the parish and not much of a showing really as we cross the Red Sea. There is a great spirit abroad, however; although along with others I did just wonder a bit one year when the band struck up with 'Lily the Pink' while we wheeled into the Baptist Church's forecourt prior for the stopover Passiontide hymn. But it was O.K. by the Carpenter of Nazareth.

The thing he really would have understood, without a doubt's shadow, was the largely unremarked event preceding the procession one year, when the big wooden cross - made by local Vietnamese refugees - was taken from its place in the church and crashed down breaking off the horizontal arms. A hurried visit to the Rectory garage followed, unbeknown to me, for a couple of bits of broken beading to act as makeshift splints. All the feel of the gospel there.

For too long Good Friday has been kept locked up inside churches. The argument for not turning this day into an excuse for an Orange Parade is a strong one. The argument for at least attempting to translate what has become encapsulated within the boundaries of a largely esoteric language system, amongst the already converted, into something practical and visible in the public arena is, I believe, a stronger one.

And then comes Easter morning's Sunrise, inspired for me by a woman who came home to our community with leukaemia to die. As she plucked strands of her hair out one day to illustrate her condition, 'Viv' gradually unravelled a visionary experience from the Californian Easters she had known. So, in her faltering steps, we meet in our hundreds down by the shore, all the gulls of whatever hues from all the local flocks, and light a fire and sing our Easter hymns and break bread and eat fish together; before, somewhat ridiculously and dottily, we return to our separate conventicles to celebrate the Eucharist. The God who moved about in a tent for a dwelling must groan.

The Western Church's problem - or one of them - is that it worships with books, unlike the Eastern Orthodox with their murals and icons. And, perhaps in consequence, it can't handle the breakdown of the liturgical train, when it happens as happen it does.

Sometimes, when I'm celebrating Communion I think of that incredibly hard-working, dedicated colleague who fainted at the altar one day. His spirit, like the Queen of Sheba's before Solomon, just emptied away, the words died on his lips, and then... splat. Bridesmaids fainting, brides, even bridegrooms: it's surprising in a way it doesn't happen more often. But for the celebrant to faint?

I've been taken short (awful reminders of a school-days' occasion during a huge concert and having to squeeze out from the middle of row six of the trebles past lots of upturned noses). But, so far anyway, I've never actually collapsed. One memorable occasion at St Martin's, gashing my hand on some broken glass during a Youth Club night and being rushed to the operating table at Charing Cross Hospital, as it then was, round the corner: that was the nearest to an 'emptying away'.

Why the anxiety, then, about fainting - or worse? Everything would adjust in due course, after all. I remember a theatre occasion in London when, because of sudden illness, one of the actors could not return for the final act. The management came out in front of the curtain, in evening dress of course, to make the disappointing announcement. 'On behalf of the theatre staff we therefore deeply regret that we have no other course than to end this evening's play at this point...'

He was trying to say something else but the words were lost in the general hubbub from the audience. What eventually emerged from the auditorium, someone acting as priest or representative on our behalf, was a clear message to the evening dress on the stage: 'You've got to tell us how the play ends.' Lots of furious chin-wagging must have then gone on behind the curtains and in due course up they went again to reveal another cast member (volunteer or pressganged, it didn't matter) who told us the rest of the plot in his own words, apologising profusely the while. 'I'm not used to this sort of thing, you've got to understand.' Of course, we weren't used to this sort of thing either but we understood him completely. We were with him totally. The other actors eventually appeared to take up the rest of the script, making necessary adjustments for their missing colleague, and when the final curtain went down the end of the play was greeted by thunderous applause.

Such it always is or seems to be. So why, indeed, worry about going splat at the altar? Why be concerned when the liturgical train either jumps the tracks altogether or runs into the buffers?

However perfect, the Order of Service can became a forbidding, spiritless recipe for desertland. A year or two ago I took my sister and brother-in-law to Evensong in King's College Chapel, Cambridge, or, rather, they took me. Very quickly we became aware of a young spastic and his support group sitting on the opposite side of the aisle from us. He made various contributions to the worship, but none more memorably than during the choir's renderings of the responses. Something about the pitch of the choir registered with this lad whose own voice rose quite unapologetically with theirs like a lark to the skies. It surprised me that there wasn't more tut-tutting or expression of irritation amongst the choir and congregation. After all, hadn't we come to witness the most perfect Order of Service? Had the occasion been not just a humble week-day one but the Festival of Lessons and Carols broadcast live to the world on Christmas Eve, well, of course things would have been different. No way would the contributions of this out of place green gull have been tolerated.

The worst derailment of my experience came during an Advent Service with a packed church at St Martin's when, after a carefully worked out Order of Service which I was largely responsible for organising, I started out on the brief meditational address from that high, swaying pulpit of unforgettable memory; where in those days one of St M.'s great characters, Vera Storey, amongst others would sit at almost eye level in the gallery alongside. 'Don't tell us about your doubts,' Vera once confided, 'tell us what you believe.' I hadn't made more than about the first paragraph, without any expression of doubts as I recall, when Robin, a youngish member of the congregation in roughly row two who was fairly high on drugs, as I realised from a brief conversation before, stood up to interrupt. Now, I know that I have that kind of appearance and style which invites such contributions from any audience or congregation; but this was going rather over the top for this particular occasion. Later on, Robin wrote about the incident and had my name published in a sixties' Penguin book on the drug culture. But stop him and his argument on this occasion I could not. In all the congregational dismay, I recall one off-duty member of the constabulary who happened to be up in the gallery, a little to the left of Vera Storey's usual perch, leaning over and shouting, 'Throw him out! Throw him out!' Whether this helped to spur on the lay ministry of the church to greater efforts I don't know, but Robin was eventually frog-marched out of the church still hurling his argumentation back at the white-faced preacher. 'Order' was never entirely restored after that. My beautiful, beautiful service had hit the buffers well and truly; or rather, it had gone clean off the rails.

Not that Open-Air worship is guaranteed to produce the goods. In fact some of the same can be as painfully hidebound as any under the tabernacle's roof.

The passers-by must have wondered about our fumbling attempts at the United Open-Air Service one Sunday evening a few years back. So self-conscious and awkward we were, so apologetic. All the normal furniture of an indoor occasion had been faithfully brought outside: portable organ, chairs, table, hymn-books, even a bowl of flowers. A few of us spilled over on to the street outside, but most of the congregation had been seated behind the Pastoral Centre's outer wall, rather like those early disciples behind their locked doors 'for fear of the Jews'; or so it seemed.

There was a feeling of awkwardness and angularity about us, all down the line. 'I just don't get it, I don't see what they're on,' said one Youth Club girl standing over by the bus shelter in the Square, in response to the invitation to come and join us. Exactly what we were 'on' perhaps wasn't very obvious, maybe we weren't clear enough ourselves. Arguably, all we succeeded in doing was to convince the few passers-by that this was indeed the nutty fringe of modern society, still harking back to its old-fashioned credentials; whilst the more rational world, come of age and mature, strolled past with a smile on its face.

And yet... Half-way through the service, some other youngsters joined us, even volunteered to come in and sit down behind the 'locked' walls. 'I just don't get it,' she said, as she strolled off with her mates. But as I took another look at her, underneath the recently acquired make-up I detected a familiar face, a ball of fire from the Youth Club and from an earlier uniformed organisation which went badly bust a few years ago, leaving a lot of its members - 'Georgie' very much included, since she was one of the life-springs of the group if not the Queen Bee herself - bruised and bemused. 'I just don't get it, I don't see what they're on.' She'd said that after another experience. The photo of her group, one of the best photos of kids I've ever seen, sits on my desk still. As a result of that bust-up, will they all be nervous now of putting their hands out to group experience, always and ever shall be world without end?

Halfway through the address I found my mind and sight floating up to the swifts circling far above us. Our earthbound spirits seemed so tight and constricted by comparison. Darting about, swooping, changing direction like radared model aircraft, lunging down and then shooting up like arrows: how free and uncluttered the swifts, as open and flexible as the skies.

But then I got to thinking of another bird, a fully grown swan this one, who some years ago flew low near our house, miscalculated her or his flight-path by some six feet or so and crashed into the church hall roof next door with a fair thud of a noise. With a rattle, rattle down the broken tiles and then a big plop to the concrete ground underneath, one irretrievably broken swan seemed possibly about to 'song' her or his last, as one large patch of broken tiles appeared in the roof above. I put through a phone-call to the RSPCA miles away, in our helplessness, and was given the assurance that we would do well to give her or him time. 'Try a trail of bread pieces towards some more open space.' The concussed period seemed to last for ages, but the said swan eventually got to standing up and very gingerly working along the bread trail, right out into the cul-de-sac road. And then, with all the grace of Concorde, after the taxi-ing round to the runway, came the really thrilling moment of engine ignition, with the long gathering of speed and flapping of wings period down the road, and eventual lift-off into the sky again.

Whether the worship is outside or in, I'm sure we'd be foolish to think of ourselves as an increasingly minority group of crashed-out swans, in contrast to our free-flying, unconstricted, swift contemporaries 'majoring' all around us. In terms of emotional and psychological damage, if not physical as well, as the Green Seagulled fringe of the post-secular society (full of uncatered for longings of transcendence still) we are no more nor less battered and bruised than anyone else. People look at our antics critically but, as often perhaps, longingly. It must be the unreformed pagan in me which still girds against their sight of us as broken-down swan crocks rather than the athletic, agile, open to the skies creatures I know I could never be, for one.

'I just don't get it, I don't see what they're on...' It needs allowances and qualifications, that dismissal. But for us to be complacent about the way we are when we go public would be a travesty of the outreaching, outsearching credentials we are supposed to carry with us. 'The Church is a school for sinners, not a society for saints,' it's often said. Not a place or group for élite, athletic swifts, but, I would plead, neither for just a collection of crashed-out swans or cygnets.

However long it took her or him, our broken-down swan looked magnificent as she or he ascended upwards again. Not swifts but swans, as St Augustine might have said, full of grace and potential gracefulness.

The outer wall has long since been removed. A magnificent Pastoral Centre has replaced the old 'Prim' Methodist Church, where both agile swifts and crashed-out swans now come and go with ease and welcome. Marvellous to relate...

The hardest Orders of Service are the leave-taking ones, outside or in. Amongst the most 'disorderly' I've ever taken was an occasion in the local cemetery.

We were standing quietly around paying our tributes. The sky looked threatening but the wind seemed to be blowing or rather bending the trees low in the other direction; no rain yet, so one tried hard to believe, especially as most of us had come totally unprepared for the elements.

And then, as it felt, up from the bottom of the sea came the most savage storm squall I can ever remember experiencing down there. At first, there was the sight of the rain falling like a curtain some distance away, but the trees near us soon started to crackle their message as the downpour spread almost with the speed of an arrow towards us; drops as big as pennies from heaven started to fall, rattling ominously on the coffin lid, quickly becoming a solid wall in next to no time, dousing and drowning us into the ground. Within seconds we all felt and looked like drenched rats. All dignity, decorum, decency down the drain. The words shouted out through the deafening curtain, "...we commit and commend the body and soul of this our dearly beloved sister to the ground..." And so the most drenched piece of ground in living memory received her into its bosom.

Is it just my Britishness which tends to assume on occasions like this that the ceremony should go on regardless? Would other cultures than our own have opted for discretion rather than dubious valour in this kind of situation, by running for shelter or abandoning ship? Two quips, as we leave the elemental stage looking and feeling utterly washed out and through, indicated at least an awareness of the issue. From someone on the fringes of her family: 'Well, she had the last laugh on us.' From one of the bearers: 'What did you do wrong?' 'Beware the humorous grave-digger' is the only maxim about pastoralia I remember from College days; but this humorous member of the cemetery fraternity had a point.

'May the angels of God welcome and receive you into the everlasting arms,' I find myself uttering on these graveside and crematorium occasions; most untheologically, and with complete disregard to time sequence, since the sentiment rather suggests that the deceased has been staying in some neutral parking-bay, waiting on the further release of ministerial words, which would be ridiculous. But the words still well up from my boots.

Circumstances didn't exactly permit them on this occasion. However, as I reflected on the hardness of her life and the struggles of caring for no less than ten children, largely on her own, I think she would have appreciated our staying by her side during the storm. She never ran for shelter or abandoned ship herself.

A memory implanted from curate days is never far away. There was ice and snow on this occasion rather than dousing rain, with the breath of the words freezing in the air, accompanied by brick-hard ground and brick-hard emotions wrapped in layers of protective clothing. And then all of a sudden came the sound of a train, as relentless as an approaching storm, at first distant but drawing steadily closer and more deafening, to the point that because of our nearness to the track, the words had to wait while the train plodded past and slowly went into the distance. I've never heard a finer funeral oration.

The worst last rites are the 'accidental' ones and the small boxed, single bearer ones. It's always a job getting the words out; the officiant simply stands there torn to shreds inside, aware of the hopeless inadequacy of anything said, dimly aware that one is representing God in the dock. 'I didn't like you at all that day,' said a man whose child I buried, in rain as it happens, a few years ago. He was putting it mildly. At few other times does the garbage collector's cap fit more perfectly. In terms of actual enjoyment it's like finishing the communion wine dregs in an old peoples' home when some of those participating have contributed rather more to the cup than they've taken.

'It makes you wonder sometimes,' people say, with the gloves still on. 'Tell me why it had to happen to HER'; even, 'How can your God allow this?' or, 'And you say God is love, parson?' These are the times when the gloves tend to come off. But, always, one senses the smouldering resentment and is aware of standing in the breach of a piece of divine equipment which once worked fairly smoothly - or appeared to, but now presents all sorts of problems. If God is not a working hypothesis for the majority of our contemporaries, any reassurance 'He' is likely to provide by a graveside is likely to be less than fully convincing. Unless, like all the statistics indicate, most of our contemporaries have really voted for keeping their options open when it comes to matters of ultimate belief, even in the bleakest of circumstances.

I squirm sometimes when I say the words because they sound like something out of a book of prayers with pretty roses on the front cover - whereas, in fact, it is an old Irish prayer slightly adapted - but they keep welling up still for all sorts of rites, last ones included.

May the sun and the wind, the rain and the storms, fall gently on our backs through all the seasons of the year.
May we be given perseverance for the pathway,
Wisdom for the work,
Friends and family for the fireside,
and love, laughter and life to the last.

Even when the storm squalls seem most savage.

The wastelands of the spirit will always remain, the experience of what those 17th century green seagulls described as being 'bewildernessed', at the end of their spiritual tether, with all hope and purpose lost. There used to be an unconsecrated section of our churchyard for those who took their own lives, 'felling themselves' as the very inadequate word means. The strains and stresses of the late twentieth century account for many more self-fellings than any section of the yard could cater for realistically. Thankfully, the sensitivities and pains of any suicidally bereaved family now deserve better than the previously cruel and barbarous tradition of unconsecrated burial.

So often I find my own assumptions about people's spiritual map references are wrong. Even in my own most doubtful, bewildernessed times, I find there's a heartbeat somewhere, a face or sound or sight to rekindle the flame. I find I live so much on what others have given me, it's always a matter of amazement to me that others find in me something which I have given them.

There have been lots of personal reference points around in this section, as if to suggest a solo rather than corporate experience of today's wastelands. Whereas the truth is, the real gut-cries of the spirit are heard when two or three gulls, 200 or 300, are gathered together in solidarity or protest round a common cause. The prisoner of conscience receiving hundreds of letters of support via Amnesty International, many of them from a completely different cultural context from her or his own; the protest marcher who finds suddenly close company with another gull from another flock quite outside their mutual previous experience; the attender of an international event or commemoration of anniversary or disaster who discovers that others around are singing a song with the same tune but in different languages: all these represent common sharing points way beyond the solo cries of the individual gull. 'My God, why hast thou forsaken *us*?' rather than just plain 'me'.

Not far inland from us many 'ecogulls' have gathered over the last few years in common gut-cry against the environmental rape of Twyford Down. One of the finest corporate prayers I know from today's wastelands has been etched either by a single gull or group of green enthusiasts on the side of a concrete tunnel entrance near the traffic lights on the former Winchester By-pass. The Twyford Down development is largely designed as an attempt to avoid the congestion caused by those lights. But as users of that hotly disputed area of present wasteland well know, close by that crucial inter-section this prayer has been winged in beautiful, colourful graffiti: CAR OR PLANET. No question-mark, just a statement as simple as BEEF-BURGER OR RAINFOREST, TANKS OR TRACTORS, AUTOMATA OR HUMANITY, GREED OR NEED. The choice is ours. Whatever else, we can't back away from our contemporary wastelands and opt for an island existence generated by the values of another age, however tempting. At times in our corporate pilgrimage we seem to come close to identifying with those green gulls from the early Hebrew flock who in their search for the truly good life used to etch out their equivalent of Winchester By-pass's soul-cry: only rather than CAR OR PLANET they wrote CURSE OR BLESSING.

As part of my own pilgrimage and search, right back at the start of my time on this present patch, I took a train to Huddersfield along with three or four hundred other gulls of greenish hue for a conference under the stimulating title, 'Seeds of Liberation'. It was mattress and rucksacks perching time with standing in long food queues, billy-cans and basic toilet facilities thrown in for good measure.

Into our midst, as we sat disciple-like all over the crowded floor, walked Daniel Berrigan, RC priest on parole for a few months from his American prison, where he was serving his sentence for burning draft cards in protest against the Vietnam War.

Part of his 'authority' came through his deep Omar Sharif eyes which spoke sensitively and with a passionate pleading. 'The only way to render to Caesar the things of Caesar's is to have very little,' he sang out to us. The youth of America was being prevented from 'any form of transcendent citizenship'. 'Ordinary people are being turned into killers'. And then, rising to his full theological height, he pulled, from roughly the same place on his personage as a Lee Marvin or an Ernest Hemingway might have kept their hip-flask, a battered New Testament. A quick flick through to a chapter in the Book of the Apocalypse, for all the world as if he were spinning the hip-flask's silver top, and then, without any apology or by-your-leave, came a long reading about the Beast. Which being translated, though by then the burden of the prophet Daniel's argument must have been abundantly clear to even the slowest gull in the gathered assembly: the Beast is none other than the conspiracy of the world's governments.

The conquering hero, a prisoner of conscience, on the side of the peace-loving angels: and we drank in his every word as if they were the ambrosian droplets of the gods. My own last glimpse of DB was of him sitting on the stairs near the main entrance with a tea cosy on his head looking totally crackers: an idiot for Christ, a Green Seagull extraordinaire, with scars, still trudging through the wastelands of his spirit.

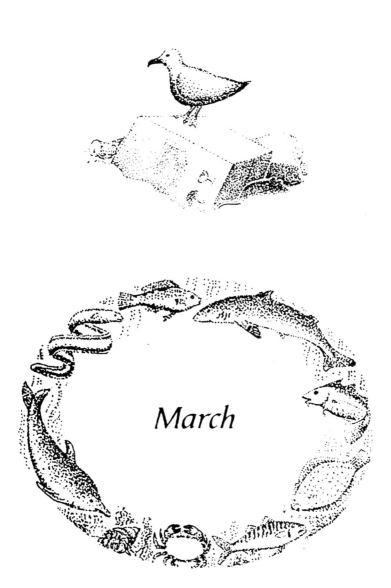

March

April

WANDERERS OF THE WORLD

No single gull of different hue has impressed us locally more than Ibrahim (popularly known as Abraham). For two years or so he came and perched in our locality. And 'perched' seems the only word for it, because his home was the top step of the disused local cinema in next door's community. He would spend his days walking nomad-like between the cinema step and some central point in town here, the home-made bread shop to be accurate, before returning 'ere nightfall to his perch: where I would frequently meet him with a cup of McDonald's coffee purchased on the standard cardboard tray with, always by request, two milk and two sugar units. And there on the cinema steps we'd sit, he sometimes waking from early slumbers, watching the very noisy world go by below.

Why Ibrahim chose this spot was beyond anyone's comprehension. Added to the incredible noise was the inconvenience of a sodium streetlight from which he never bothered to shield his eyes. He never used a pillow, never accepted a blanket or clothing. In fact, I still have in my possession a magnificent over-rug which someone left anonymously on the perch one day when he disappeared. And disappear he did quite frequently in order to refresh his spirits down in Southsea, where Abraham spotters regularly sighted him, sometimes on the front, more often than not in a bus shelter, once again right in the thick of some of Pompey's busiest traffic.

I remember once while we were nattering on his perch a car drew up and out jumped a very kindly disposed woman who came up the steps to offer him a coin. To my amazement, Ibrahim refused the offer, saying that he had quite sufficient already.

Rumour, of a kind which made me fairly angry, claimed that he drank. Occasionally he was seen knocking back a bottle of whisky, but I don't believe be was a habitual drinker. From the little he ever revealed of himself and his background, he had been on the road for twelve years. And sometimes in the depth of a severe frost, like many others I would marvel at his body temperature being able to adjust to existence without benefit of even the thinnest of blankets. His shoes were virtually non-existent, just strips of leather hanging loosely together, with holey-looking socks and a menacing, festering big toe which he regularly showed me. But when pressed about getting some medical treatment he always waived me aside with, 'It's alright, no problem.'

In fact, the foot did become a problem and he disappeared altogether. Eventually, by dint of a local hospital computer, I managed to trace that he had been in Portsmouth's Queen Alexandra Hospital for a two-month period. But then he'd vanished - back to London; even back to Cyprus, his birth-place fifty-three years ago? Probably we shall never know. But the Abraham supporters' club will never give up hope that he will one day return.

The risk I took in carrying my Abraham visual aids kit around with me all over the local place here was that of romanticising his condition: the happy gentleman of the road, of his own apparent free-will, wanderer of the earth in the footsteps of his biblical namesake, amazingly tough and resilient, never complaining, surprisingly all there after so many years.

In fact, I had reason to believe that Abraham's road pilgrimage was not entirely of his own free will. He never spoke of it, but every now and then there were just hints that he was on the run from some unhappy previous circumstances in his life. He was not such a free agent as popular legend had it. Sometimes the green gull on the doorstep brings out a battered family photo to refer to past areas of pain; it's a convenient shorthand, no further words are needed. But Abraham kept all his cards and photos - if he had any - very close to his chest.

No sooner mention this sturdy wanderer of the earth, though, than thousands of others, like the massive chorus of a Notting Hill Carnival, come flooding into mind. Very locally I think of the Bed and Breakfast families whose cramped existence was instanced so vividly for me in my friendship with June and Jock. Portsmouth has really changed out of all recognition in my twenty-five years here. Once upon a time people used to stay in one of the dozens of holiday hotels and homes along or near the seafront. One of these big hotels now houses over sixty semi-permanent Bed and Breakfast families or single people, some of them coming out of care or prison. Portsmouth itself has been in the national B. and B. division one league.

June and Jock lived in a single room with their pregnant daughter Janet, in a so-called hotel off the seafront. We used to meet either in their room or another B. and B. residence and talk heatedly about all that needed to be done for the local homeless. Once or twice we even penetrated into the inner sanctum of the City's Department of the Environment to complain about the glaring Health and Safety omissions in many of the hotels and hostels which offer perches to the hundreds of families on the official waiting-lists. Some of these stay on housing hold, as it were, for up to five years or more; their children know only home spaces barely the size of locker-rooms. Through a Housing Trust we've managed to get some kind of immediate relief off the ground in the shape of a Day Centre. But the problem remains, despite the assurances of our local MP who at least had the grace to listen when a group of us lobbied him in the Commons, recently. In the last two years, a first for our parish, eleven families have taken up B. and B. residence amongst us, half-a-dozen of them in a local main road hotel, formerly patronised by business executives and area representatives. That particular establishment, run by a Muslim couple from Pakistan, will play a part in the Green Seagull story at a later stage.

But for June and Jock, life has moved on quite a bit: the last time I heard from them they had been rehoused in an area of the City's outer estates, there was the prospect of some work and Janet had had her baby. The picture of them leaving the City offices' car park, after one of our encounters with the D. of E., in an old banger which sent out clouds of smoke everywhere, their whole home inside packed to the last crevice, somehow typified the homeless experience. And the Word was made flesh and *tented* amongst us, indeed.

In about year ten here news came of a sudden forthcoming visitation through the skies of a whole flock of green gulls from another world and another culture. The first batch of Vietnamese refugees was arriving on Thorney Island next door to our community.

To say that we weren't really expecting them would be a considerable understatement. After the sudden announcements in the local press about the Home Office's plans to use our disused adjoining RAF Station as a Refugee Centre, a flurry of comment, rumour, anticipation followed, all of it coming to a head in a tightly packed public meeting held in the church hall next door.

The police had been tipped about the possibility of a National Front protest, but in the event the meeting both respectfully heard the Centre's future chief, a gentle former army 'Majorgull', called out of his retirement by the Home Office, and then eagerly responded with their questions and offers of help.

And so began one of the strangest chapters of all in the whole history of our community.

'What about *our* needs?' The question was clearly in the minds of those who attended an angry public meeting some while later. Only a handful were expected for a quiet Discussion Group (as billed). But the room was full and tense as we arrived; a far cry from that headily encouraging public meeting of only a few months ago.

'The Vietnamese Refugees and the local community's response' was the preferred title of this little educational exercise. Others present clearly saw things differently. My colleague, the gentle Army Major, led off on the recent history of the Vietnamese people and why the refugees felt they had to leave their homeland. There was a fidgeting in the audience. People were looking at each other. Eventually the head of steam could hold back no longer. 'What I want to know is, how can they afford to buy our spirits?' Quite a jump there from the war-torn history of a far-away people to our own fragile situation here. Others threw in their weight. 'How much money are they getting?' 'It's not fair. They're taking our jobs.' 'Have you seen them handling our fruit in the shops?' 'Why can't they all live on some island?'

The anger and bitterness had been around for months, ever since the refugees were seen to be 'not as poor as we'd been led to believe'. But the thing which gradually emerged was the reason for everyone turning out that night. 'We'd heard a rumour that you were trying to get the Vietnamese into the empty houses behind the garage.'

Reassurances, corrections, attempted answers were all really to little avail. People started leaving, shaking their heads. One man went out saying, 'Well I'm off to work, underpaid.' One of the only laughs of the evening came when I added, 'Like me, I know it, underpaid and under-appreciated.' One final attempt I made to stress the positive side of the tense confrontation: 'It's been good to have it out anyway.'

The most revealing moment in a way came from a young Mum: 'What are we going to do? My husband's been sacked from his job because of his heart attack, we're having to get rid of all our savings to survive.' A look of panic came into her eyes in the discussion afterwards. She looked large with further life, too. I'd seen John in hospital some months ago when he'd told me about the long-distance driving and his lifting tons and tons of onions, and how the whole situation had got him down.

'Where's your compassion?' asked one of the better off members of the group. 'Charity begins at home,' came the reply. And in the case of John's family, she was right.

The refugees started to come to our services, in very small numbers admittedly. Because of all the language difficulties they sat for the most part looking rather lost or bemused; but their being with us felt strangely good; I trust for them, too.

The old man with the wrinkles of ages all over his face used to come quite regularly. He sat with his cap on throughout the service; when he knelt at the rail for communion his cap was still there firmly on his head. Only a bold, and probably rather stupid, gull would have told him that in this country men don't normally wear hats in church, even supposing an adequate form of understandable communication could have been found to reach him. After the service all the wrinkles used to break into a smile, as he gave the Vietnamese greeting and toddled down the path with two members of his family.

Transport was a major problem. The inventive youngsters amongst the Vietnamese managed to cobble together something approaching a bicycle. For most of the refugees it had to be a two-mile walk to the shops and back. Unless, that is, they happened on a lift. Sometimes my car felt as if it was driving on four hub-caps, with eight or nine tightly packed passengers on board.

Just occasionally on these journeys, we were able to strike up some form of conversation. My Vietnamese couldn't survive more than an opening word or two but one of the three people in the front seat on one occasion managed some English.

'Are you a Catholic?'

'No, I'm a Confucianist.'

'Does that mean you feel very close to your ancestors?'

'Yes, the spirits of our family are always close to us. When someone dies we believe that he goes to his ancestors.'

'This must be very hard for you now then, living so far away from your ancestors?'

'Yes, but when we die we shall go back to Vietnam.'

And as one very laden vehicle swept round the corners of the bird sanctuary world between the camp centre and the rest of civilisation, I wondered whether the mind of the soul-bird beside me had already taken wing over the marshes to start the long migrating trip back to where he really belonged. Did he leave his real self behind when he fled from Vietnam?

'Here we have no abiding city. Our citizenship is in heaven.' 'We are strangers and pilgrims.' Saints Paul and Peter could have been speaking for him.

The rooms of the refugees down at the Centre had a strange simplicity to them. A family of five or six occupied two double-beds, arranged as bunks one on top of the other. There was a table, a couple of chairs, a few personal effects round the washbasin, but, apart from a transistor or tape-recorder, very little sign of any other luggage. Most of the families arrived with precious little other than the things they happened to be wearing.

The decorating of their temporary nests appeared all the more moving and remarkable because of this enforced poverty; as did the cleanliness and tidy appearance of the 'birds' themselves. Over the chair, or under the wash-basin, were signs of plumage washed and ironed for future use. Round the mirror or in a jar on the table very often was a spray of twigs full of paper 'twists' to represent, one can only hazard a guess, the dream of better spring and harvest times to come.

In the entrance hall for one festive occasion paper decorations reflected the same dream and longing. One enormous branch stood there, but decorated in such a way as to suggest it could have come straight out of some Eastern painting. The same paper twists covered the entire branch, festooned every twig, only this time in different colours; the whole effect suggesting a kind of corporate prayer for the future.

Or maybe the branch and spray decorations prayed the same message as one of the posters in the refugee children's school: 'We may have arrived in different boats, but we're all in the same boat now.'

One evening at the Refugee Centre I shall never forget. The guests were all welcomed, including a group of top brass from the London HQ. The lively meal was aided by liquid refreshment which all the guests were invited to bring (they don't sell alcohol on the Centre's premises). The liquor question continued to rumble on as a local issue. 'Isn't it our money they're spending?'; occasionally even,

'They shouldn't be allowed it'. But the point wasn't entirely a fair one. It's hard to imagine 700 Brits cooped up in a similar Centre on the outskirts of Hanoi or Srebrenica, say, without some of them at least wanting to break the no-alcohol-sold-on-the-premises ruling with an occasional visit to the Off Licence down the road.

After the meal we sat back for the entertainment, all of it supplied - again with much excitement - by the refugees themselves. Some of the items betrayed signs of under-rehearsal, others suffered from slight embarrassment on the part of the singers and actors. The public address system could well have been turned down several decibels or, better still, switched off at source. But the evening was saved by the children's dancing and then by some fine piano playing by a very talented young performer who managed to coax an untuned 'honky-tonk' into some very plausible renderings of Mendelssohn and Beethoven.

During the entertainment I found my mind drifting off to another refugee concert recently experienced at one of the other Centres in these parts. The two memorable items on this occasion were, firstly, a drama sketch involving a capture scene in which a member of a refugee family was summarily removed by a very aggressive police presence, never to be seen again - or so one was led to believe - despite the heart-cries from the family's other members. The poignancy of the scene needed no translator's note, it could only have broken surface as a result of painful first-hand experience. Did its enactment provide some kind of purging for the participants? One was left wondering.

The second memorable entertainment item came from a group of young Vietnamese girl dancers. Down went the house-lights and then on to the stage moved the dancing lines, their steps so minuscule they looked like two continuous flows or streams. In their hands they carried simple night-light candles in low glass bowls, which they then proceeded to move elegantly in the darkness, by far the most expert movement being the small circle in which each hand appeared to revolve round and round like a slow Catherine Wheel. All this while the minuscule, tiptoe movements of their dance were maintained to the haunting off-stage music of a single flute repeating its tune over and over again.

The whole effect was so heady one felt almost drunk by the end. I guess that the really moving thing about this candle dance was that it had survived its long flight from another culture and appeared to be so alive and well, as if through some ancestrally coded message, in these young performers.

The fragility of our parochial response to the coming of the refugees really hit me at times. On one occasion heavy rainstorms had caused bad flooding through the roof of the old house we used for the Support Project. 'Que Huong Moi: New Homelands', the notice in the hallway somewhat shakily proclaimed; the shakiness made explicit when we got heavy rain, because then the water dribbled through from the attic, collected in great puddles on the landing and in certain of the first floor rooms, then percolated through whatever cracks and fissures it could find, and so down to the ground-floor either in big droplets which sounded ominously and hollowly as one entered the building, or in streamlets down the walls and over any notices or pictures it found in its path. 'Que Huong Moi'. Welcome to rainy Britain: that seemed to be the message on some days.

We had our lighter moments round at the Support Centre; like the day when Harry the plumber called to try and fix one of the myriad waterworks' problems.

Some weeks before, Harry had walked into the Centre. He'd been sent by 'the Office' (which he invariably mentioned with a look heavenwards) to check on the water situation. It didn't take him long to assess the position: one of total chaos and something well outside his normal experience. I was just sitting in one of the front rooms reading or scribbling, but we got talking and Harry teased out some questions about the Refugee Project - dipping his toes in, testing the water, as it were. From that time on he got pretty involved with us. We rang each other up like buddies. 'Hi! Harry.' 'Hi! Dave.' He was always dropping round at the end of his day after the routine calls. Harry was a man under authority, 'the office' and all that. On this occasion he chose to come over and give his Sunday time as he staggered in with all his equipment, blow-lamps, cold chisels, Big Bertha, the lot. Two young friends' arm sizes turned out to be very helpful getting through the floor holes. 'Makes you think of the kids going up the chimneys in the olden days,' I offered.

'Where they should be still, an' all,' replied Harry.

I guess he did give them a fair old run; his kids, I mean. I don't suppose Harry at home had much time for the natural failings of youth, or of his wife, come to think of it. But he still came over in his free time; there was no money in it, either.

And then there was the extraordinary Wild West day round at the Centre, involving a meeting with a splendid Organisation rejoicing in the grand title of 'The Commancheros'. George and Harry, two regular helpers, had come with their 'Wild West' colleagues. George seemed to spend most of his life with a cowboy hat on his balding top and a pair of spurs on his boots, with a cigarella or something which bounced up and down on his lips as he talked; giving every appearance, especially when he could be persuaded to remove his hat and reveal all, of a Buster Keaton character on some late twentieth century 'loner' trip, with a gentle snook cocked at the conformist society he found increasingly around him. Harry, his immediate No. 2, apologised for his deafness in almost every sentence.

But today, with a thunderous drumming of horses's hooves, it was Commanchero time. Out from their rather crashed-out looking vehicles they all piled, in their remarkable garbs. Big, barrel-chested Bob quickly emerged as their leader, stamping on the occasion the clear insignia of his office. 'Sheriff', said the badge over his heart. Round to the back of his car he moved, or rather swaggered; with a punch of his thumb up flew his boot, to reveal one belt lined with bullets and, in their midst, two pistols in holsters. On went this impressive leather ephod with a snap-click of the buckle. Thumb and fore-finger adjustment of the velvet hat (rather better quality than George's), and then, guns both in place, we were ready and off. Two officials eyed each other over, Sheriffed and Dog-collared, and business commenced. The big question: could they use the Project's land to build a 'Street Scene'? 'For our gun-fights.'

Well, the gun-fights never really came off, because very shortly after this the Measurers from the Ministry arrived with their dreaded marking sticks. In no time we were under starter's orders for the big dumper-trucks and bull-dozers.

A good many moons have passed now. The Support Centre I've described has long since closed; the beautiful old building was knocked down, leaking waterworks and all, the ground flattened out to pasture a few animals: prior to the arrival of the motorway pioneers. We are now part of T.S. Eliot's twentieth century memorial, a tarmac road.

Partly to console myself, no doubt, I often reflect somewhat ruefully on the extraordinary fact that our cardboard notice proclaiming the refugees' presence was never once vandalised or decorated. It positively invited the attentions of the spray-can artists but, despite its delicate message, even at the height of the refugee backlash times in our community, no-one ever tampered with it.

Such I believe was the quiet and largely unspoken recognition of the holy ground we were occupying.

All the same, I often wonder where the Commancheros took their beautiful euphemism of a 'Street Scene'. Harry I still see about in his Water Board togs; George and Harry's green seagull-hood, I trust, operates well someplace else.

We had our not so light moments, too. On another occasion the Centre's hall was packed full of refugees, reminiscent of the crowded pictures of Hong Kong's camps, which I was later to see and witness for myself. The New Year Tet celebrations were in full swing, with the public address system, yet once again, many decibels too loud. I looked down from the balcony, surrounded by children hanging over the side, with feelings of 'all of life' before my eyes: a fragile old lady with wispish hair and inscrutable lines; a babe blissfully unaware of all the surrounding noise and excitement, quietly sucking away from Mum, whose eyes looked expressionlessly towards the stage; a child standing on a chair, mouth and eyes wide open, arms just dangling in total absorption.

And then all of a sudden a scuffle broke out following the singing of the popular 'Vietnam, Vietnam'. As if out of a cloudless sky, fisticuffs started with accusations flying fast and loose. Trieu, our New Homelands Project foreman, was on it like a flash, trying to cool things down, still with his warm smile. One of the people involved in the scuffle had worked in the workshops with us. Eventually, after a lot of persuasion, Trieu and one or two others - his wife(?) by his side, too - managed to calm him down.

'What was the problem, Trieu?'

'Oh, it was an argument between someone from the North and someone from the South.'

Once upon a time the argument was thousands of miles away the other side of the world, with guns and bombs rather than words or fists. Small wonder that the flashpoints still come, that the attitudes of years and years were still there not far below the surface, rumbling away. 'Vietnam, Vietnam', everyone sang lustily - but whose Vietnam? That was the point. And, amazingly, it was still being settled on our doorstep. Thank God, it was now just with words and fists.

The Vietnamese children's games fascinated me: their marbles and skipping dexterity (the finger flicks and balanced jumps from one foot to the other), the engrossed look on their faces somehow inviting the onlooker to put all her or his preoccupations to one side and see the world in their grain of sand. The petiteness of their bodies and the openness of their facial expressions were a world of delight. My really big regret about their time with us, as this gradually drew to a close, was that not more of our community had had the opportunity to stand and be engrossed, too.

Geographical difficulties and Ministry of Defence regulations were responsible, understandably in both cases. But what more could have been done to let the children marble and skip in our community? It's a question which their time perched with us left blowing in the wind.

The one solution which seemed a non-starter was to organise a playing space in the High Street. This kind of engrossed playing just can't come under starter's orders.

So, eventually, came that evening barbecue, when farewells and end-of-chapter feelings filled the air. For two years the Refugee Centre had been right in the forefront of my mind and development; and now, because of cutbacks and government policies, this Centre too had to close. We couldn't possibly take any more refugees from the Far East, enough was enough.

What a dreamlike affair the whole sequence had been! For long afterwards faces kept coming to me - briefly met, smiled at, responded to, with memories of many encounters. They left their poems and messages for us like twisted pieces of colourful paper on our hedgerows.

Migratory birds land periodically on our shores, and none more notably than the Brent Geese on their regular flight-paths to and from Siberia. These bold venturers, as they appear, are often the subject of local farming complaints, not least because of their corporate power of crop destruction.

The contrast between these seasonal travellers and the vulnerable human migrant gulls who dropped out of our skies and on to our shoreline from the other side of the world could not be more striking.

Here she stands, representing the greenest ones of all in the world community, with her brave little smile and flimsy dress, the wrenched-from-home gull revealed.

AWAY FROM MUM

Thousands of miles apart from you
On the other side of the earth,
When can I see you again?
You have looked after me day and night
From Childhood to Adolescence.
You wanted me to have freedom and peace
And a bright future,
So you let me escape.

Please don't worry,
I have been given good accommodation
And proper education.
From now on, and maybe forever,
Britain is my new homeland.
Britain has come into my life sweetly,
As beautiful as rice stalks,
As lovely as branches full of Oranges.

While I am missing you,
My dear Mum, please don't worry,
Britain has been taking care of me instead of you.

Those words were written by Dao Huong, aged fourteen.

I met Huong at one of our local schools. She had come with a small group of other refugees, at my invitation, to meet a fifth year class of English students slightly older than her, though she looked far beyond them in years and maturity. Which might account for the rather stupid class-room question I asked through an interpreter; Huong's English in those early days being just a matter of 'Hello' and 'Goodbye', the two words one heard constantly in the long corridors of the Centre, as if in practice, to test out the audience reaction.

'Are you married?' I asked Huong. Her face seemed ageless, if that's the right word to describe that delicate, fragile blend of almost birdlike frailty which is the Vietnamese aspect through and through. The children playing in the corridors, ingeniously devising their own games, seemed so fragile and tiny compared with their English contemporaries; even their fathers had a slight, wind-tossed appearance. I've yet to meet a really portly Vietnamese. Delicate, fragile and meticulous. Every line and detail of their faces was fashioned with exquisite care, one felt, like the arts and crafts and poems they produced with their hands.

'No,' the interpreter hastened to answer my class-room question about Huong's exact status, with a smile which suggested he was doing his best to suffer fools gladly. 'She is not married, she is only fourteen.'

Huong has a wonderfully open smile, another common characteristic amongst the Vietnamese, one of the first things our local children here noted when the refugees started arriving. 'They all smile at us.' Surprising again when you think of what they'd been through, over the last twenty years to go back no further, not to mention the living hells of their more recent boat journeys to 'freedom'. Did they find *us* a nation of smilers? I find it hard to believe so.

But behind Huong's smile there were pleading eyes which seemed to beg, 'Please, I'm very vulnerable and frightened, be gentle with me.' The sun would come out, her whole face light up, but, never far away, the threatening clouds in her mind soon sent the sun back in as the ground she tip-toed on began to feel insecure.

'Could you tell us why you left Vietnam?' But my second question to Huong never got an answer. Before even the interpreter could handle it, the deputy administrator from Thorney who had come to the school with the refugee party had deftly fielded the question and, quite rightly, ruled it out of order. Some things can be asked, some things cannot; one can enter someone else's private world, albeit ever so gently, but only so far. Beyond a certain point not even the angels dare to trespass. 'Away from Mum', Huong called her poem later. Only fools would have entered that territory without further invitation. I was near to being such a fool.

'You must understand,' the deputy said, 'Huong left Taiphong province, Vietnam, only three months ago. She's here all alone and it's really too emotional and sensitive an area for her to speak about.' There was no rebuke in his tone. The explanation was entirely acceptable. What he might have said but didn't, was, 'In ten, twenty, thirty years' time, ask Huong why she left Vietnam.'

I wonder where Huong is now, and Phan Phui and Trieu? I knew what the future held for Phoum, Phuoc and their son Tomh, one of the most professionally qualified families of all the refugees (she a gynaecologist, he a GP before they left Saigon), because they still write to me each Christmas from their home in Cambridge. But what of so many others?

And so we bade our farewells. The staff members in the Thorney camp were a remarkable scratch gathering of green gulls who had flown in from all over the place; some of them wearing their own only too obvious refugee status (in flight from domestic or job situations) fairly near their sleeves; many of them students on placement for a year or so from universities. It was good... What next for them? 'We've got a job in Jakarta.' 'I'm looking for a job in Mozambique.' 'We're off to a camp in Malaysia next month.' 'I leave for Thailand in three days' time.' 'First I'm going to have a rest and then they want me out in the Far East again for a few months.'

The global village has rarely been made plainer to me. Jakarta, Mozambique, Malaysia, Thailand - the staff speak of these places as if they were up the road, over the next hill. Almost as if they were referring to a world map which related only very dimly to the normally accepted boundaries and frontiers of our globe. Where most of us see countries and continents, members of the Refugee Staff Community of the World see only camps; or perhaps dumping-grounds for the refuse of humanity, the places where people are put when they have nowhere else to go. A good part of me envies their vocation, their priesthood, their commitment to the flotsam and jetsam, the casualties of the planet earth. 'What are you going to do when you grow up, Jill or Johnnie?' 'I want to be a human rubbish collector.' It must require a certain courage to come out from the back rows of their peer groups with that kind of commitment.

The dreamlike affair broke up, we part as friends. Whatever their feelings as they left us for the next camp, I knew mine were sorrowful. The heady days of wonderment at the sight and sound of those first refugees arriving on our doorstep (unbelievably, as it seemed at the time) now feel light-years away.

Dreams fade with the dawn of the cold light... but the dream was vital for us. The local community stretched its response, in fact over-stretched its response initially; local opposition to the Vietnamese presence in the tense housing and job situations was expressed and felt openly; but the thin line held.

The dream died, long live the dream!

Before leaving the British refugee scene we encountered from our community, I turn briefly to two foreign parts. But it's worth referring to the hard experience behind the resettlement process. The Home Office's vision was that all the Vietnamese taken on board by Britain should be resettled in very small clusters round the country, to ensure their absorption into our culture.

I always had considerable misgivings about this official line and still do. Absorption into our culture? But what about the sustaining of their culture?

'Britain has come into my life sweetly, as beautiful as rice stalks...'

Could Huong still say that now? Not if a newspaper comment at the resettlement time is anything to go by:

'They are still here, trying to carve out a new life in a country that has largely forgotten their existence. There are, indeed, nearly 15,000 such refugees already in this country, with others expected to come on from transit camps in Hong Kong. But "people no longer know who they are, or why they're here - and don't care," one welfare worker commented.'

The delayed reactions were inevitable, the trauma of deep loss, of having to adjust from the painful past, the distance away from their ancestors: it didn't require great prophetic insight to predict that there would be problems. The hardest part to bear - far worse in a way than all the frustrations because of lack of jobs and language learning facilities - must have been the coolness many of the resettled families found around them in response to their presence, to put it mildly.

'The only people who seem to take a close interest in the Thamesmead refugees are local youths who shout "Chinky!" at them, throw stones through their windows and scrawl obscenities on their walls,' the paper comment went on.

It's a hard judgement but, far from being totally to blame for their inhospitable behaviour, I believe those local youths were merely acting out parental and grandparental attitudes; they were the true Brits representing our island mentality, repelling the boarders on our behalf. The doctrine of Original Sin seldom makes more sense than when racial attitudes are under consideration. Years ago I remember meeting a very different group of 'youths' from a place of education none other than Eton College. So enlightened on every subject under the sun they seemed, with the one exception of immigration. Then everyone present reverted to parental and grandparental types in a trice.

I am a true Brit with a very 'Off-shore Island' mentality. Despite all my posturing I am as nervous of the foreign boarder coming on to the goodship Britannia as the next person. I don't throw stones through their windows or shout 'Chinky!' at them. My good self takes over and organises workshops and Cooperatives, even magazines, on 'their' behalf. But I am a sinner, underneath it all, and the sin lives on. I always take disclaimers of racism, particularly from politicians, with a large pinch of salt. I remember coming out of the house here to find two Chinese girls, offspring of the Takeaway round the corner, looking rather sheepish and embarrassed because two local youngsters had fled in giggles at the sight of their lacquered fingernails. 'They're teasing us,' one of the girls said.

. I find it doesn't take much in me to identify with those Thamesmead refugees, though, because of the past pain of a young teenager experience. I did not belong to the local village gang and having to pass them to post a letter was sheer agony.

'Chinky!' Oh, my God! Must it go on until the end of time? 'Britain has been taking care of me instead of you.' May your dream continue, Huong.

Sometime after the refugees had left us I visited the war camps on the North-East borders of Thailand. A nurse from our community had been working out there some while and I had become so enthused by her vivid accounts that a visit grew from imaginary flights of fantasy through to eventual hard fact. One of the visual aids Nurse Andrea had brought home on her last furlough had been a white stole, fashioned beautifully over a period of six weeks in the most primitive conditions by a leprosy refugee patient called Chou Lou. "Hut 28, Row 48, Chou Lou", said the stitched tape on the back of the stole.

Thailand's refugee problem is, to be sure, one of the most acute and complex of all amongst the world's total fifteen million displaced persons' population. The hundreds of thousands of war victims have fled from Cambodia, Laos and, most recently, Burma. Their journeys in flight from war take them frequently through desert pilgrimages in length anything up to two or three weeks by their accounts, without food other than berries and roots, right up to the Mekong River (in the case of those fleeing from the East). Once at the river's edge they wait in hiding for a chance boat on a moonless night in order to escape detection or, more dramatically, a hazardous journey clinging to blown-up bags, most of the hill people being non-swimmers; with their children and babes tied on to the adult or older children's backs in a drugged condition, again lest their voices and screams of panic raise the military alarm.

Safe arrival on the Thai side is followed by detention in jails or holding-stations, in the former case with the men strictly separated from the women and children. After some degree of rather spasmodic sifting and sorting, eventually the refugees are allocated a more permanent camp where they stay in cramped and primitive conditions more or less indefinitely. At the Banvinai camp we visited, down a long dusty track a good number of miles from Nhong Khai, the nearest northern town, out of the world's mind and sight, one couldn't help feeling that many of the present 50,000 refugees have been there for five, ten, fifteen, even, in some cases, twenty years. Banvinai is their home; here they have married, had children and grandchildren; and here - short of some UN or Thai government miracle - they will die.

The Hmong people at Banvinai and in the jails and holding-stations Nurse Andrea took us to see come from the hills of northern Laos. Why they felt forced to flee their country is still by no means clear. Their stories of crop and livestock destruction, of killing and rape, pour out through the Thai interpreters. They stand looking vacant, with one or two bundles as their sole reminders of home; they lie on rush mats bunched together tightly under the single canvas canopy, endlessly waiting and yet with an apparent sense of relief. 'We are together,' they say. A family relation looks after a baby after his mother has been killed; a mother is given some soap by Andrea after she had revealed that her baby suffering from skin rash had been born twelve days previously there on the rush mat we were standing on and that no-one had yet visited her medically; a boy suffering from malaria is prescribed some pills for the first time in his life, 'to be taken morning and evening', with three medical fingers in the air trying to spell the message out to him as clearly as possible.

And there they wait, the world's Green Seagulls, displaced and islanded in their seemingly '*perpetuum immobile*'. I was impressed by the UN personnel's care-ful pastoring of their ever-growing flocks. In Banvinai there had been a fire in one of the camp's sections the night before our visit. A dozen straw and bamboo huts had gone up in a trice, leaving only a few pathetic pots and pans in the charred wreckage. 'When you have lost everything it doesn't take much to start again,' commented one American worker in the camp's sewage department.

At Banvinai, as if to act as a symbol of hope in the valley of total loss, they have the most beautiful butterflies. At the end of an extraordinary visit, my son and I separated outside the bamboo hospital in an attempt to recoup our shattered emotions. Earlier in the day we had met Chou Lou, the maker of the stole, and been shown round the Leprosy Centre. 'It's the most perfect marriage,' Sister Pierre had said to us in one of the well-ordered huts. 'He has no feet and she has no hands, they do everything for each other.' Whilst, outside, a young lad with a shrivelled hand practised his superb handwriting with the aid of a pencil strapped to one of a pair of wrists which ended in stubs. The stoles I now wear for Communion services came from the same hearth; in many cases their makers work with needles similarly strapped to their finger-stubs. And yet there at Banvinai, in this heart of darkness at the world's end, in amongst those thousands of abandoned seagulls, the laughter of Sister Pierre flitted unforgettably like a brilliant butterfly, bringing hope, purpose and joy to God's forsaken ones.

But no more moving picture of the world's wanderers has come home to me than from the experience of seeing a day in the life of the Hong Kong detention centres, where the boat people arrive, often after harrowing weeks of starvation and privation at sea, to await the world's decision as to their future. The most amazing thing about these centres is their cleanliness and freedom from human stench. 3,000 people occupying a former factory building, hundreds of people huddled together in almost total dark and airless Nissen huts, rows and rows of square-boxed dwellings, three or four storeys-worth, stacked on top of each other, with only a blanket at most to provide a shred of privacy and the communal ladder for passing up or down: and yet the washing is still done, children play under the stand-pipes, the colourful clothes still look colourful. Shortly before my arrival there had been a fire. A blanket had gone up, the flames quickly spread to two or three other dwellings: buckets from stand-pipes outside had worked overtime and now there were just the charred, waterlogged remains. Two sights of this boxed world quietly proclaimed the triumph of the human spirit: one, of a babe in a tiny hammock being rocked by an attentive father, which felt about par for the stable in Bethlehem; the other, of a young couple who had prepared an elaborate meal for the visitors out of their slender pockets. As we sat cross-legged on rickety storey level three and shared their chop-sticked provision, I felt that nowhere in the world that day could the communion have been holier.

To put it negatively, the one thing all the world's refugee gulls have in common is that they remain, in most cases probably for ever, light years away from Jonathan Livingstone and all his ilk. The really worrying thing is that the gap between the high-flying and the low-flying members of the flock gets ever wider.

POLL-AXED IN POMPEY

And so to the eighties. It was said of Queen Elizabeth I that, if and when her heart were opened up after her death, the Cinque Ports would be found imprinted there; so vital was that issue to her political survival. The Faith-in-the-City report of 1985 still has that feel about it for me. Coming as it did from the heart of the Jonathan Livingstone Seagull decade, where get-rich-quick, winner-takes-all were the banner cries of the day, that report for me spoke with complete authority and conviction on behalf of millions of our contemporaries who found and still find themselves increasingly cast as green seagulls, grounded if not trampled on by the world around them.

Waiting one day for the 5.50pm from Waterloo at the tea bar, pigeons all around, I looked at one of them again - and it's not often I actually look at a London pigeon. I saw that both 'his' feet were lame. At first I thought I was seeing things. I lost 'him' but then he strutted back and I could see him more clearly. Sure enough, no toes on either feet, just club ends. He was a seasoned campaigner, obviously, he had learnt to adapt, a survivor. But the gait was awkward, rather halting. What story lay behind his 'clubbing'?

The Faith-in-the-City report spoke for all the citizens in our oil-rich land who found and still find themselves 'clubbed' or walking with awkward, halting gait.

During the last nine or so years since the report first bravely travelled through our skies there has been a range of responses. Some have praised it, others have vilified it. Some have warmed to the report's recommendations about the wastelands of the inner city or outer estateland, as well as supporting the Church Urban Fund and its projects. Others have seen behind the report a darkish if not demonic move to the left on the part of the Church's leadership with their frequent accusations about mixing religion with politics.

Personally, I think the charge of leftness levelled at the episcopal bench rather misses the point. The bishops remain much as they always have been: if anything has lurched politically it is society itself, and very much in a rightwards direction, however hard the attempt is made to deny the evidence.

Almost 70% of the nation is now home-owning, North Sea oil wealth has produced a better standard of living for the majority of our citizenry, most of us have never had it so good even in direst recession times. What has manifestly happened, for all the easy speeches predicting otherwise, is that the trickle down effects of the new-found wealth have not reached the parts of the body politic where no other wealth has reached before. The rich have got richer, the poor poorer. The board room's astronomical pay rises have had only the faintest of echoes in the boiler room's pay packages. Inflation may have been checked, as against the banana republics of popular mythology. Unemployment remains unchecked, scything through even our own flatlands' community during the last few years.

At this point we go back to the vexed question of personal responsibility as raised in the introduction.

The question remains much in the contemporary air concerning the issue of criminal behaviour. Are the joy-riders of Blackbird Leys, the race rioters of St Paul's, Bristol, the wild youth of Newcastle, responsible entirely for their actions; or have their circumstances driven them to act as they do? Muggers and murderers, thieves and vandals: are they born entirely responsible for all that they do, or are they bred by circumstances beyond their control? The James Bulger tragedy, and some acts of political terrorism soon afterwards involving the loss of young life, brought the issue sharply to the attention of the whole national flock. Should the perpetrators of these crimes be hung, locked away, treated as sick, given a pat on the head and told not to do it again? So, I asked a group of teenagers in a fairly basic area of Portsmouth just after James Bulger's murder. One lad indicated he thought that his murderers should be hung, most thought they should be treated as sick, none thought they should be given the pat on the head counsel.

But when Prime Minister John Major jumped in so quickly with his talk of 'condemning' rather than 'understanding' the perpetrators, he did the debate no service at all. Not the least virtue of the doctrine of Original Sin is its reminder of the common condition we share with every member of the flock. Condemning some gulls as totally responsible for their actions, with no circumstantial reckoning or understanding at all, is the verbal equivalent of putting them in the stocks or burning them at the stake - or, indeed, hanging them. The Prime Minister was clearly appealing verbally to our vestigial past.

Something that has puzzled me is the way, as a society, we have so often assumed - aided and abetted by a very conservative press - that our present vastly unequal, newly-wealthed and under-wealthed, State is largely unassailable and part of the divine order of things. The speech-giving gulls blame the recession and remind us constantly of the condition of the worldwide flock. Their references to the wider picture would be welcome but for the fact that the focus of their concern is invariably on those European or Western or Northern hemisphered members of the flock who already have the power and hold the purse-strings. Naturally, the First World didn't relish the recession; no-one in power wanted the existing systems changed, let alone upheaved.

The puzzling thing, I find, is how the rest of the flock - as reflected in national election-times, for instance, over the last fifteen years - has been prepared to go along with Jonathan Livingstone's ideology, without more than perfunctory murmurs of disapproval on occasion. One of the biggest things to account for the nation's complacency, I've surmised, is the home ownership syndrome. To my surprise, I discover that a majority of the houses in Paulsgrove, one of our City overspill areas hitherto, in pre-1980 days, solidly council run, is now owner-occupied.

That is a matter for rejoicing, only but the most enviously green, bitterly motivated gull should agree, surely? For too long the Christian stress on the virtue of poverty has been misused, albeit unconsciously for the most part, as a subtle ruse to keep the rich in privately owned castles and the poor at their council-run gates, in some awful phoney eternal scheme of things.

My difficulty is, firstly, with the manner that home ownership has been introduced into the body politic, with all its manifold problems of repossessions and credit-living, as well as the gross neglect of the affordable rented housing sector, which have followed relentlessly in the introduction's wake; and secondly, with the overall appeal of this subtle ruse new-style to the less than best in us. The plain fact of the matter is that over the last fifteen years we have become less compassionate and more individualistic; more concerned about home management and garden maintenance, less concerned about our communities and their consequent breakdown. The race now is increasingly to the swift and God help us if we're left behind.

Popular mythology has it that Tories wash their milk-bottles out, Socialists don't; that Tories pick up litter, Socialists drop it; that Tories pull themselves up by their own bootstraps and Socialists rely on others to do their boots up for them. I find myself an inveterate washer of bottles, an almost pathological picker up of litter - believe and see the expert as he trudges round the churchyard of an evening in the wake of any local celebration: a natural Tory am I by so much upbringing and inclination. But whether or not it has to do with my first school report ('He is slow at doing up his shoelaces'), what brings me to near apoplexy now is any suggestion that there should be no safety-net or state welfare or support system for many millions of other gulls who find themselves either pinned to the ground or unable to fly by their own efforts entirely.

I say the going along with the prevailing flock wisdom of the eighties has baffled me. A small group of local green gulls started meeting in 1986 to thrash around together on social issues. We talked about debt, the credit problems, homelessness, powerlessness, hopelessness and lots of more positive things. We have met together at least four times a year for weekends. The 'greenery' shared is heady stuff, even if for some of the time we feel as if we're rattling the bars of a very tightly controlled cage.

For me and I suspect a lot of other green gulls the get-rich-quick, fly-yourself-into-the-record-books decade came to a juddering climax with the issue of the community charge, which I now turn to, with some passion as well as blood-spattered feathers on my wings.

It was an extraordinary time in the life of our body politic. For much of the period I felt transported to my beloved seventeenth century, moving around our locality for all the world like some Muggletonian or Leveller or Shaker or Fifth Monarchist. After my own refusal to register for the dreaded Poll Tax on grounds of conscience, because I didn't agree with the lack of account taken for people's means, locals would stop me or shout across the street with sundry observations, like 'Still not in prison, Vic?' or 'What's the latest from the Wat Tyler front?'

The injustice of the Poll Tax touched our society's nerve ends. As a nation we are not easily roused. Even the most fulsome or provocative media headlines ('Gotcha!' from the Falklands, 'Our boys go in' from the more recent desert campaign against Iraq) leave gaps and question-marks in the popular mind. Phlegmatic, dryly humoured, for the most part tolerant and certainly not prone to opt for the revolutionary barricades: the British character is not given to deep political persuasions. It takes a lot to shift most of us from our armchair or pub-stool opinions to activist street marches and 'cause' membership. Since the advent of the Poll Tax only a very small percentage of the population volubly or visibly protested. But by all the poll survey accounts the vast majority of people (well over 80%) believed the Community Charge tax system to be wrong and unfair. The cause for comment and dismay is that our parliamentary representatives, most notably on the Opposition benches, did not sufficiently appraise or anticipate this popular 'uprising'. Demonstrations in Toxteth, Liverpool or Brixton, London, were one· thing. Demonstrations in Southampton, Newbury and even Tunbridge Wells, were clearly quite another. We've had race riots in St Paul's, Bristol, my home town; but what really staggered everyone was the Poll Tax riots on the College Green outside, and for some inhabitants inside, the Council buildings, in the shadow of the Cathedral, in the heart of Bristolian establishment. And to explain away this and other popular 'uprisings' as the work of the Militant Tendency or the Trotskyists or the Socialist Workers was only to explain away a very little.

In amongst all the local toings and froings of letters various, the most critical from well-established members of the local congregations, a sermon stood. For the first time ever I found myself appealing politically to the gospels and finding evidence there for a green seagull in a very tight corner. Jesus as the first pacifist or socialist? - the arguments for those claims fall flat on their faces on the grounds of unacceptable historicising. Pacifism and socialism are 20th, not first, century phenomena. But Jesus as the possible first non-payer of the Imperial tax? That's much nearer to the bone.

'Render unto Caesar the things that are Caesar's'. The text stared out at me the first Sunday back after holiday under the theme of 'Those in authority'. I had previously resolved not to take the Poll Tax issue to the pulpit, but the combination of the searching readings for the day and the powerful head of steam which had built up unwittingly during the holiday reflective time combined to blow my cover. And so out it all poured.

The sermon majored eventually on a sharing of my somewhat startled rediscovery of the opening of St Luke's 23rd chapter. Fifty-five verses later it was all over, the threat to the nation, the would be disturber of the peace, was safely in his tomb, the crisis had seemingly passed. But the opening lines of Luke's passion narrative fairly crackle with political tension: 'And they began to accuse him saying, "We found this fellow perverting our nation, and forbidding us to give tribute to Caesar, and saying that he himself is Christ a King."' Alone amongst the evangelists, Luke itemises the charges against Jesus. With Matthew and Mark he reports the 'Render unto Caesar' incident; only Matthew refers to the strange little tale about the 'Community Charge' coin in the fish's mouth.

Not for the first time, I detected a rearing back or at least a dropping of heads in certain sections of the congregation at the suggestion - as clearly hinted by all three evangelists - that Jesus found the taxation question a pain in the neck. 'Knowing their hypocrisy,' writes Mark of Jesus. 'He perceived their craftiness,' says Luke. 'Why do you set this trap for me?' asks Jesus in Matthew. If he'd said, 'Don't pay a penny of your taxes,' he would have been quickly disposed of as a secular insurrectionary pure and simple. If he'd said, 'Pay your taxes down to the last penny,' he would have lost out on all the alternative kingdom he had struggled and worked towards so passionately. And so, with a mixture of angry petulance and despairing frustration, he called up the dreaded drachma coin and straddled his options: to Caesar these things (undefined), to God those things (undefined).

The reared backs and lowered heads tend to occur at any smidgen of a suggestion either that Jesus was not wholly in control of every situation he ever encountered or that Jesus was not always wholly in control of himself. But on this occasion especially, the problem appeared to be with the pulpit argumentation that, whether or not the charges were false, Jesus was clearly heard to be encouraging others towards non-payment of taxes, in exactly the same way that he was heard to be perverting his nation and proclaiming himself a Messiah. Anyone who goes round the place dreaming aloud about another upside-down kingdom 'not of this world', where the rich would be poor and the poor rich, has only herself or himself to blame if the hearers of the dream start drawing their own conclusions about such mundane matters as the payment of taxes. Jesus may not have proclaimed civil disobedience in so many words. As Luke's list of charges bears moving witness, this was still amongst the key messages the general populace of his day received.

But the resistance in the churches to this even latently disobedient Jesus shows no sign of abating.

Jesus's whole ministry was absorbed in the 'things of God'. The Beatitudes indicate the topsy-turvy values of his dream kingdom. It seems hard to believe that he intended these values to be interpreted only in a spiritual fashion, that never in his wildest visions did he entertain their practical or political application. Why, if not out of corporate cowardice or threatened identity most dastardly, do the churches keep Jesus and political action at such debilitating arms-length? If 'the things of God' were so substantially concerned with such key human areas as justice, compassion, mercy, love, as the prophets through the centuries had claimed, it is a strange attitudinal stance which holds that a law so manifestly unjust as the Community Charge should cause no flicker of resistance amongst Christ's followers today.

Whatever is the most convincing interpretation of Jesus's rendering to Caesar counsel, the whole force and point of his counter to the scribal trap lay in the second half of the sentence. By good Aramaic linguistic custom, the second part of Jesus's pithy and memorable utterances was invariably stronger than the first. 'You have heard it said of old... but I say to you,' that was the stamp of his preaching trade. And thus, without any forcing or strain, we can understand the poll tax text in similar vein: 'You have heard it said of old (ie this is your custom), "Render to Caesar the things which are Caesar's", but I say to you, "Render to God the things which are God's".'

In each case 'the things' are left unspecified, with the same little word to cover both. The things of Caesar and the things of God: in the same sentence, in exact parallel, with no hint of a whisper as to what each might contain or describe or refer. No wonder the world has been puzzled by what he meant ever since.

Christians differ as much today about the precise description of the caesarian and godly things as (clearly) those who stood round Jesus with the original question. If payment of Caesar's Poll Tax had not been a hot potato, the question would never have been asked. It is customary for the Church to interpret the different categories in terms of supposedly watertight compartments, as if no overlap or shared areas of concern could ever be contemplated; and this all the more remarkably in view of the gospels' very open-ended answer to the taxation question.

The fiction of the withering away of the centralised State in Britain, with more and more power and control passing to local government, gives way gradually to the realisation of what huge inroads Whitehall bureaucracy has made into virtually every corner of the kingdom. For the churches to continue doffing the cap to law and order, without heed or care for the basic ethical issues like the citizen's ability to pay and the ever widening gap between the 'can' and 'can't' payers, is quite unbiblical as well as constituting a dereliction of the gospels' credentials.

Let Caesar be paid our dues but only according to the means of each. That is and will continue to be one of the things of God which we neglect at our spiritual peril.

In our Faith-in-the-City Advisory Group we have talked often about Kingdom values; the ethic of the Sermon on the Mount, in other words. For me the Poll Tax issue brought this to the top of my consciousness as nothing else. The issue was Kingdom - rather than Church - sized. We were facing a crucial debate about the nature of our society: was it to be Jonathan Livingstone or Penny and Percy 'Green' who had the final say?

Over the months the court cases proceeded, mostly in fairly desultory fashion. In this area at least the threat of bailiffs activity, so much talked about and feared, turned out to be little more than 'the frighteners'. The publication of names of Poll Tax defaulters in the press proved a strange form of retribution. I can't imagine that the local reporters attending courts were all that much interested in the long lists of names, by far the majority of the people behind them choosing not to appear in court. So who can have been responsible for all those column inches but the Community Charge departments themselves, seeking to make public local defaulters in a somewhat bizarre echo of the Bastille's heads-on-poles-in-the-market-place policy?

The court cases I attended were lack-lustre occasions betraying all the signs of pathetic amateurism. The members of the Bench almost without exception appeared completely out of their depth, as if they were the ones who drew the short straw on a hiding to nowhere. The power and control of the proceedings remained firmly in the hands of the Clerk, sometimes bossily and officiously, sometimes with great sensitivity. On one occasion I witnessed the woman Clerk on duty save the day as one defaulting member chose to cut up very rough when asked to remain standing. 'Why should I when you're not?' he bawled to the tight-lipped Bench. After fairly strong further altercation the Clerk had the wit to point out to the somewhat rattled ones above that, because the offence was a civil and not a criminal one, it was perfectly within the Bench's right to allow the defendants to remain seated during their case.

Why we were herded like cattle into the courtrooms (in some cases very makeshift ones at that) was never made plain. I imagine it was because large numbers of defendants were expected, when the vast majority of those summoned, in their anger, frustration, boredom, fear, whatever, chose to stay away. But no adjustment or flexibility in coping with the very few who opted to attend seemed to be on hand: cattle we were and cattle we should remain.

However correct the woman Clerk was in her face-saving distinction between civil and criminal justice, confusion over the matter generally abounded. Would the Poll Tax default go down in police records, affect one's Passport, be set against one's future employment prospects? Answer, no. Except that public perceptions never saw matters so clearly. In the eyes of many, law-breakers we were, 'can't' payers and won't' payers all, with no benefit of doubt or distinction; with, never far away from the frustrations and fury involved in the euphemistically styled 'adjustment factor', the resentment of having to pay yet more for the sake of those unpatriotic so-and-sos who have let the national and the local side down so heinously.

The charge of lack of patriotism comes strangely. Not only my country right or wrong, as it implies, but my country even when its elected representatives for the people's interest are so misguided, bewitched, blinded and brow-beaten, as to vote into legislative being a taxation system totally at odds with the principle of preserving those for whom all rightful laws are designed to protect. When the law of the land manifestly shows itself to be not just an ass but quite unjust, and the elected legislators incapable of fair policies and practices, what price all traditionally conceived patriotism? Who are the true patriots: those who doff their caps to the law of the land however corrupt, or those who rise up against legislative malpractice even in the highest courts of parliament?

More personally, one of my own crunch moments came soon after a local news report when visiting a long-standing parish connection. We've always had a straightforward relationship and been able to say things to each other honestly and humorously. 'I've been thinking about it for a long time,' she said, 'but I'll say it straight to you. I'm not prepared to take Communion from law-breakers.'

I was surprised that my request for a tribunal to consider my non-registration plea was honoured. My case rested on a conscientious objection to being registered on the Community Charge lists against my will. Countless millions of pounds were spent in setting up this registration process.

My concern in all the foregoing has been about the role and the place of the Church in times of social unrest. When the churches remain silent in times of social unrest something is indeed rotten in the state of Denmark. It's possible to argue that they haven't done in our present context, as all those who have followed the progress and the out-workings of the Faith in the City report, as well as the reports of other churches, will rightly affirm. For all the correctness of that claim, though, my judgement remains that the churches should have been far more galvanised into protesting action about such a manifest injustice as the Poll Tax than, with certain honourable exceptions, proved to be the case.

For all that it went against the grain of the times, thank God, many people took a stand after the introduction of the Poll Tax; the voters 'forced' the government to change its mind. The Poll Tax was a 'Kairos' time, 'a moment of truth', during which the whole people became politicised. Would that the heart of that historic opposition had beat with more Christian blood in it.

A friend, who resigned her magistracy over the Poll Tax, and I, produced a pamphlet about the issue as we'd experienced it locally. We ended that pamphlet:

'Pompey gave birth to Charles Dickens who grew up in its streets, knew its sufferings and wove its stories into his tales. If this brief account has brought to the surface at least some of these stories it will have served its purpose. The people behind these stories are those we wished to represent.'

The introduction of the Council Tax sent no similar shudders of protest though the limbs of the body politic. But now, in the mid-nineties, the new Criminal Justice Bill stands close to the statute book and many of the protesting gulls are taking to the streets again.

Our own Criminal Justice concern has concentrated on the plight of a group of Travellers who have been perching on a tiny patch of land in the midriff of our community. All kinds of tussles have filled the local press with the Travellers' tales during the last six months. Still the issue of the future is unresolved. Close by to where one of our more politically aware students scrawled his "Stop the Poll Tax" headline aloft on the side of the railway bridge (in letters still legible and unremoved), another Justice issue sits and stares us in the face. Where next for the perched gulls in our midst?

The base-line for my present conviction is that a lot of the Travelgulls we hear so much about today are not Travelgulls at all: they're Settlergulls rather than Nomadgulls. Our own so-called Travellers haven't 'travelled' anywhere. And there's nothing particularly 'New Age' about their apparent belief-systems. Like a lot of their contemporaries in other contexts elsewhere round our islands and beyond, these localgulls come from a very immediate situation, with friends and families just down the road or in the neighbouring estate. They were born here, bred here, schooled here and - contrary to much popular legend which would have these localgulls as 'scroungers', 'not contributing to society', 'not paying their way' - they work amongst us if only on a part-time or seasonal basis.

Their greatest 'crime' is that they just happen not to want to earth their present vision and pilgrimage in the vagaries and anxieties of the local Housing List. They have opted instead, however long or short the perching time, for the vagaries and anxieties of an old charabanc or lorry or caravan; rather than the bricks and mortar life-styles and 'nests' of the more conforming majority of the flock.

Just shunting the non-travelling localgulls on from their present perches into foreign parts, beyond the reach of all known contacts and resources, is no way to run a rail-road let alone a society, and certainly not one still with semi-christian or pluralist pretensions to it.

The Criminal Justice bill is now well and truly on trial here in the flatlands. 'No such thing as society': did *she* really mean it? Maybe she was joking? But we now know too much to believe she was.

May

June

CONFESSIONS OF A KILL-HOPE

The 1982 Falklands War was instrumental in causing many hitherto unremarkably coloured gulls to realise their greenness as if for the first time. I found myself willy-nilly amongst them.

Normality is a slippery concept and dangerous to define, not least because of its implications of sub- or ab-deviations. But in my own case I became acutely aware of a sea-change in my attitudes to issues of war and peace during the weeks of the Task Force's expedition to the South Atlantic. From my National Service days in the Royal Marines I had a fair idea of what was going on eventually at Bluff Cove and Goose Green. Six months spent doing commando section-in-the-attack exercises in North Africa and Cyprus had drilled something of the Falklands War basics into my system, even though there were clear times when that late fifties' system found the war - or practising for war - syndromes hard to take. Any ideas of harmlessly playing at soldiers for a limited period of time during which one could see something of the world entirely at Her Majesty's expense were swiftly shattered during a crucial Cyprus exercise when the helicopter involved gyrated out of control, causing a blade to snap and travel faster than the eye could see just above ground level until it came to rest the other side of the thighs of the sergeant-major standing next to me. Perhaps some seeds of my own greenery were planted near the helpless face of my dying neighbour on that anything but 'playing' occasion. Why him and not me? I came out of the Royal Corps wondering and I still wonder about that question.

Otherwise, though, there was nothing particularly green or unusual about my attitudes, say, to the Aldermaston marchers or to any protest marches for that matter. Except that I did have a vague feeling of being in the wrong place at the wrong time during the great and unforgettable October, 1968 march through London. I had known a small section of that huge crowd through the Flower People community who were squatting in the unused former school next door. But on the day itself, as the crowds swept past St Martin's like one enormous human tidal wave, I was buried right up to the top of my psyche in the church conducting a Folk Service. Seldom before or since have I had the sudden painful awareness of looking and feeling a political eunuch.

My Damascus Road experience came with the sinking of the Belgrano. I had never been happy about the Task Force's sailing; the whole *raison d'être* for the extraordinary displays of nationalistic fervour which rippled through the body politic after that fateful debate in the Commons seemed to rest on such totally shaky foundations. The hostilities which followed left me tossing on a strange spiritual dilemma: nothing less than how to pray in public and within a naval parish's context which involved the commitment of a lot of local husbands, sons and lovers, not to mention their families and relatives back home. And this is where I stumbled into the issue of war and peace for the very first time. In the aftermath of a Sunday night television programme, when my own contribution had tried to spell out this dilemma along with sundry other observations about the nature of war and peace, I found myself requested to stand down from the chaplaincy of the local Nautical Training Corps, a much valued post to which I have since been reinstated. The pain at the time, though, was considerable and not least because of my apparent inability to distinguish in public with much degree of success between praying for our boys in the South Atlantic and praying for all the people and parties involved in the conflict.

I have never been happy with Pope John-Paul II's heavily conservative teaching about sexual ethics; but I shall always be grateful to him for his courageous stand, just before the Falklands' hostilities began, in regard to the inadmissibility of war as a means of settling international territorial disputes. In amongst all the surrounding hollow appeals on behalf of the sanctity of life and the subsequent sleight of hand apologies for the necessity of the Belgrano's sinking, the Pope's words beamed out like a beacon of sanity and hope.

How exactly it could be that in 1958 I stood with apparent equanimity beside those who two years earlier had been dropped by helicopter from the commando ships at Suez, some of them with the wounds and scars of that conflict still fairly fresh about their bodies; whereas twenty-five years later I had such heavy ethical problems with a commando exercise not really so different in kind, I find it hard to explain. Equally hard to account for is how I could stand in an official capacity at the foot of Nelson's Column in Trafalgar Square during the late 1960s, apparently unbothered by the Trafalgar Day serried ranks of flags and weaponry in front of me. The nuclear dimensions and escalations since the late fifties obviously accounted for a lot of the sea-change; as did the growing conviction in me that gunboat diplomacy no longer made any sense in our world. The Falklands War proved to be only one of a hundred and twenty since World War Two. And yet, that we as a nation could be so swiftly and summarily involved in the fighting of it seemed like a total betrayal of the nuclear age. For all the 'God bless 'em', 'Gotcha!' headlines locally and nationally, the case for a sober assessment of the meaning of patriotism seldom seemed stronger than during those dark weeks.

Quite as disturbing, if not more so than the sinking of the Belgrano, was the still unsatisfactorily explained presence of nuclear depth charges amongst the Task Force's hidden stowage of weaponry. Ah, but they were never used; ah, but they mere removed from the bowels of the ships during the Ascension Island stopover. Both explanations still remain inadequate. Their presence on the weapons' inventory could scarcely have been unintentional or overlooked, even in all the frenzied packing up operation down the road from here before the Task Force sailed. It would be of some reassurance to know that a bout of something like an altogether higher moral order than naked, bare-knuckled patriotism overtook the consciences of the powers that be as the Task Force sped towards the Ascension Islands; which led in turn to a signal down the line for the removal of the depth charges on the grounds that any ensuing conflict in the South Atlantic should be fought with conventional weapons at all costs and on no account be allowed to cross the nuclear threshold for the sake of the world's future. No such reassurance is ever likely to be given on this point. If the improbable 'genuine error' theory about the mistaken nuclear weaponry inclusion can be dismissed (it seems unbelievable that anyone anywhere near the Task Force's Ops HQ could actually have forgotten the difference between a nuclear and a non-nuclear ship's inventory), we are led to the shabby conclusion that the cloak and dagger removal of the depth charges under all the blanket security of the Ascension Islands' haven was purely and totally a self-interested gesture. The future of the world was not the issue which pricked the tender consciences of the Ops HQ; the future and safety of our own ships was their sole concern, full-stop.

If one of our nuclear ships had been hit, well, it could have presented some local problems in terms of contamination and radioactive fall-out. But equally, we can only assume, if a good many of our ships had gone to the ocean bottom of the South Atlantic, then the nuclear option was still there safely stored away in the mid-Atlantic haven. Before the whole world our country stood and still stands condemned as apparently prepared in all conscience to consider the nuclear option; and this, even in such a grossly inequitable contest, with one side armed to Goliath's teeth with state of the art weaponry and the other, save for a handful of deadly imported European or American planes and rocketry, sailing around in rusty, forty year old boats or standing there shivering in their David-like, ill-fitting equipment with pathetically inadequate, clapped out rifles. We were dealing with a crazed High Command, yes; but for Goliath, even 8,000 miles from his home-base, ever to have considered crossing the nuclear threshold against such opponents in such a cause borders close on national insanity.

That was the beginning of the slippery slope so far as future so-called conventional warfare was concerned. The nuclear insanity clearly spread to other parts of the global flock. By the time of the Gulf War almost ten years on, it seemed to be taken as a matter of course that nuclearized weaponry would be stowed away in the Allied Forces' inventory without so much as a parliamentary by-your-leave. And by then the sophisticated lethal weaponry launched at the Iraqis - precisely targeted and civilian friendly, as was quite falsely claimed - were making the once dreaded exocets look like nursery toys. The dividing-lines between conventional and nuclear warfare became weaker and weaker from the Falklands on.

And so to patriotism. Did the 1982 conflict in the South Atlantic see the death-throes of old-style nationalistic thinking, with its pre-nuclear assumptions galore? My country right or wrong, drunk or sober, crazed or sane, in nuclear or non-nuclear conflict, and regardless of the merits of the issue at stake: clearly that would be tantamount to mindless patriotism. But whither the mindful patriot in today's nuclear jungle if not in frequently lonely wildernesses over against the prevailing and, at times like those fateful days leading to the Task Force's sailing, Gadarene wisdoms of the hour?

I love my country too much, the mindful patriot's credo struggles out, not to question its every move in the dangerous waters of international relations. I love my country too much to pay any heed to the calls for gunboat diplomacy in any circumstances. I love my country too much not to see her stripped of all preposterous pretence at ruling the world's waves and to regard her as one of many others in a world community whose myriad conflicting interests can only be settled now by jaw rather than war.

At times, I know, it is a seemingly lonely credo. The eventual hope of the whole Falklands episode was the discovery of so many other 'I's' turning this lonely credo into the beginnings of a faint but firm 'we' statement of conviction for the nuclear age.

It is relatively easy to write about my 1982 sea-change now; there have been many other issues since the South Atlantic episode ended and all kinds of anti-nuclear and Peace occasions have occurred to move the argument and agenda on. But never before or since have the differences of conviction within the Church been thrown into such bold relief for me. From the then Bishop of London right across the board to the naval wives and parents within our own congregation (whom I endeavoured to support and encourage through their dark hours), I became aware as if for the first time of the still very lively Just War convictions abroad in all of the mainline churches.

On one occasion recently I found myself sharing an exercise with a naval Captain at a War and Peace workshop when we were bidden to draw pretty or not so pretty pictures. I've completely forgotten the nature of my own drawing, but his was a simple rendering of Epstein's Risen Christ. 'His two hands represent our two different points of view,' he commented.

The other unforgettable eye-opener was sitting by my own father's sick-bed just after the Belgrano sinking. He was gradually slipping away from us and this was really my last deep conversation with him. Other members of our family somehow managed to be more forthright in their exchanges with father. I seldom produced anything to indicate a difference of opinion between us other than my occasional choice of tie. But in this last discussion, weak though he was, his hand came out from under the bedclothes in response to one of my Task Force observations as he said with clear and total conviction, 'You can't let anyone get away with the unlawful invasion of territory.' Other means than the Task Force option for settling the dispute we didn't consider.

A good part of the green seagull's progress, I have learnt somewhat hardly, involves the acceptance of others' differences.

The pity of it is, we caricature our positions. 'Pacifist' or 'Pro-nuke'? Take your choice. But the real debate trudges through every member of the flock - well, any member, that is, who has lived consciously through all or part of the so-called post-war era. Subsequent historians will doubtless see more clearly than we can, even years on from the Falklands, after the official ending of the Cold War, just how programmed, duped, hoodwinked and brow-beaten we became during that long, long exile in Babylon - for such it was. The trillions and trillions of wasted expenditure on the nuclear and conventional stockpiles; the huge proportion of the western world's Research and Development scientific commitment in the service of the military and the antics of the politicians whom we elected to spend our money in the cause of defending our precious islands and cherished western freedoms from the Russian Bear who was waiting to pounce on us for forty-five years: before, thank God, even at a tragically late hour, one Eastern leader had the courage to write his passionate Perestroika and cry out, 'Enough is enough.'

But just how deeply programmed and brow-beaten our whole national flock had become came home to me only last year - ten years after the Falklands, eight years after Perestroika, seven years after Chernobyl, two years after the first and almost certainly not the last of the world's resource wars in the Gulf. Fifty theological students came from London for a day in the flatlands, to sample our spirit and discover what made us tick, in a part of the world where at least 130 local firms have to do with either Ministry of Defence work or the arms industry. In the evening, under a theological college roof of all places, we met to discuss war and peace matters. I had invited a local retired Admiral to share a platform with me under, as it turned out, the watchful female chairing of our diocese's World Development officer.

The evening started with a well-prepared statement by the Admiral which basically supported our existing defence policies and commitments. Then it was my turn. Apart from the frustration of not finding the right place on a tape which was fairly crucial to my plea for alternative defence policies, I became increasingly aware of a growing restlessness amongst the student gulls. And rather to my surprise, when it came to the discussion time, far from the good

Admiral getting his comeuppance from all those free-thinking, liberated, modern young theogulls, I found myself in for one of the least pleasant roastings of my life.

It wasn't that they were all in favour of nuking Russia or blowing any potential enemy out of the water. Of course not. What bothered them - as I heard it - was the credibility of any nuclear, let alone conventional, warfare critique. For ever in my mind now when I go on a peace ticket is the telling point from a lively female gull in the front row: 'You convince me emotionally for Pacifism but not intellectually.'

I don't remember now whether it was I who introduced the 'P' word into the discussion, but very clearly from the heat of the roasting discussion *that* was the flash-word uppermost in people's minds. Such, I say, was the effect of the Cold War propaganda; it changed the colour of our minds as well as our plumage. We spent forty years or so wasting the world away in Babylonian exile. Not only were we robbed, we were thoroughly duped as well. Staggering out of crude and blatant propaganda, we still can't really believe the Exile has happened or ended. As we desperately try to find our way back to some even remotely rational vantage point, the infamous category, the origin of which goes back to another era altogether, has now surfaced mysteriously again, but only with questionable relevance to our own very different agenda. 'Pacifist' or 'Pro-nuke'? The debate has to be more subtle than that.

A year or so before the debate with the theogulls I found myself 'coming out' on the Peace subject through the long-suffering pages of our parish mag. The Focus article caused virtually no comment at all, probably because most readers were quietly thinking, 'Here he goes again, par for the course, we've heard it all before. Boring, boring.' For me, as I waited with baited breath for the lively, even red hot, responses to drop through the letter-box afterwards, it seemed an important watershed.

A good part of my defence against using Pacifism with a capital 'P' to describe my position has relied on the old historical argument: the concept belonged to the period of the First World War. Pacifists, like Suffragettes, were rooted in the early 1900s. 'Pacifism' could not possibly address the very different responses to war and peace issues required of the 1980s and '90s. As an instrument it was much too blunt to use about more or less anyone; today's very complicated war and peace agenda required something much more precise.

But, now, no sooner put than I see the hollowness of that argument. Pacifism may well have been a child of its time, but doesn't the stance it describes have ramifications and reference points relevant to any age and not least our own? Answer: yes, very probably. So what was and is the source of my unease? And now it comes home to me, almost for the first time, how extraordinarily emotive the very term 'Pacifism' is. In my case it goes right against the grain of my upbringing (not that we were a particularly warlike family), my schooling and my commando training in the Marines.

Pacifism has more to do with emotional experience than rational deductions: a state of being rather than a state of mind. For so long my whole 'being' had been persuaded that to be pacifist was to be untouchable, a pariah, a leper, someone beyond the pale of respectability and acceptability. All my past had led to the conclusion that Pacifists were wets - and weirdos as well.

Conversations over the last ten years with people in the services have convinced me that there are many peaceful and peace-loving members of the armed forces whose 'being' and way of life function on a very unwarlike basis. 'We are peacekeepers,' many people have said to me. 'Our primary task is to prevent war.' And several have confessed further, 'I didn't join the service with any idea other than to contribute to the peace of the world.' Which is why the experience of being pitched into a Falklands or Gulf war and required to fire a gun or heavy weapon with intent to kill can be so traumatic for them and their families. (We have only just begun to hear about the post-Gulf War trauma and shock experienced by many thousands of people involved in Desert Storm.)

I have the utmost sympathy, too, for all those in the front-line situations of our society and world faced by huge decisions about how to respond in the face of violence and aggression. Someone who had served five tours in Northern Ireland was speaking to me recently of the agonising problems that confronted him on patrol. 'What would you do,' he quizzed, 'facing a teenager with a rifle when it is your life or his? Worse still, what would you do when you're protecting your troops from a gang firing metal bolts from their catapults which can easily kill?' I found myself playing for time and asking all the obvious questions about loud hailer announcements, even warning shots. 'And then?' he pursued.

Pacifism can be unearthly, unrealistic. It can also be found in the most unexpected of places. The pacifist soldier and policeman exist. The time has come, surely, to move beyond the use of capitalised labels to describe fixed, entrenched positions: all Pacifists on this side, all Warriors and Aggressive Militants on that side. If my own story reveals me to be a very mixed bag of internal experience and self-argumentation, I can't be so different, it must be so for others. Even the most dedicated Just War theologian had doubts about the ethics of the Gulf War. Even the most ardent Pacifist had and still has to struggle with the question of what to do when a Kuwait is invaded, with appalling suffering an immediate consequence.

But mixtured and mixed up though we are, there still remains the basic attitudinal question: can we or can we not contemplate the use of force either in our families or in the international arena? Probably the majority of us would want to say, 'Only very reluctantly and at the very last resort.'

The Pacifist questions that 'last resort' - along with the arguments to justify nuclear deterrence and arms exhibitions because even then the price in human life is too high.

The moment the Belgrano was sunk I knew I could only belong to that group of questioners from thenceforth.

In fact, before that rather grunting apologia, I found the Chernobyl aftermath to be one of the greenest times of my life. I remember sitting slumped one cold Remembrance-time in front of the Peace Globe in Portsmouth Cathedral, following a small fracas in the Guardian newspaper with Geoffrey Taylor, one of their erstwhile feature writers. 'As a grand universal theory, pessimism is no good,' wrote Taylor in the wake of a heavily downbeat offering in the letters' column from me. I still scribble letters, with many rejections. One in four is printed, roughly. When the three others only make the wastepaper basket I try to console myself with the thought that it's being part of the debate that matters, not whether you're published; rather like the old chestnut about playing the game, not minding about winning. Which worthy counsel the unreformed bits of greenery in me still find hard to accept.

Anyway, I was sitting in this rather gloomy corner of Portsmouth Cathedral, scribbling away in the aftermath of Geoffrey Taylor's broadside on my pessimism, when I became aware of another figure who had crept in silently beside me and remained on his knees for an impressively long time. Eventually out of the corner of my eye I realised the kneeling pray-er was none other than our Bishop. There was no rebuke implied in his praying as opposed to my scribbling presence. At least, I was too dense to see it if there was. But it struck me at the time: before the peace globe some of us light our candles prayerfully, others remain inveterately scribbling. Both are necessary, I believe.

Chernobyl had happened not long before. Black pessimism seemed to stare the globe in the face - and still does. Only a fool or very stupid gull would pretend things to be otherwise, that the nuclear issue is safely over, end of story. This is how part of my scribbling came out on that episcopally presenced occasion.

———————

I have been charged with pessimism. I find myself on the receiving end of similar observations at the slightest hint of a suggestion that a lot of our present corporate hope (if such a sum of parts really exists) rests on facile optimism and illusory sleight of mind. Even approach a multi-lateralist's balloon with the hint of a pin (viz. 'Disarmament will never happen, we're far too embedded in the military-industrial research and development complex for anything to be reversed now') and the disdainful response is almost assured. On one such occasion recently a clerical colleague, whose strong suit could scarcely have been history, threw the theological book at me with a dismissive, 'You have a too low doctrine of Man' (sic); and, later over a conference meal, 'You have a too low doctrine of God, too.' From which I concluded that some constructs of our current predicament, whatever their internal provision of solace and comfort may be like, are perhaps best left undisturbed by anything approaching the facts of the matter. Except that this sealed system kind of theology is precisely the danger now.

In the group experience, however, as opposed to some one-to-one confrontations, I find that matters cannot easily be left so sealed off from reality. At just the point where nuclear discussion flags up signs that we are approaching the final synthesis (on the lines of, 'We've almost cracked this one, give us a few more years, the post-nuclear age is only just round the corner'); at just this point some visceral gasket in me seems to blow. Kill-hope I may be, but on to the carpet flows my outpouring about the abyss and the worst (and most probable) case scenario ahead.

Visceral offerings defy easy analysis. All the same, I can detect the following seven strands of reasonably identifiable pieces of gut. Their sum hardly makes for a watertight or particularly cogent theology. Their individual parts all seem crucial to me now.

A theology of pessimism:

1. Reaffirms the distinction between propaganda and truth, between alarmism or fatalism and realism.

No place here for detached stoicism or hot-headed extremism. The theological pessimist listens carefully to the hints of any prayer or insight from any source which bears the trace of the divine whisper as distinct from ideological reinforcements posing as truth (viz. the free, Christian West over against the unfree, atheistic East models of unreality). Too much propaganda on both sides of the East/West divide has passed uncriticised for too long. Now more than ever we need the sober truth, and nothing but the sober truth, about Chernobyl; but also through to the wider fears and anxieties, concerning the aspirations and weaknesses of both communism and capitalism.

2. Considers the worst case scenario rather than the facile optimism dream.

How we ever dreamt that with so many thousands of nuclear warheads in the world there would never be an accident, miscalculation, holocaust, now passes understanding. The hope which could continue to keep us on this optimistic, imaginary path, is illusory; it defies past and present evidence, it is *mauvais éspoir*, because such day-dreaming effectively blocks off the possibilities of facing the alternative. The survival of our planet now can only come from a clear-headed passion which should be forthcoming from an awareness of our terminal condition and is at present being dissipated by the false hope of an unlikely best case scenario.

3. Explores the possibilities of sharing common subconscious and dream anxiety.

Apart from occasional handling of the subject in the media, worst case planetary scenarios have been relegated to the world of sick jokes. Species or planetary end has replaced sex and individual death as taboo subject *numero uno*. For most of the time today's theology is little other than an elaborate design to prevent us bothering ourselves with any other end-thought than 'All will (somehow or other, DV) be well.' Theology has become detached from the comic and therefore the tragic. It no longer speaks to our real angst. The frequency with which we are said to reflect on sex has itself been more than adequately reflected in the reams of theological offerings about personal morality. But what is there now to minister to our quite as frequent holocaust anxiety but almost total theological silence? If nothing else, Chernobyl blows the whistle finally on the supposedly comfortable thought, willed for the most part from a pre-nuclear age, that 'it' could never really happen. If God doesn't meet me in my angst and terror, I do not meet God.

4. Looks for the hope which comes from facing corporate cancer and structural sin.

Analysing, identifying, naming our present condition, calling a corporate spade a corporate spade, will ensure against complacency and hoodwinking. The world train may be ultimately driverless but at least the attempt to sort out the sequence of events and the dread resultant effects of mutual fear and suspicion which have put us on our present track can hardly be less than worthwhile. The unholy alliance of a political-scientific-military conspiracy continues to hurtle the train forward at ever-increasing speed. Questioning the rights and roles of each member of the conspiring triumvirate can only be wholly justified. No single pull on the communication cord against the madness of the present journey is likely to stop the train. Multitudinous pulls to the would-be drivers will at least ensure that we go raging into the night. The crimes against God, which have hijacked the world's train, the structural sin which now so easily and direfully besets us, cannot be left unremarked. No reading of the Genesis account of our responsibility for the care of the planet can possibly let us off the communication cord duty. And, then, something approaching hope springs defiantly if not eternally. How so? We have only one guarantee: the human experience, even in our dire present condition, of still being able to distinguish between phoney hope based on propaganda, lies and mutual terror, and real hope earthed in a steady concern for the facts.

5. Accepts the chaos of Creation and the hopelessness of Redemption.

For too long traditional theology has overstressed the evil and wickedness of the world, on the one hand, and the need for personal salvation on the other; the order of the original creation, on the one hand, and the individual pilgrim's journey towards the haven of heaven on the other. The ecologists have reminded us of the sacredness of all life; the women's movement has signalled a heavy question-mark against any complacent acceptance that order and peace will inevitably triumph and that our planet is destined to become the heavenly Jerusalem, however long it takes to build. The chaotic potential of Creation now stares us in the face, the radioactive future hangs over us, the glory of ordered theology has departed for ever. Under that hanging cloud the cross symbol inevitably becomes the despairing last throw of God rather than the hitherto simply acceptable statement of his final triumph. God's kingdom comes to rest in the cry and anguish of the nuclear family, shielding themselves and their children yet to come from the food and water of contaminated cloud matter. In the aftermath of Chernobyl the hopelessness of God is laid bare.

6. Challenges the individualistic, pietistic moral ethic and the false Christian modesty about the pointlessness of social and world action.

St Paul: 'For we are not contending against flesh and blood, but against the principalities, against the powers, against the world rulers of this present darkness...' God's political tryst with humanity in the life, death, resurrection and ascension of Jesus, becomes the source and inspiration for today's struggle; and the struggling with him becomes for the politicised Christian the only remaining hope. No passengers on the train can stay uninvolved or detached from the unfolding nuclear drama. The experience of resurrection hope comes when the struggle seems hardest, like the unearthly taste of angel's food, like the whisper of the divine Breath. Small wonder that the heavenly vision is still so vital for us corporately.

7. Lights candles in the prevailing darkness whenever and wherever.

The only coinage of hope now worth anything comes through the cries and heartache of all who hold out for justice and peace, whatever the personal cost. As the darkness deepens their candles flicker out the little, fragile, unassuming message of the new earth and new heaven dream that will be there to the world's dying gasp and the final Breath of God for us.

Many times I have been moved at the experience of looking into the eyes of someone who acknowledges and accepts a terminal condition. Every expectation would suggest that the beholder of those eyes should find there the spirit of hopelessness and defeat. I find that it is very rarely so.

The last saving grace of a theology of pessimism lies with a simple conviction: namely, that the open acknowledgement and acceptance of our planet's terminal condition will bring with it immeasurably greater degrees of human spirit, responsibility and courage than the present fatalistic compromise with phoney hopes for the world's future can ever allow. A theology of pessimism enhances hope by accepting the abyss ahead.

———————

At no point since that piece have I really felt the need to rubbish the theology of pessimism. The nuclear problems remain long after the ending of the Cold War. Other people have certainly helped me out of my own black holes of despair, and not least those gloriously green gulls one has met on picket lines and protest marches and peace councils over the last ten years.

They have stopped now, or rather have been moved up-country to Aldershot, but for a number of years we in the flatlands used to host the bi-annual Arms Fair based on Whale Island. Amongst lavish hospitality laid on by the Ministry of Defence, potential salesgulls, almost all of them male and many of them duskily hued, used to come from round the world - Iraqi procurers well to the fore - with a view to purchasing arms and equipment for their country's defence. I used to have occasional arguments with service people in our congregation and community over the question of how far these military 'toys' were for eventual and actual 'defence' purposes. Weren't they ultimately just fuelling the world's wars, compounding the world's problems, and spilling yet more of the world's blood? Discussion remains fairly lively on the subject in these parts, with so much investment tied up in the arms trade.

Matters came to a head in September each second year when a small group of us found ourselves in the business of futile gestures. The dark clerical suit and the fisherman's smock used to have a long discussion in the wardrobe beforehand as to which should be worn for the occasion; the issue being finally settled by the growing persuasion in me that the crucial ground to be won or lost here concerned the 'ordinary' and 'middle' sections of our society as opposed to its lunatic fringes. They know about the fisherman's smock brigade outside HM's Naval establishments all over the land; they need to see more of the established dark suits, clerical or lay.

I'm not a natural placarder or marcher. Others have many more gifts in this area. A sneaking feeling of admiration came to me once at the sight of two religious placarders in Oxford Street, London and near Waterloo station. Their taut, withdrawn faces rather indicated the solitariness of their calling, as well as the hardness of the Judgement Day they both evidently felt should be proclaimed. Batty lunatic fringe or courageous minor prophets? A bit of both probably. I don't have their courage anyway.

One year the occasion outside HM establishment at Whale Island felt like Homer's Odyssey. The 'rosy-fingered morning' had barely made her presence felt over the house-tops, 'the dawn risen from her marriage-bed', before a tousled ginger-head appeared from nowhere, sandalled bare feet and all, to become my companion for the day. In the Galilean Appearance stakes his won hands and feet down over mine. Unemployed, he always seemed to put the time on his hands and sandals to good use. 'I've got time to support the things I really believe in'. We made an oddly assorted pair, as the bemused faces which passed us in their cars at the Royal Naval entrance rather confirmed.

Shortly we were joined by half-a-dozen middle-aged if not senior citizened Quakers from a market town somewhere up-country. If they'd arrived in Shaker hats and plain white spats it wouldn't have been at all surprising. 'Are you a pacifist?' one of them questioned me closely. My credentials beside hers didn't look too impressive. From their midst a brother with a leadership streak emerged; his impeccable Pacifist credentials were tested 'in the Last War', as his good wife (seated on a portable camping stool) was quick to divulge. 'We've got to get this properly organised. I vote we hold a meeting to discuss our tactics,' offered Super-Shaker - his face, unlike the more relaxed ones of his colleagues, showing the strains of responsibility. Whether it was his suggestion I don't remember, but eventually we resolved to move our picketing site to what was generally deemed to be a more advantageous pitch, aided by two burly members of the constabulary who now joined us, approaching us first with a question, clearly meant in jest. 'Are we likely to get any trouble from you lot?' A less troublesome 'lot' it would have been hard to imagine. Super-Shaker issued out the protest boards which we all duly draped round our necks. Our number had now grown to the biblical twelve. Looking along the line of us one had more than a passing suspicion that we gave every impression of trying to outbid Dad's Army. A caricature confirmed in the local press the following day - the photo taken presumably by a newsman who stopped his car at a distance from us, jumped out quickly to get his shot in, and then sped past as if to dissociate himself as quickly as possible from the act.

By now the rosy-fingered one was well advanced, the dawn from her marriage-bed had long since risen, and one dark clerical suit began to wish it had stayed behind in the wardrobe. To my surprise the passers-by were remarkably restrained in their comments. Galilean Ginger-head proved to be a fearless pamphleteer. Any form of life which appeared anywhere near us on foot, bicycle, dumper-truck, whatever, had a piece of paper outlining the purpose of our presence offered to it. '60% refuse, 40% accept - so we are communicating with some,' he calculated after a while. Sometimes we heard the passers' comments, sometimes they were reported back to us through our pamphleteer, with a delightful smile on his face. 'IRA,' some youngster shouted from the opposite pavement, indicating that he hadn't given his target too much thought or, indeed, visual study. 'What did he say?' we asked our tireless missionary on one of his return journeys after contact with a very naval-looking gentleman with a rather portly gait and a sweeping right arm movement which travelled to and fro across his personage as he strode past us on the other side of the road. 'He said our campaign was quite ludicrous and that he knew the facts.' Even the rosy-fingered lady, I guess, smiled at that one. It's remarkable, though, in view of all the unemployment and Dockyard tensions in the air, that the comments were so mild, or at least so largely unspoken. Not that we were presenting a very threatening aspect, any of us. One of the Shaker brethren wore a saintly, wouldn't-hurt-a-fly face beneath a Panama hat, another was topped out with a pork pie which gave him a strangely monklike appearance. 'Is this going to be a peaceful protest?' I remember a man from the News asking me earlier in the day. The question, with its implied suggestion that we might be hurling half-bricks or heaving paving-stones at passing Admiralty cars, did take me rather by surprise. Panamas and pork pies just don't seem to make very violent barricade-stormers.

The climax of the day - the arrival of the London Press coaches from the local railway station collection point - turned into something approaching a farce. We'd been waiting and waiting for these said coaches for sunbaked hours. A great shout went up as they rounded the corner, all our banners went aloft. But the spirit, stuffing and soul drained out of us in a trice at the discovery that only three members of the London press chose to risk the journey, which left the two fifty seater coaches with a fair number of empty places. Soon afterwards our little Community broke up and we bade each other congregational farewells, like friends of many years' standing. Picket-lines, peace presences or marches, turn tiny steps into miles.

For me the most memorable meetings of the day - apart from that with Galilean Ginger-head - had to do with two different priesthoods. One involved a young family from a Roman Catholic congregation who were professional picketeers, obviously. 'Andie and Sarah (aged four and two) are quite expert by now,' said the mother of the two in the push-chair behind her. She and father had a set, determined look on them - they'd been on this kind of pilgrimage before. 'My husband started an international Anti-Whaling lobby a few years ago,' she revealed when he was temporarily out of earshot giving the push-chair a breath of air. 'And it really works, this kind of picketing,' once again said with total conviction, as she recited her impressive catechism of achievements. 'We made one shoe firm stop buying whale oil, another said it wouldn't import any whale products, a big international combine did the same - all because one or two individuals took some action. They really do listen, you know, it really works.'

The other form of priesthood concerned the burly constabulary. Why they'd been detailed off to look after us lot I wasn't entirely clear. Surely they had better things to do with their time and energies? It can't have been to keep a check on Panama and Pork Pie in case they cut up rough or started reaching for the paving-stones.

Whatever their job specification sheet for the day actually said, the more communicative of the two clearly had his own credo. 'I believe in the beat, nothing like it. You can get lost with all your panda cars, for all I care. Nothing to replace the walkabout round the community. Criminals? I know them all! Watch their every move, just by strolling about and everyone knowing me.' Our own local bobby would have echoed his credo to the letter. The quiet disappearance of the panda car and the return to the bicycle age is the best thing that's happened in the Force for a long time. Most revealing in the picket line testimony, though, was Burly Constabulary's word about football matches. 'It's quite different on the terraces when my mate and I are on duty that end. Why? Because we know them all, their Dads, their homes. The trouble only starts when they bus in police from outside. Not when we're on, though. You can see them looking round before they start up on the "Sieg Heil" chanting - to check whether we're on.' So much for an interesting, nay vital, priesthood along the perimeters of the sacred rectangle.

'I know my sheep,' as the gospel said. Nothing to replace it. But contrary to one of his other musings, the only policeman without honour seems to be the one from another part of the country with an unknown face.

Some years later I came across Odysseus again, this time in a much more involved way. We had kept in vague touch since that day outside the Naval Establishment. In the year that followed he became very committed to a protest group on the site of a local weapons firm. I saw his occasional outbursts in the local paper and he joined us as a regular attender at our area Peace Council meetings.

Our closer involvement came as a result of a letter Odysseus received from the Borough Council informing him of the illegality of his forthcoming Peace Music Festival. Did he realise that he was planning to use Council property to stage his festival without permission, that be would be liable to arrest along with all the other organisers? We thrashed out the issue at a Peace Council meeting and then I offered to be the 'muggins' go-between and wrote a letter of concern about the whole matter to the Borough's Mayor. As I sensed things, this festival was going to take place, nothing could stop it; and yet if it went ahead on the proposed Council site a lot of innocent people could get badly hurt in the ensuing confrontations.

I don't know whether Homer was watching over our progress from then on, Gilbert and Sullivan could well have been; because at this point in the proceedings everything began to take a kind of bizarre turn not uncharacteristic of 'There is No Alternative' British society. The more Odysseus waxed about his music festival, the more the Council authorities waned in their enthusiasm for anything approaching the hint or suggestion of long-haired, layabout musical chimes. 'And you call yourselves Peace People? You make me sick,' as one Councillor vented his severely stretched spleen.

Odysseus and I were summoned on two occasions to meet the Council's various representatives, I in a resurrected former City suit, he in open-necked shirt, jeans and trainers. Through the Conciliar eye we must have once again seemed an oddly assorted couple, indeed: he, Galilean Ginger-head, with every shred of hair he possessed standing out like a very wild gorse bush; I with my collar and breast-pocket handkerchief and well-combed hair, for all the world as if I represented the Ecclesiastical Pru.

The Ecclesiastical Pru description seemed doubly apt as I noticed how several times the meeting's Chair referred to me as 'our good friend from the Church'; on at least two of these occasions he added, 'who has been offering us his mediating services in the hope that we can find a solution'. The Church as piggy-in-the-middle seemed to be the way he saw me.

On reflection this ploy could well have been an attempt willy-nilly to prise Ecclesiastical Pru apart from Galilean Ginger-head. The placatory gesture in my direction normally seemed to be a kind of prelude to further conciliar onslaught against the ranting, ridiculous Peace People of whom Odysseus seemed such a typical example. Except that along with the deferential bow in my direction for my supposed 'good offices' seemed to go an equal respect for Odysseus's intelligence. 'You're a clever man,' said the Chair grudgingly, as he sized up the far from woolly-hatted opposition in front of him.

Gilbert and Sullivan would have had a field day, yes. And the matter for dispute was precisely that: which field? Where was this Festival going to come to rest? As the arguments flew it must have dawned on most members present that, with all his unsuccessful efforts in the role of piggy-in-the-middle mediator, Ecclesiastical Pru was proving somewhat of a non-starter as a political eunuch; any divine assistance or assurance under this particular prudential policy was now clearly resting on rather shaky foundations. Some of his contributions were beginning to sound distinctly less than 'good' and 'friendly'.

Another hot outpouring from Odysseus, with equally temperatured ripostes from all sides, and he and I found ourselves walking towards the Council door with a brisk dismissal. 'Thank you, that will be all!' It felt almost like something out of a black and white 'B' movie film.

Much huffing and puffing through the local media followed these abortive meetings until the great day for the Festival arrived. Despite all the sundry forebodings and conciliar precautions (trench-digging, security patrols, and, by far the most frustrating, steadfast refusal to the end over any possible water or loo provision), the event itself could hardly have gone more peaceably and with better humour, in the circumstances anyway. Roughly two thousand people made the Festival at some stage, despite the shaky weather and the primitive conditions. All confrontations were avoided, not least because of a sane and very low-profiled police presence. My own wild surmising of another Stonehenge battle on the flatland's plain proved to be well wide of the mark, *Deo gratias*.

All credit to wily Odysseus for his realistic choice of some fields next door to the disputed area for the Festival's site which certainly took a lot of the potential steam out of the issue. To the whole Borough's sad discredit the tragedy of the event - apart from the lack of suitable facilities - was that it took place to one side of all our normal life, down a dingy path in a well-nigh abandoned wasteland, away from Market Place, High Street, Community, Church, everything. Negatively, it felt like an unacceptable pimple on the face of suburban respectability. More positively, as one listened to the night-time music and walked amongst the dozens of little groups huddled round their bonfires, it had all the feel of the Exodus people's desert experience.

No-one else was there to witness it but one moment about this little tale I shall always carry with me. Back in the council chamber for round two I found myself parked alone in a large committee room waiting to be summoned. As I sat on one of the many leathered chairs, just musing away, Odysseus suddenly arrived and came running in excitedly to sit in the chair immediately next to mine, along with his plastic bags full of files and paper cuttings which he then proceeded to pour out over my lap.

In more sober times the choice of such a proximate chair would seem remarkable. Somehow on this occasion it seemed like a mark of our mutual need of each other. Some issues just seem to make all the normal differences of dress and outlook between Ginger-heads and Prus rather beside the point.

The seasons have come and gone. In all weathers our thin little band has stood outside the Dockyard, come Ash Wednesday, come Remembrance-time. At our most spiritual times we have marked each other with a charcoal cross from the fire on the beach-head in front of the enormous black shadow of the Warrior's wooden hulk. In fact, that hulk, now part of our revered local heritage, met its own comeuppance eventually. After decades of successful warmongering - all in the unimpeachable cause of the nation's defence, naturally - the good ship Warrior at last became unseaworthy; not because of its leaking bottom parts or through wounds inflicted by the enemy, but due entirely to the activities of thousands upon thousands of little creatures boring into its woodwork. Where canon gunpowder failed, the death-watch beetle triumphed. A parable there for the peacemongering gulls, indeed.

At Remembrance-times we share our White poppies. Sometimes the sharing is a bit bashful, because of the fairly vulnerable memories some of us have of struggles not so distantly past. Red poppies are seen on the ground of our flatlands in greater profusion than most other parts, very probably. Service people past and present abound, as do Remembrance Sunday parades. It still takes a certain courage for the green peacegull to wear the white poppy amongst a sea of red.

I detected a slight waning of the Remembrance traditions in the middle and late seventies, but we're now back in the thick of them again, thanks no doubt to boosts in the Falklands and Gulf campaigns. The general sensitivity to war and peace issues has increased amongst the service personnel, I'm sure of that. A group of sailors, whom I met outside the Dockyard en route for the Gulf just before the onset of hostilities, seemed well aware of the strange role they were being called upon to play. At the same time the acceptance level of our present Defence policies and ideologies seems almost universal. Our Remembrance Sunday afternoon service for the local uniformed organisations is now always packed. Which makes the journey of any would-be white poppied, war-questioning gull flying even in a fractionally different direction fairly hard graft, to put it mildly.

At Ash Wednesday times, along with a few other madcapped gulls, I have customarily stood, with a big purple banner bearing the one word REPENT on it at the Dockyard gates. This fairly useless gesture has brought forth a range of gesticulating responses from members of the travelling public as they've passed. The odd friendly thumbs up has been more than evenly matched by finger signs of a well-known kind indicating something other than friendliness and sympathy. I liked the man who came up with an embarrassed apology one year. Pointing up to my REPENT banner he said, 'When I first saw it I thought you were in the decoration business.' But I guess the current conventional defence wisdoms and policies require rather more than the respray treatment he was suggesting.

Let the final word of the Kill-hope's confessions provide something by way of a sting in the tail for all Christian gullery. Whale Island again, and I happened to be one of the only eye-witnesses of Astrid's arrest after what the paper described as the staging of her 'noisy protest'.

In view of the ear-splitting sound of low-flying craft scything - and showing off shockingly - through the skies above at intervals during the Exhibition, as heard from miles around, the charge was ironical, indeed. Astrid's 'noisy protest' involved the beating of a single drum and the singing of a chanted mantra.

We had crossed at low tide to Whale Island a few days previously, prior to the Exhibition's opening, for a picnic sharing, under the watchful eyes of the police and military.

Astrid's crime was that she chose to attempt the same crossing during the near sacred rituals in the Exhibition's temples of worship. While the rest of us stood silently at a safe distance before the wondering eyes of the arriving worshippers, Astrid chose to be more activist. She had had previous arrest experiences, she knew the risks. Off eventually she was swept in the police van to spend a day in the cells whilst the rest of our evidently more programmed presence later dispersed to attend to our daily round.

'I have people I can't let down,' I found myself muttering from deep within my becassocked defence system, in answer to my peaceful neighbour's query as to whether we should follow suit with a solidarity gesture on behalf of our arrested colleague. Heavy deflection from the diary's demands is hard to entertain, even on the Christian picket-line.

Some six hours later Astrid was released, collected from her cell and homed again by members of our peace presence. Another futile gesture, or was it? She just happens to be a Buddhist nun.

Astrid helped to restore my belief in the efficacy of useless gestures.

July

August

CANDLES IN THE DRAUGHT

The media is forever trying to persuade us that charismatic leaders make history rather than people movements, and not the other way round. In the instances already quoted, Wat Tyler, rather than the thousands of 'peasants' around him, ended the fourteenth century's poll tax. A chastened but for ever cool and calm Michael Heseltine brought its twentieth century equivalent formally to a close, rather than the citizens of an outraged Britain. Gorbachev's Perestroika and leadership ended the Cold War, rather than the voices and cries of many millions of people around him.

The green seagull doesn't accept this interpretation of history. Like everyone else she or he sits in front of the box, listens to the radio, reads the paper or periodical, picks through the bulletins' entrails. The highly edited, arbitrarily selected newscasts are fed relentlessly into our systems all. Some independent-minded gulls refuse to have anything to do with the media circus, choosing instead to listen to the messages on the wind if not from their walkmans.

I was never entirely happy with the counsel of Harvey Cox, the American theologian, who in his Secular City days stated very clearly that he'd have nothing to do with the telephone at home. He simply didn't have or bother with the damned thing. I know the phone can be massively invasive but to put oneself beyond the reach of outside messages is, in my view, a bit on the arrogant side. Alright, people can write, they can visit rather than intrude with the phone. All the same, the marooning away from every possible message on the wires came strangely in Cox's otherwise massively impressive plea on behalf of the un-Godforsaken City.

Switch off, unplug, forget the world: or handle the news as presented with the greatest of care, and perhaps with *the* greatest care when it comes to the most respectable parts of it, even those with the most thoroughgoing credentials. That seems to be the choice. When the 'World at One' programme on Radio 4 finishes with its incredible end-line, 'And that's the world at 1.40pm,' I always want to add, 'Apart from the millions of stories you haven't mentioned, I guess you're about right.' Green seagulls need to do their own heavy sieving with all critical faculties alert. On which side of the barricades were the cameras? Through whose eyes was that reported? Was this really the story? What was edited on to the cutting-room floor?

The people movement version of history needs time to surface, to be sure. And perhaps nowhere more so than where news of any kind is hard to come by, in any case.

In this chapter I look at one particular part of the world which I've been fortunate enough to visit twice: Russia. We now know something of the enormous economic pressures the Soviet Government was under to bring the Cold War to an end in the mid-1980s. We know of Mikhail Gorbachev's crucial role in humouring the grizzly old Russian bear. Since 1945 that bear has become armed to the teeth like its American preying counterpart, with between them an armoury large enough to blow the world to pieces at least fifty times over.

By chance my second visit to Russia came during the crucial year of 1985, when Soviet policies reached their watershed. After much inner tension and crisis during that year, the Politburo eventually resolved to wind the war game down and cry 'Enough is enough'.

From the way all the subsequent summit meetings and treaties were reported, a visitor to the planet could be forgiven for thinking that only two people were involved. And but for their far-sighted and visionary desires for the world's peace, nothing would have been achieved at all; no SALT Agreements, no nuclear weaponry treaties eventually, no end to the Cold War itself or the destruction of the Berlin Wall. Were Presidents Reagan and Gorbachev pushed or did they jump? The extra-terrestrial visitor could be forgiven for thinking that it must have been their sole, unaided initiatives and efforts which 'jumped' the peace process into action.

Obviously, the leaders of the flock play a role. But perhaps only subsequent historians will be able to detect just how far the flock itself was responsible for altering the course of things in the instance of the Cold War's end. We heard much in the media about the peace movements of the UK, Europe and the US; but virtually nothing about the enormous commitment of the movement for peace in the former USSR. Economics may have driven Gorbachev and the Politbureau. It's my belief that millions of green seagulls 'pushed' them, too.

Since the Falklands' chapter I have found myself involved in a number of anti-nuclear protests. On all occasions the thing which has come quietly and sanely through to me has been the gentle sensitivity of my fellow-walkers and companions. During the October, 1983 Cruise protest in London I remember standing for what seemed like an age in the huge sea of people along the Embankment as we waited for the start of the procession. Immediately in front of me in the ocean was a family which included three youngsters, none of whom could see much more than the skirts or trousers of those around them. Listening to their talk about potties and bananas and drinks made the whole occasion feel strangely familiar. No way was this the batty, woolly-hatted brigade. Later in the same procession I walked briefly with another Mum (or, maybe, guardian because of the difference in her charge's colour). It was on the tip of my tongue to ask whether the child was hers. As if reading my thought and taking it on further she commented, 'It's her future, that's why I'm here.' And there she was, at most two and a half feet of her, plaits and all, singing and clapping away as we strode into Trafalgar Square.

It's the incidentals, the sub-agenda, which come home on these protest occasions; the reassuring looks and odd remarks, too, all of which seem to confirm the worthwhileness of the journey, the existence of much other green seagullhood. There are many ways to peace, no doubt, and it's nothing less than tragic arrogance for any peace movement to assume that its way is especially by divine right. But, still, to find other kindred spirits amongst so many different members of the flock is hugely encouraging. What others say in a crowd or conversation or by letter or in the press is so often balm for the soul.

One Sunday morning I remember going out from our Family Eucharist to a US air base twenty or so miles up the road. There was nothing unusual or remarkable about the occasion - the same tents and fires and cups of tea and smoky conversations were all in evidence - until the time came for us to walk up to the perimeter wire of the base. How, exactly, it happened, I can't exactly say, but as we approached the perimeter, one or two friends asked me to conduct a short service. The contrast between the highly structured church service I had just come from, with its books and clearly ritualised progress, and this completely unstructured, open to the winds kind of 'worship', could not have been more obvious. In the event we stood round in a circle, held hands, sang 'We shall overcome', kept silence, and put some symbolic sprays of flowers in the circle's centre. I felt then and have felt subsequently on one or two other similar occasions the sense of returning to something very simple far back at the human dawn. Whatever else, the anti-nuclear protest brings out the simplicity of our basic common agenda; when survival is the common concern a lot of the normal liturgical super-structures and the need for the same fall away. The songs to express the voice of the people shouldn't need sheets.

As time moved on, I found my peace and church commitments had come together in a madcapped scheme which eventually involved the mailing of a letter to the Metropolitan of Minsk, inviting him to send a representation of Russian Orthodox church members to Portsmouth Cathedral's November Remembrance-time. The letter was sent near the last day of the year and for the next three months the silence was deafening. Until suddenly a reply came back inviting me to go over to Moscow to discuss the project further, with barely three weeks to organise everything. I understand that's par for the Russian hospitality course.

What follows is the attempt to describe at least part of a people's peace-making process, at the dawn of Glasnost and Perestroika. Let me precede it by saying that it was my good fortune, quite by chance, to have one of the greatest green seagulls of all as my travelling companion on the Moscow flight: Arthur Scargill. He had a stinking cold, but to my surprise seemed more than willing to talk throughout the journey. His copy of 'Private Eye' for the week in question had a cartoon of himself on a catafalque in place of the Russian leader Chernenko, who had just died. The end of the miners' strike was only a few weeks old and by all reckonings he should have felt utterly defeated. Through his voluminous pile of Kleenexes, and allowing for whistling-in-the-dark bravado talk, I got a very different impression of him. He seemed more than ready to talk about his home roots, the new-found role of his wife and of many other mining wives during the strike, as well as his own passionate convictions about nuclear disarmament. 'What does it feel like,' I asked, 'to find yourself constantly cast in a demonic role?' By way of reply he instanced the experience (known to many other green seagulls) of going into a public meeting or gathering and feeling the hatred and animosity beaming out through every eye present and then, after a few loosening stories and jokes, seeing with some degree of relief those same uptight faces gradually relaxing their muscles into a smile, even eventually a laugh. Some green seagulls have their greenery thrust upon them.

Contrary to some media speculation, Arthur Scargill was not fleeing his British nest of defeat and shame with a view to a Communist migration; he was addressing a Soviet miners' delegation rally and, to my amazement, intended to return home the following evening. My own motivations for a Soviet trip were less precise. Apart from a general desire to return to Russia after an interval of some twenty-five years, I had long felt the whole extraordinary East-West confrontation to be based on mutually illusory assumptions, such a welter of figmentary half-truths and false perceptions, that anything any individual or group could do to expose these to the test of something approaching reality would be of value in however small a way. For this venture I had hoped to travel with my eldest son and a Cathedral colleague. But in the absence of their visa provision being allowed, one of the two vacant seats on the airplane had obviously been snapped up in a fairly last minute fashion by the secretariat of the NUM. Hence my Scargullery tale.

When we eventually landed in Moscow my green seagull companion was whisked away by officialdom, leaving me and the rest of the passengers to face the long exit queue. After what felt like an interminably long time two lads scrutinised me, again for what seemed an age, through their glass screen. Their uniform gave them a military appearance but their faces had all the marks of vulnerability. My passport was clearly giving them problems. Both of them sat wrapped over it as if in meditation. Every now and then their four eyes looked up and stared unblinkingly at me. One of them held up the passport eventually, to show me the photo, with his forefinger indicating disbelief. Is this really you? seemed to be his question. As I came to reflect on it myself, the photo, taken some years back - well, only two actually - did raise some identity problems.

More meditation followed. The large queue behind me grew increasingly curious and restless. My immediate successor in the queue turned out to be a wag, though, with clear experience of the system. 'It's all quite normal,' he kept indicating in a jovial way which helped me relax considerably.

Eventually the long meditation came to an end and a button was pressed. The intention of the button-presser obviously was to let me through the exit gate and on to the next stage of the Customs procedure. But to both the lads' surprise the pressing of the button produced no result at all. The exit gate stayed firmly shut. More buttons and knobs were pressed from deep in the recesses of their little booth, with both lads now indicating clear concern at this simple technological failure.

Rather more agitated meditation now, until a phone was eventually picked up to report the matter down the line. The phone was replaced and both lads rose immediately, switching out the light of the booth as they left through the curtain. The bewildered company behind me were left to find their way to another queue, while I was beckoned to follow the senior of the military-looking lads.

To my great surprise he took me, not to a detention centre as part of me was beginning to expect, despite the light-hearted banter of my friendly neighbour, but through a large iron gate, releasing the problematical passport as he went with a wave on to the next stage of the system.

My mind went back to a previous entry into the Soviet Union, this one far more dramatic. We were travelling by bus, a double-decker one, this time. At the Brest-Litovsk border-point we had to pass under a triumphal arch of flags which had clearly not been built for the likes of double-decker buses. Our driver, the son of the inventor of the hovercraft as I recall, had brought us painstakingly all this way from England and showed no signs of quailing at the challenge now in front of him with this beflagged *arc de triomphe*. With a great roar of his engine he went at the task with such verve and determination that the whole arch was lifted bodily out of the ground until it landed with flags and all in a great crash ahead of us. It wasn't exactly the most respectful entry into the Great Union of Soviet Republics.

No doubt the lads had something to report down the line that day, as well.

But the queue for the passport check had nothing on the Customs line. Once again the boyishness of the officials was notable, although they operated without their hats for some reason this time and, maybe because of this, with their youth more emphasised than ever. Once again there were technological problems with the screening equipment. After a longish period of unhurried meditation, once again a phone call eventually produced an older official who seemed as puzzled as his protégés. The thick queue grew more restless, not helped by the arrival of more travellers from Frankfurt who infiltrated themselves into our ranks to general cries of protest.

While the customs staff struggled with the screening crisis - except that it wasn't that, it was just a small hitch which could one day be sorted out, don't worry, we've got all the time in the world - two girls who seemed to be involved in the Customs' ritual sat down on their inspection table showing remarkably little indication that this small technical hitch was anything but utterly 'normal', too.

When my turn eventually came - after a good hour - the lad seemed only interested in one question. 'Have you brought any roubles or bibles?' My visage and answers didn't convince him obviously and so he went through my case and hand luggage closely. 'Any bibles, any roubles?' and at one point for good measure, 'Any political pamphlets?'

It was the best possible introduction, this whole entry into the USSR, to the custom of apparently timeless queuing as part of the web of Soviet life.

But Mstislav (pronounced Meeshlaav, roughly anyway) was there to greet me. 'Moscow Patriarchate', he had written on a piece of red paper. 'The dog collar helped me to recognise you,' he said jovially. 'I'm very sorry to have kept you waiting so long,' I apologised. 'No problem,' he said, 'it's just the system.' I was to see the broad shrug of his shoulders and hear his big laugh of dismissal many more times during my stay.

The hotel was vast, with high and elaborately decorated ceilings and huge hanging lights at every turn. 'This was built after the Revolution, in the same style as the famous restaurant where we are now.' An evening meal was in process as we arrived. A lot of youngsters and families helped to make the enormous dining-room look reasonably full. Suddenly the air was filled with the deafening sound of dance music, the signal for everyone to take to the floor rather than attempt further conversation.

Mstislav struggled to continue answering some of my questions. 'American music?' I offered at one point, a trifle teasingly. 'No,' he parried, 'it's general music, isn't it?' Despite the dancing invasion he seemed surprisingly ready to discuss the weaknesses and failings of the Soviet system. At first I couldn't help feeling that his frankness might be because of the music. I could barely hear, sitting a foot away from him, so what chance for the KGB ears, possibly, on the next table? But gradually I came to realise that this was fantasy: Mstislav was genuinely open and ready to discuss, wherever we were and with or without the deafening accompaniment. The only time I noticed he baulked somewhat was at my suggestion in Red Square after we'd come out of the obligatory GUM (State) shop visit. 'Could we just have a brief interview together here with my tape-recorder?' 'Another time,' he replied as he steered me back towards our car, 'otherwise we shall be late for the Monastery.'

Whether it was because my responses in the dining-room to his dissertations about the nature of Soviet and Orthodox philosophy were becoming increasingly senseless, or not, Mstislav eventually dried up. Maybe the music defeated even him. He and Tatiana, who worked at the Church's Publicity Department, made it clear that Lenten observance prevented them from dancing. Every now and then there was a brief pause between the dance numbers, allowing for a quick question and answer; otherwise we spent the rest of the meal gazing round the room and, in my case at least, exploring the remarkable decorations above. As if reading my thoughts, Mstislav threw in the odd bits of between-the-dances details: 'A very fashionable pre-revolutionary restaurant this... Rasputin was involved in a scandal here, did you know?... Those people up in the balcony? They are diners, too.'

The hotel was used by the Church quite heavily, it would seem. I'd seen several bearded and be-cassocked characters in the corridors and even bumped into a splendiferous Metropolitan of Kiev in the front hallway. 'Good day to you,' he said as I struggled uncertainly into something between a bow, kneel and embrace by way of a greeting. From Mstislav's impeccable responses I gathered now that anything from an Archimandrite upwards should be given the kissing of the hand treatment; which from then on I learnt to perform with reasonable dexterity.

Some more study of the glass-clinking rituals in the dining-room indicated that every re-charge of the wine-glass ('but not beer,' my thought reader reminds me) merited a clink all round. The politenesses of the dance invitation routine seemed to be observed meticulously, as well: even by one over-enthusiastic male who prowled the whole room looking for partners, with a rather gauche but terribly gallant wave of the hand and bow as he approached each very suspecting female. Most of those on the receiving end of his invitations obviously knew his advances fairly well. But he was so keen I even found myself holding my breath as he passed our table, half expecting him to invite me to the dance-floor in sheer desperation.

I wished Mstislav goodnight as he left for his house a few steps away up the street. Snow was still thickly piled on the side-walks ('it snows here from October till April') and the streets seemed extraordinarily dark at night. No lighting seemed to be provided for any but the main streets.

I retired to my room, No 328, past the floor attendants who kept changing shift, perhaps guard as well, with great regularity. Did they just do three hour stints and then go home, or did they do other jobs? Their impenetrable facial expressions left me wondering.

Some of Mstislav's facts and figures kept pounding away in my mind. 'We have no unemployment here in the Soviet Union, everyone works - or is supposed to' - the last throwaway comment said with one of his teasing smiles. I don't suppose he'd be so sure or smiling now.

'You keep asking about the numbers in the churches. We don't count them. It's impossible to know. There are 17 million Communists - or there are supposed to be 17 million Communists - in our country' (said with the same slightly mocking smile). 'There are about 50 million Orthodox believers, say, the average between an estimated 30 or 70 million, though who's in the Church you can never tell.' Once again, no doubt the patter of statistics has had to adjust a bit since Glasnost and the official demise of Communism.

Is the Church persecuted? 'The persecutions are exaggerated. Since Kruschev's time the Church and State have got on alright and understand each other.'

How many believing people are there in the Soviet Union? 'We have Baptists, Roman Catholics, Lutherans, Jews, Muslims, Buddhists - not Anglicans, but lots of others.' So two or three out of five people in the Soviet Union would claim some religious affiliation? 'Yes, that's true.'

I wondered whether Mstislav's employment by the Moscow Patriarchate hadn't perchance deafened him a little to the cries of the persecuted Church. It might well be that my base-line question about the relation between the official Church and the underground Church could not be altogether answered. Is Holy Mother Russia now really within the acceptance of the official Kremlin ideology? Are many of her dissident children still shut away out of earshot in places like the former Lubianka prison?

And was it a Freudian slip that made Mstislav forget to point out to me the Lubianka prison site when we passed it in the car on the way to Red Square, despite my request that he should? But on another occasion he proudly quizzed me on our IRA problem. 'Our country would solve Northern Ireland in a fortnight,' he beamed.

Metropolitan Philaret surprised me with his keen questions about the proposed visit of the Orthodox delegation. At first the matter for surprise was the way he kept yawning and stroking his long beard. But Mstislav later pointed out to me that the Metropolitan had just come off the overnight train from Minsk. 'It's 800 kilometres away and he does the journey overnight twice a week.'

His diocese is probably the size of Great Britain and he has no assistant bishops. 'You keep asking me about numbers... I should say there are at least 10 million people in his diocese. He is responsible for 369 parishes and has the charge of the Foreign Relations Department of the Moscow Patriarchate.'

I stumbled through all the greetings and gifts I had brought. Tea and chocolates were brought in and I noticed how the Metropolitan tucked into the latter with a verve. Every now and then he got up to ring someone at his desk and I began to fear for the rest of our time together. But then, helped possibly by the chocolates, he stopped yawning and really concentrated on the business to hand, with clear and precise questions at every point.

Later in the day at the St Daniel Monastery in Moscow I noticed the same careful handling of my questions by the Archimandrite in charge. Since 1982 the Church had been granted the redevelopment rights of a large piece of land, near the centre of Moscow, for the whole Monastery with its complex of cathedral, churches, new offices and buildings (with even two old factories pulled down to make way for the exciting new project). 'Yes, it is a time of great hope for the Church', said the Archimandrite whom I liked and warmed to enormously. My question about one side of the Church's role - 'Does the Church ever criticise the State?' - he parried rather defensively; but still he found it possible to give me a bear-hugging embrace as I took my leave. Earlier I had laughed with him about my surprise at not finding the bear-hugs I had more than partly expected everywhere. His hug was another careful answer to my question.

I left the Metropolitan's office after a possible over-stay of welcome to the extent, as I quickly discovered in the corridor, of at least two archimandrites, as well as a Bishop and his chaplain, not to mention a fluttering of assorted other cassocks. No chairs in the corridor, everyone stood - as they do for worship. 'Would you say that the iconostasis screen in your churches separates the clergy from the laity, the priests from the faithful?' Yes, Mstislav says. To my amazement, too, the Metropolitan had kindly agreed to see me again in a couple of days' time.

5.30pm on Tuesday, 26th March, 1985. As on any other weekday of the year, Vespers was being sung at the Patriarchate Cathedral with a hundred or so in the congregation, partly gathered round a chanting deacon who seemed to rattle through a lot of prayer, for all the world as if he were auctioning tobacco or cattle. No pews or seating constraints hindered other members of the congregation from walking the icon routes or finding some appropriate bit of ground to kiss or lighting a candle or simply standing and crossing themselves repeatedly. 'For a Eucharist, yes, the building would be full.'

'Round these corners as well?'

'Of course.'

Up in the minstrels' gallery behind, one could dimly detect the Vespers' choir who broke into the auctioneer's chanted patter when they were allowed to, which didn't sound like very often. The whole building was heavy with gold and icons. Earlier, in the new Monastery's icon-making room, I was firmly put in my place by the Monk and my eager thought reader: 'I'm sorry, Father David, you cannot take any of our old icons out of the country without the State Department's permission.'

Later Mstislav reminded me, nay rebuked me, for my lack of charity. He only seemed to call me 'Father David' when he made a firm point of what turned out to be a limiting kind. 'Shall you need the car tonight again, Father David, or shall you not?' No Fatherly preambles this time but, as if to soothe my Protestant hackles over the auctioneer, he threw out over his shoulder from the front of our car: 'The chanting is better, isn't it?'

'One goes as a pilgrim to other churches, don't you find?' I say rather lamely in response.

5.30pm, Tuesday 26th March, 1985. But it could have been any day, any time - as the Archimandrite at St. Daniel's reminded me, too. 'The Church worships God eternally.'

The GUM shop came as no real surprise; although its size and the thickness of the crowds seemed quite as bewildering as they must have done 25 years ago. Then I tackled the fur counter. This time, with a more environmentally up-to-date hat on, I was much less ambitious and settled for a few items of the wood trade; with the awful feeling afterwards that 20 of my preciously acquired roubles could have been far better spent elsewhere. 'It's roughly £20,' as my thought reader uncomfortably reminded me.

There was more colour in the clothing, some of it, with occasional flurries of style, and a greater range of goods generally, than I recalled before. But, hang it, this was 'downtown Moscow', in Mstislav's repeated map reference phrase. And comparing GUM with London's West End stores seemed an embarrassing exercise. The bareness and the brownness and the shoddiness and the general lack of finish hit one in the eye on all sides. 'But you mustn't judge us by your criteria. Our criteria are different. Our history, our culture, are different.' Full-stop, end of embarrassing exercise.

On another occasion: 'Besides, the countries of Western Europe are very difficult for Russians to live in or find acceptance in: which is why so many of our defectors return eventually.'

Perhaps Russians abroad hunger for the trudge of the crowds and the crushing round the Metropole entrances in the peak hours ('Rush hours? No, we call them peak hours'). The sheer loneliness must defeat most émigrés. 'There are well-established Russian Communities in Australia, in Canada, even in America; but not in European countries.'

We agreed that if your name is Solzhenitsyn or you're a famous ballet dancer and have a recognised community in the reception country, that's one thing; but if you're a couple of private soldiers fleeing from the action somewhere on some bleak frontier of the Empire, then that is quite another.

There were far more cars here than I remember before. But most Russians still seemed to trudge everywhere - and for six months of the year on icy side-walks.

Tatiana was there to greet us at the Publicity Department. She was very personable and I noticed her warmth towards Mstislav and,

by the end of our visit, her warmth towards me (and mine to her).
She and Mstislav have much more humour on them than the
conventional Russian myth might suggest. Russians are chess players
rather than poker players; they work from step to step, whether it's
building a new monastery or arranging an official visit from their
country. But there's humour in the chess-playing evidently, too. In
Mstislav's case, he so often spoke with a roar of laughter and one of
his big shrugs. 'We shall see. If I don't know I can't tell you. No
problem. We shall see.'

Tatiana's humour seemed more playful, although Mstislav
frequently left me wondering whether my leg had been pulled without
my realising it. 'I'm only teasing, Father David.' He and the car
driver, Alexander, who wore his big Russian cap at a slight angle, had
a good laugh in the front seats every now and then; I wondered at the
possibilities of humour they found in their curious visitor behind.
'What are you laughing at?' I found myself saying. 'It is nothing,
just something of no importance, Father David.' The limiting factor
at work again, possibly.

In Tatiana's case the humour took a slightly edged turn. 'You
could have brought in your tape-recorder, but you didn't.' 'You could
have sent us some examples of your Diocesan magazine, but you
didn't.' She said it with a playful smile and eyes, but with just a hint
of how-unorganised-you-British-people-are in the not so distant
background, as well.

She was proud of their new building. This, coupled with the
proposed Foreign Relations Department just nearing completion on the
St Daniel's Monastery site, was a sign of the detectable new spring in
the Church's step. 'When will the building be finished?' I asked the
young, elegantly coiffeured monk with his sartorial cassock worn
rather like a kimono, who was showing us round. The question was
asked as we trudged through the slurried chaos of a building site that
seemed to stretch for miles ('About 6 hectares,' in fact). 'In two
years,' said the monk. 'What are you laughing at?' he asked. 'You
don't believe me?' While on our progress through the slurry a worker
came up wearing a protective hat made out of a piece of Pravda,
which he hurriedly removed before half-kneeling to kiss the monk's
hand. The gangways, stretching right to the top of the huge Cathedral
dome, seemed unbelievably flimsy. A worker passed overhead and a
pile of mud droppings descended on us; no comment from the monk

or Mstislav. 'How many have lost their lives on this site?' I was tempted to ask but didn't.

Tatiana showed us the pictures on the Publicity Department's walls. Mstislav had obviously seen them many times, so wandered on ahead. 'You take the remembrance of those who died in the Wars very seriously.'

'But of course. War is a serious business.' Once again, there was the slight suggestion that only the Russian people appreciate the point.

'But look at this child here standing next to all these clergy. She's a member of Komsomol, and yet here she is next to the Church. How can that be?'

'War makes no distinction between atheists and believers. If war comes...' Her sentence was left unfinished. We had a very playful exit with hand-kissing and embracing. But I was left wondering whether Tatiana would have liked to finish her sentence with the sentiment that any war would be 'our' fault. Just for me to think about, in case I hadn't before.

From the Journal of the Moscow Patriarchate one really gets the impression that Patriarch Pimen, who has since died, was the most peace-loving person in the world. Every sermon and speech he delivered was studded with references to peace and the cause of peace. But just when I was about to close the journal in total admiration and praise, a passage like this sprang out from the page: 'We are deeply satisfied that this desire of our people for peace, for ridding mankind of nuclear and other annihilating weapons, finds due expression in the consistent peace-loving policy of our government. An irrefutable proof of this is the invariable readiness of the USSR to negotiate on just principles and its constant peace initiatives which find positive response among wide circles of the world public. We trust that the goodwill of our people and of our government will meet in the end due understanding on the part of those statesmen who are responsible for the fate of their nations, but who are deaf to them at present.'

Mstislav was merciless in his leg-pulling about the unlikelihood of ever hearing over the BBC station ('which we can get normally') that there had been a Revolution in Britain and that all members of the House of Lords had been incarcerated and the Chinese People's Republic had taken over as the one lawful government.

In response, it was clearly time to test out Mstislav on Pimen's own apparent deafness to the possibility of even a margin of error in his government's approach to the peace-making process. Does the Church really have to pay such court to the State's peace-loving infallibility?

It was a lively breakfast together, broken by the arrival of two or three of his colleagues from the Foreign Relations Department. I was fast beginning to think of their hotel building as a glorified Church House establishment. The rooms were huge and spacious, well equipped except for minor blemishes like missing basin plugs; the food was good and well served. The Orthodox Church looks after her clergy and visitors in style. Money? Roubles? I asked about the coffers of the church. 'No problem.'

'Is the Church supported by the State?' That has become one of our little jokes together. He used to answer it heatedly. Now Mstislav no longer bothered.

What really sparked him into an extraordinary outburst, even before we'd had a mouthful of breakfast, was when I showed him the offending paragraph of the Patriarch's speech. At first he read it through slowly, his finger travelling along the line to make quite sure he'd got the general gist of the matter, and then reading on a little further, no doubt to make sure of the context.

A brief period of silence and then, with that quizzical, semi-humorous look which I'd come to expect of him whenever he found my thought processes hard to follow, he asked, 'And what is your problem?'

Before I'd had time to state what was in my mind he continued, at first calmly but gradually getting more and more excited.

'Well, yes, I'd query one or two things in Pimen's words. The reference to those who are "deaf" to peace is a trifle unfortunate, in terms of history anyway. Because it was the Russians who walked out of the last Arms Talks, wasn't it? But what you Westerners just cannot understand is that Pimen speaks for the people and so does our government. Our people are not like you much-travelled Westerners with all your beliefs in a plural world. We're bus drivers and workers, we're not intelligentsia' (this last almost said with disdain or derision). 'Take our driver. Do you think he can understand what's going on in the wider world? No, of course not. And so he trusts Pimen and he trusts our government in its search for peace. Pimen belongs to the people and our government belongs to the people. You've got to understand, we're a vast country, with 15 republics and 100 different languages. Don't judge us by your democratic criteria. Is it really so surprising to you that the Church and the State stay in harness together - for peace?'

His friends' arrival prevented any further flow. Perhaps it was just as well because I had more than a passing awareness of finding my own 'problem' either not being addressed at all or being made to look like a minnow in a whale-sized pool.

To Zagorsk, through the unremarkable Muscovite suburbs, past the great Economic Exhibition which brought back so many 1959 memories. 'It was popular in the fifties and sixties but now - well, it's lost its novelty a bit.' New to me, though, was the huge Telecommunications tower ('about the largest in the world') and the Monument to the Astronauts which soars into the sky with a grace and thrust that is at once impressive and moving. The graceful, thrusting 'soar' could be interpreted as a very aggressive symbol, but its spirituality, the human quest for transcendence, said something to me, too. 'A wonderful symbol', as the Metropolitan said yesterday with a dancing eye, when I showed him the rather travel-weary dove made by some of our local children as a gesture of peace and friendship. The sheer grace of that upward thrust had something of real wonder about it, too.

I guess I had prepared myself for possible disappointment at Zagorsk, the home of Holy Mother Russia as it's sometimes known. The original monastery was founded by St Sergius in the fourteenth century on the site of a 'holy water' spring. Was this going to be just another tourist attraction visit? I fell in love with it as a student. Surely, today's visit could only bring a rather jaundiced eye to what on earth had been the cause of such smittening all those years ago?

On the way Mstislav pointed out the churches with just one or two words. 'Functioning', for those still open or in business. 'Not functioning', for those which were neither. For a building once used for worship, in some cases for centuries, now to be used as a museum, evidently presented him with 'no problem'.

And on the way, as if reading my thoughts again, he provided me with the present run-down of Moscow's 'functioning' churches: 'forty-five Orthodox, one Baptist, one Roman Catholic, one Adventist, one Synagogue, one Mosque, four Old Believers.

Altogether in the Moscow region there are a further 132'. The
arithmetic of the matter was rather beyond me.
'The Old Believers?'
'They're 17th Century off-shoots of the Russian Orthodox.'
'And are all the churches full?'
'Of course.'
Zagorsk itself seems to be a microcosm of the Russian Church's
history. For centuries it produced priests, monks, icons, frescos,
prayer, liturgy, millions of faithful. Then in the years after the
Revolution, 'up until the War', it was closed completely. And now it
has risen again, full of pilgrims, visitors, students, icon restorers; and
is still rising.

The deputy Rector of the Academy entertained us very splendidly,
with apologies for the fish diet of the monastery but before a table
immaculately set out and with three more courses still to come. The
Academy has 520 students who stay for four years. It is one of three
theological seminaries in the USSR (the others being at Leningrad and
Odessa). 800 correspondence course students are on the books. At
least 1,800 students are currently training for the priesthood or
monastic life. 'We have three ordained orders: monks, celibate and
married clergy.' Only the celibate clergy can become Bishops or
Metropolitans.

I looked round at the large week-day congregation as they heard
the sermon part of the liturgy, with frequent crossing (the Orthodox
are the most manual branch of the church by far, as well as the most
dramatic - to judge anyway from the floor and icon kissing). So
frequent and regular is the crossing through the congregation, it
became abundantly clear that the vast bulk of people present were
pilgrims rather than passengers off the tourist bus, and pilgrims of all
ages. The singing and chanting had a natural wail and joy to them.
In fact, Orthodox worship generally has a ducks taking to water feel
about it. No books; priests miles away up behind their iconostasis for
half the time at least ('It's traditional, that's all'); icons so thick and
fast around every nook and cranny, to cramming and dizzying points:
more or less every canon of Protestant liturgical understanding broken
to smithereens, and a good many Catholic ones, too - and yet, damn
it, the Orthodox worship remains as natural and easy as falling off a
log. Without so much as a by-your-leave, Mstislav went off to kiss St
Sergius's remains through the pane of glass over his tomb; while next

to me our student guide joined in the wail of intercession led by the priest at the foot of the tomb. In between his offerings and during the congregational response various hands reached out to him with pieces of paper and rouble notes.

The clergy's cassocks were downright beautiful: exquisitely made all of them, styled and fitted, with varying decorative touches depending on the rank and importance of the wearer. It's only a small consideration, but it seemed to speak volumes about a Church confident of its place 'in the social system' (another of Mstislav's 'no problems') and of its roots in and near the people. 'How much are the cassocks?'

'100 Roubles - paid for by the Church, of course.'

Ahead of me as I sat on one of the few wooden seats was a cowed babushka. She seemed to be kissing the floor for a great length of time but eventually got up and made her way through from near the iconostasis where she'd been worshipping to hear the preacher's sermon. He stood close to the people, without notes, having emerged through one of the iconostasis doors. Throughout his remarks he kept crossing himself and the congregation followed suit. The old babushka made her way towards him. It was only as she steered steadily towards my brief-case on the ground that I realised she was blind.

Zagorsk left me too full of wondering questions to be disappointing.

Vespers at four parish churches in Moscow: St Nicholas (built in 1682), St John the Soldier (1712), The Joy of all Sorrows (1790) and St Nicholas (1681): in all cases the service lasts, almost every evening, from 6.0 to 9pm. There's a constant coming and going, purchasing of candles from booths at the back of each of the churches, as well as lighting and tending of candles by the ever present babushkas, who seem especially on hand to deal with these tokens left by the faithful; sometimes with the aid of small steps in order to help them reach up to their vast charges.

The chanting and singing goes on apace, whilst two or three or four hundred people gather tightly round the principal characters in the evening ritual.

'But don't the congregation ever sing?' I asked after listening to the four choirs in the churches we visited. 'Sometimes, on certain occasions, yes'.

I was struck by people's stillness and the way they stood upright with their hands and arms to their sides; except when the liturgy bids them bow down or cross themselves, sometimes with great elaboration. 'They know the service by heart.'

One woman stopped me on the way out of the last church. Mstislav had gone on ahead but eventually he was able to speak at some length to her. She appeared very concerned and upset. 'Please apologise to her if I have offended her in any way,' I asked. He waived my apology to one side. 'There's a difficulty. I'll explain later.'

It appeared that she saw my dog-collar and wanted to involve me in an uncomfortable situation that had arisen between her parish council and the State's representative. Apparently, each parish has a council of 20 laity ('the priests aren't involved') and one State representative is appointed to keep a watchful eye over areas of the Church's affairs at roughly a Deanery-size level. 'She should not have approached you, nor her clergy, nor her bishop. She should take this matter, through her council, to the proper State authority.'

And later: 'It's all very complex and she was obviously very upset.'

At about this point in our dinner conversation a girl of evidently somewhat different persuasions was ushered to our table by a waiter who then engaged in rather heated conversation with Mstislav who managed to persuade the waiter to move our visitor to the next table. 'I just want to let you know I love you,' the electronic music boomed out from the end of the room.

'It was a misunderstanding.' Both of us seemed wary and a trifle put out. 'I feel sorry for her.'

'But we can't feel sorry for the whole world, can we?'

With our composure more or less restored, I quizzed Mstislav a bit more about the nature of the parish churches.

'Nothing is presumably allowed outside the actual buildings.'

'Right.'

'So the Church has no social life or activities, it is simply a place where one worships?'

'Right.'

'We've seen four very old churches this evening. Are there any new parish churches?'

'Not in Moscow. They've got enough here already. In certain other parts of the country, yes, there are new churches being built.'

'What really amazes me is how people can live this dual life. During the day they work for a State and government avowedly atheist; in the evenings they come to worship in their Churches. How can this be?'

'People are people and that's the way they are. Be amazed.'

'But how about all the government's atheistic propaganda?'

'It doesn't work, does it? People are in the churches, so the propaganda can't be very efficient, can it?' The huge guffaw followed.

The Metropolitan received us again with gracefulness. He looked a little less tired and more relaxed than before.

This time we talked generally about the Orthodox Church. He handed me two books, one of them a general history of his Church. It had a picture of Zagorsk on the front showing thousands of pilgrims gathered round the churches and cathedral. 'That's only a few,' he laughed, 'sometimes there are many more.'

The other book was the record of the 1982 World Conference, 'Religious Workers for saving the sacred gift of life from Nuclear Catastrophe', which he chaired in Moscow. '600 delegates came from all faiths and none, with representatives from the State as well.'

The Metropolitan spoke with passionate conviction about his commitment to World Peace. 'The sacred gift of life' occurred frequently in his speech. Every now and then there was a reference to multilateral disarmament or the 'no first strike' principle of his government, which indicated that he was well aware of the contemporary agenda, that he wasn't just mouthing Ortho-ecclesiastical platitudes. Earlier Mstislav had put me right about the Russian attitudes to unilateralism. 'It's a non-starter, looking at it from our point of view anyway. We have to get agreement about arms reductions by all sides.' The Metropolitan's peace convictions echoed his sentiments almost exactly.

One point in our conversation disturbed him and he leant forward, with many more hand notions and his whole face - now only inches away from mine - lit up with a kind of hurt excitement.

'Some people in your country talk about the dissidents in our system. Some people criticise our Church for working so closely with the government. But we are the Church of the nation; we are the heart of the nation. The State needs us. So, is it any wonder that we stand to mourn our State leaders alongside all the other mourners? What do people expect of us? We have baptised the leaders of our nation in many cases, so we should see them leave this world, too, shouldn't we?'

'How old is he?' I asked Mstislav afterwards. His beard and long hair gave Metropolitan Philaret a timeless appearance. 'He's fifty.' 'Will he be the next Patriarch?' But I could have answered the question myself. It came with the largest shrug and laugh of all. 'Only God can tell!'

The overwhelming feeling in me as I left was that here was a remarkable Church leader and person who just happened to be rather short of Western friendship and acceptance.

But the last sections of this short saga must belong to my remarkable thought reader. He has lived in Moscow all his life; he has travelled to 45 countries; he has never seen any of the Leaders of his people. A government car passed in front of us with its curtains drawn, preventing the view in or the view out. 'But of course,' is all he said. 'I think your leaders keep a lower profile than ours.'

'Maybe you are right.'

Mstislav has walked, wined and talked with Archbishops, Patriarchs and Emperors. 'Only one Emperor,' he corrected me. And yet standing next to him in a parish church and being aware of his crossing in time with the people around him, one can appreciate the force of his comment: 'I am a Russian, a member of my nation. I am a believer. So what's your problem? I have no problem.'

We had a long and lively final meal together with wide-ranging conversation to do with our differing understandings of the Church's relation to the State. Mstislav spoke very personally. 'Please don't publish any of this part of our conversation.'

Earlier we had stood and queued with thousands of others in the Kremlin for a glimpse at the famous Churches. It was a moving reminder of a former pilgrimage of wonder. 'They are museums but not museums, you understand?'

It was only a peep inside part of Mstislav's varied experience, but at one point we met a party of children in one of the churches. He listened to the guide, a woman in her late thirties or early forties, and came back full of praise for the delicacy and reverence of her discussion with the children. 'She's using all the correct theological terms to describe the Church as the spiritual Body of Christ.'

'Look at the children's faces,' I marvelled. Without any obvious exception they looked full of wonder and interest as they followed their sensitive guide's hand gestures round the beautiful sixteenth century icons and frescoes.

Their faces were so compelling I reached for my tape recorder to catch something of the sincerity in her voice. Mstislav stayed my hand. 'Don't put her off,' he said. 'If she thinks you are a government agent coming to check on her she may change her talk. Twenty years ago what she is saying wouldn't have been allowed.'

In that brief moment I sensed at once something of the buoyant hope for the future and the still very frightened looking over the shoulder at past memories experienced by unknown numbers of Russian believers today.

If Mstislav had any problem it was near the cross-roads of that moment, I guess.

We said our farewells at Moscow airport, my gentle thought reader and I, with the biggest bear-hug I anyway will ever be likely to experience; before I left for the customs check. Not such a long queue this time but as it came round to my turn I almost fell over with surprise at seeing the same pair of lads who had the technology and identity problems with me before. So many millions of people, and the very self-same lads hoved into view.

The bear-hug routine would have been inappropriate, but no amount of official duties could hold back the smile of recognition. Before the inevitable questions came: 'Any bibles, any roubles?' Only now with a really thorough search of my case in support. 'Any icons?' they added this time.

The purpose of my Russian visit had been to arrange for a delegation to come to our Cathedral's Peace Celebrations. Sometime after my return, with several phone-calls in between, I received the following telegram from the Metropolitan:

"Informing you, dear brother in Christ, that unfortunately working schedule of our department does not permit us to receive you in September neither send to you our Church delegation in November Stop with love in Christ Archbishop."

The Metropolitan's 'gram arrived at an unfortunate time - just prior to the publicity about the defection of a leading KGB spy in this country - and it was tempting to make some connection between the cancellation of our inter-church exchanges and the extraordinary game of 'Sneaks and Leaders' in the aftermath of the KGB defection. Having caught some glimpse of the pressure of work in the Metropolitan's under-staffed and primitively housed department, I still preferred to take the 'gram's wording on its face value. Mstislav was insistent on the phone that there was no connection between these cancellations and the 'spy' and foreign personnel expulsions which followed the defection ballyhoo. 'We had heard about it,' he said down the phone as if grateful for the crumbs of information falling from the Russian media table.

'...for saving the sacred gift of life from Nuclear catastrophe.' By western standards of acceptable forms of communication the Metropolitan's credo sounds and reads now a trifle over-flowerily. But the phrase has become part of my own life's rosary, part and parcel of my own pilgrimage as much as for the members of today's Orthodox Church. Not 'human' life but all life: I like that, it has the right vibration about it. And 'sacred gift': that feels increasingly right, too, especially in the face of all the evidence which would point to the expendability of everything. And it links in with one of my School Assembly aids: the sliced melon, in unequal parts, coming together again in the cupped hands to form a broken attempt at one world.

The night the Russian party should have been here visiting, a small group of us huddled round the Cathedral's wrought-iron globe lit up with candles. It felt like a Bethlehem stable experience. Many of the handful present belonged to no particular church or creed, some of us belonged to distinctly other traditions than the mainline Christian ones. And yet there we were, in all our common lonesomeness, huddled round a stable of light; rough-hewn shepherd characters, visitors from far beyond the well-worked normal liturgies of the Church, in the cold light of a candled night, clinging to the dream of a world where peace may still be possible. The musicians who happened to be playing behind us seemed to be offering their beautiful gifts of frankincense, myrrh and gold at the stable door as well.

For all her or his waverings about like a candle in the draught, today's peacegull holds to the simple conviction that 'out there' are many other lights, from many different languages and customs, holding and clinging to lights of hope in the darkness, too.

The visit from the Russian Orthodox Church never did get off the ground, to my great disappointment, or not as I had envisaged it anyway. Under the new order of things, and with by all accounts much better, more open relations between the Kremlin and the Church's leaders, it could well be possible - come, say, in the Jubilee year of 1995 - ten years on from my green seagull trip, to organise visitations of many hues between our churches, God willing.

My own disappointment about the Orthodox church's cancellation was considerably sweetened some time on by the sudden announcement over the phone by two keen local peacegulls that a Russian Archbishop was due to land on them. Could I organise a programme for him? Having recovered from the shock, I set about going off to Heathrow Airport to meet his plane, with one fairly big question hovering in my mind throughout the journey. What on earth would a post-flight Russian Orthodox Archbishop actually look like? The journey turned out to be an abortive one. The flight from Moscow arrived. His Arch-nibs was not on the flight. I paced around the arrival building with its sea-full of different coloured gulls somewhat frustratedly, wondering whether he might have been on an earlier plane. At one point I even went up to a very black-robed, distinguished looking cleric. 'Russian Archb...?' I started. But no sooner had he turned in my direction than I realised he could only have been a Chief Rabbi.

Back to the airport on the next evening, after several fairly frantic phone calls during the day to track down the errant Archgull. And to my great relief, this time everything went as smooth as a whistle. As I stood at the arrival point with my RUSSIAN ARCHBISHOP board, looking at the exit for His unmistakable presence, it was one of the surprises of my life when someone casually walked up to me, while my gaze was still pinned roughly twenty yards away, wearing a cloth cap and raincoat. The Arch had arrived in person, dressed in western-style mufti, no less.

The programme for his time with us involved a big Ordination Service in the Cathedral and several services in the parish. Everywhere we went, indoors and out, his Arch-nibs wore a beautiful velvet blue head-dress and an immaculate cassock. And everywhere he went he wore his broad smile. And everywhere he went he spoke the same message, with a deep guttural voice: 'I do not come to you with snow on my boots, but with the warm greetings of many Russian hearts.'

Some peacegulls are just naturals.

Each Transfiguration Day (August 6th), a small but very committed local band of peacegulls meets by the millpond to float our candle-boats in memory of the atomic bomb dropped on Hiroshima, most of us very mindful that our country's Trident submarines now possess a destructive power many times greater.

The candle-boats are full of flowers as well as lights. Some of them include imitations of the Japanese crane, the worldwide symbol of Hiroshima and Nagasaki, made by a young gull who died from leukaemia (as a result of the bombs) while she was making her hundreds of paper birds.

The boats take to the water of our millpond at 9pm (or at 2100 hours, as some nautical members of our flock prefer). One year my young niece from Canada joined us for the candle-boat floating. She wrote afterwards:

'I launched my boat. It floated. When many were launched they blew down the millpond. They reminded me of people...

some were fast;
some caught on fire and burned themselves and others out;
some blew out by the force of the wind;
some sank;
some floated on unlit;
some blew the wrong way;
but some, a few, floated on, lit until the end, when they came up against a wall. Then we went home to bed.'

Alison wrote these words in 1985. It was her own Perestroika, her own candle-in-the-draught.

TIGERS IN THE THINK-TANK

I remember a local Baptist Minister telling the well-known tale of the two people in a train compartment, one of whom spent the whole journey tearing up pieces of paper and throwing them out of the window. Eventually the other could contain her curiosity no longer. 'Excuse me, but can you tell me why you are tearing up those pieces of paper and throwing them out of the window?' she asked.

'It keeps the tigers away,' the other replied.

'But there aren't any tigers round here.'

'I know, it's effective, isn't it?'

So much of the Exile in Babylon has felt like that. For all these years we've been keeping the tigers at bay, or waiting for the Ruskies to land with snow on their boots. As a student visiting Russia in the late fifties I remember being approached by a couple of earnest youngsters. We had travelled by double-decker bus, as I mentioned earlier. On one side of the bus was an advertisement for Guinness portraying a crocodile. 'Is this a piece of government propaganda for the abolition of crocodiles in English rivers?' asked the youngsters. The green seagull phenomenon positively pales into insignificance alongside the fantasised world of enemy tigers and crocodiles we inhabited, or allowed ourselves to inhabit, or were persuaded to inhabit, for all those years.

Others know the anti-nuclear speaking platforms and broadcasting waves much better than I do. My flight-paths have tended to be at lowlier altitudes, involving occasional journeys to murky church or public halls in the back of beyond. One I remember up-country where my opposite number on the panel happened to be a distinguished theologian who has since flown up to much higher things. I rather dreaded the occasion because although I have admired his recent offerings I also knew his analytical style. In other words, I thought he would take my argumentation to the cleaners. In the event, my task as the second speaker was made considerably easier by the surprising discovery that the distinguished theologian in question chose to pitch his remarks almost entirely round the year 1945, as if nothing of any consequence in War and Peace matters had happened since. We have to hold on to nuclear weapons in case... Stockpiles? No problem.

Other uses for the trillions and trillions of pounds we've wasted in an increasingly hungry, ecologically destroyed world? No matter, our guard has to be maintained. The enemy is always there.

I'm guying my co-debater's position a bit, but as a general rule of thumb I've found it to be true that intelligence, with otherwise great political and worldly wisdom, in theologians, amongst even the highest flying statesgulls, is absolutely no guarantee against the 'Here be dragons' (tigers or crocodiles) factor surfacing, often in the least likely places. My father spent much of his latter years convinced that Tony Benn would become Prime Minister and lurch our country irretrievably leftwards. He was equally convinced that the Russian submarine fleet, even many years after the Cuban missile crisis, was waiting to pounce from vantage points all over the world and would one day do so.

Not that the deterrent argument always had a walkover with no contest. Even at my altitude of flying there were always lively debates around; allowing, too, for the undoubted fact that many of these tended to call out the anti-nuke members of the flock rather than their tiger-believing colleagues. I've always believed that if the bulldozers came in to knock our church buildings down, the first people you'd hear from would be those who never darken their doors. Ditto, I'm sure, for the great silent majority of the flock over the hardware varieties of War and Peace issues. So long as the 'building' of Trident goes on apace, no problem. Greenham Common and Faslane may present mild irritants to the body politic, as the anti-nuke gulls turn out in their tiny grouplets, even their thousands on occasion. Such is the power of the 'Here be tigers' propaganda, though, it would need something little short of heavy corporate convulsive electrical therapy to create an anti-Trident campaign in the present political climate. The ruling gulls know this and play on it. Even when no enemy exists we have to be prepared for one. Elizabeth I's and Elizabeth II's Englands differ little in their need for outside foes.

American Presidential elections provide a sharpening time for the War and Peace debate. At one such time I was really convinced that everyone bar a good number in the churches, by and large, was actually keyed into this debate and making their contributions. It wasn't really like this, but after the furore over the 1984 "Church and the Bomb" report from the C. of E. General Synod, the churches seemed to go to sleep over the matter: as if to say, 'Well, we've done our bit, and from now on, it's "No comment."'

The Church in general still seems to be urging us to leave the War and Peace issues, please, at the door. As you come in, hang your real intelligence on the coat-rack and put all thoughts of possible mushroom clouds in the umbrella tray. We've got plenty enough on our private (ie sexual) morality plates to be bothering about issues of public morality.

Convinced that the paper-tearing exercise needed to be at least challenged, however ineffective the chosen flight path, I once agreed to be part of a War and Peace panel on the Isle of Wight.

'What sort of occasion will this be?' I asked the evening's host as she collected me from the ferry-head. 'Oh, we shall get over a hundred people. We're meeting in a small theatre building.' At which I quailed, partly in anxiety but equally at the reminder that the Isle of Wight really does seem to turn out for the key issues, even on a cold winter's night in late November. Quite a stronghold of political protestation is the IOW Nuclear, Housing, Third World Development lobby: for all these issues the Muggletonian, Levelling, Quaking sisters and brothers are never far away.

Three hours later, on the return trip to the mainland, I felt rather like some Somerset Maugham character, jaded but still just ticking over after a foreign escapade. Over the longish drive to and from the 'theatre building', my companion proved to be very dedicated and committed to the cause but human with it. She told me how she was just off to Russia, one of four mothers from this country on an exchange visit. 'If we can just go and tell the people we meet we really believe in peace for our families, we'll have done something.'

Our meeting place turned out to be a vast building in the back streets of nowhere. There was a stage for the panel, about forty to fifty people were scattered in the auditorium: quite a range of age and social groups, some punks, one eighty-nine year old complete with war medals, quite a lot of students, some sensitive mid-forties' couples, one or two clergy. In the ice-cold temperature, no-one took their coat off.

A bespectacled student opened the proceedings and we were off. There were terribly nervous answers at first but, to my surprise, no-one was concerned about taking the Church's lamentable record in the area to task. Obviously that didn't feature in people's minds as the key issue. One of the panel, the only woman, reminded us of the temperature of the hall by speaking with a lot of cold anger in her voice. I found the occasion very open and stretching and even tried feeding in a little humour. Peacegulls are long on theory and words, I still feel, and short on human spark; at least we were from this platform.

In a way the most impressive contribution of the whole evening came from a white-haired seasoned campaigner, his wife beside him, in about row six. 'We fought for CND in the late fifties and early sixties, and we failed. How can we ensure we don't fail again?'

A cold night - and yet some forty or fifty people felt it worth their while to sit in a fridge-like building in a small town on one of this country's off-shore islands. They didn't stay at home. And that was what stuck in the mind at the end of the day.

The lights of the abbey were all twinkling when we passed in the car earlier. At 9.30pm as we passed on return they were all off. The monks were in bed, presumably, getting ready for their night offices, leaving the rest of us to struggle out the world's issues. Or so it felt.

The problem is that three years into the Berlin Wall's demise and we're still in tiger land. The debates have been held, the Arms Treaties are in place or trudging their way into the history books, at least four Tridents are on the order books, all three major political parties fall over themselves not to offend the pro-nuke consensus. So, where now? Equally important, where have all those Muggletonian, Levelling, Quaking flowers gone? Why have CND's numbers declined so dramatically? Have the Trident fantasists won the day?

Protesting sisters and brothers of the anti-war faiths turned out in plenty at the time of the lead up to the Gulf War. In our hearts we must have known that once again the persuaders had done their work on the flock: territorial invasions can't be countenanced and certainly not when oil interests are at stake. The Chinese invasion of Tibet was one thing; the Iraqi invasion of oil-rich Kuwait, quite another. It suited the world to do nothing about a Namibia or a West Bank situation. Only with the greatest reluctance does the UN get off its backside and tip-toe ever so gently into a Bosnia or Rwanda crisis. But when oil rather than bananas is the threatened resource, then heaven and earth have to be moved, as move they did. From November, 1991 the die was cast. In response to the August 2nd invasion of Kuwait, three months later the US military took the reins into their own hands. The UN, and most pathetically its Secretary-General, didn't get a look in from then on. When Perez de Cuellar was finally able to fly his green seagull trip to Saddam Hussein in mid-January 1992, the military on both sides could be contained no longer. The gods of war were appealed to from both sides and battle commenced.

So the protest marches in early 1992, locally and nationally, knew they were flying in the face of hopeless odds. In the general shambles the anti-war cause never really got more than the flock's partial ear. There remained clear avenues for resolving the Gulf crisis other than by military means: much greater UN willingness to take action on the West Bank issue, much earlier and more intensive diplomatic activity than proved to be the case, the pan-Arab or regional resolution of the area of dispute, to name but three. As it was, with many previous suspect arms deals with Iraq clanking about in the background, including, without doubt, the procuring of all that equipment over the years from our very own Whale Island, as well as much shabby recent history - not least over the lack of support for the Kurds and the befriending of Saddam Hussein as a would-be puppet; with all this around, the US took us into the war which ended so unsatisfactorily two months later with its awful aftermath: at least 200,000 Iraqi civilians and military dead, much still untold suffering, the Kurdish and the Marsh peoples' problems, and a host of environmental and ecological disasters, which damaged the whole region irrevocably.

The hardest thing to swallow from the churches was the way the Just War theory was trotted out to bless the whole calamitous enterprise in the Gulf. Far more depressing than the sight of newly fledged Prime Minister John Major rallying the British contingent of troops on the Saudi Arabian soil was the sound of the Just War theologians doing their spade-work back here on home ground. I did a mid-term clergy course with Bishop Richard Harries of Oxford, way back in 1974. During the course we each had to produce a paper on a subject of our choice. His I remember was on the Just War theory. Little did the rest of us mid-course gulls realise then how tremendously influential the thinking behind that paper would become in the life of our nation. The learned bishop has since published endless letters, articles and books on any number of subjects, but none so crucial as those written in episcopal support of the nation's war machines and ventures. When the tiger persuaders and the paper tearers have been given the theological OK, there's no stopping them - in so far as an ecclesiastical thumbs-up counts for anything. And judging from the way President Bush spent the last day before the Gulf War in the company of Billy Graham; and from the way, further back, President Reagan never had the Almighty far from his lips or thoughts when referring to nuclear weaponry, his fated Star Wars project included; and from the way, right back at the start of the nuclear age, the first bombs off the US assembly line were given Christian names quite literally: by these yardsticks alone, it's clear that the theological icing on the nuclear cake was deemed to be not unimportant. Presumably this is still the case. Let's watch the naming of the Tridents 2, 3 and 4 space with care as well as interest. And who will do the blessing bits? I wonder.

Roughly a year before the Gulf War debacle I found myself inveigled into taking on the Chair of CANA (Clergy Against Nuclear Arms). I had attended two of their Annual Meetings in London and Birmingham, but always had some reservations about the organisation's *raison d'être*. It wasn't that I didn't recognise fellow green seagulls, flapping around very often in the teeth of the storm; many of them with brightly coloured plumage which made my own look distinctly dowdy. My problem was with the word 'Clergy'. The origin of the organisation or group went back only to 1982. We were Falkland's War children, offspring of the first Thatcher government, when characters like Michael Heseltine were muscling about the country in their flak jackets. But why just the clergy? If we wanted to retain the acronym with its good biblical feel, why not Churches or Christians Against Nuclear Arms, instead? What about all the other Muggletonians, Levellers, Quakers and Co, in other words?

It wasn't just a name problem. Sometimes I get to thinking so congregationally about the Church - and I'm referring to the deep convictions of the United Reformed Church in its previous existence - I wonder how on earth I survive in the hierarchical C. of E. Priestgullery or clergyhood for me has increasingly become a functional thing rather than a matter of essence. Leadership, but from the middle rather than square-jawed from the front, 'enabling' as non-directively as possible to use the near-sacred parlance: that's where I feel most me. Which is why I arrive on our local Quaker meeting on the second Sunday of the month with such profound and soulful relief. After functioning in pulpit, behind altar, up front all day long, I find it a matter of balm and cockles to sit in a circle 'levelled' with other gulls, not necessarily all of the green variety, where we can just be ourselves without bell, book or candle. The priesthood of all believers it has to be or nothing.

So the concept of the so-called leaders of the Church - and our little CANA flock of five or six hundred raises a few bishops as well - delivering the peace goods to even a semi-ignorant laity is totally anathema to me. Whether it's the women at Yellow Gate, Greenham Common, still there long after the cruise missiles have been packed off back home to the US; or the ever-vigilant Nuke-watchers who track and follow the hazardous journeys of the warheads back and forth from Faslane to Burghfield; or the peace and justice workers in any number of places like Iona, Barnes Close, Birmingham and Sheffield; or, back on home soil, the totally committed members of our congregation who wear their white poppies without apparent flinching: whoever and whatever the peacegulls, nine times out of ten they come to me as the real leading lights. The peacegulls amongst the laity empower the clergy, not the other way round. So often anyway. The other problems about Clergy Against Nuclear Arms is its seeming negativity and narrow focus. Why against rather than for something? Why just anti-nuclear and not anti- all forms of armaments? Why not for 'Peace, Justice and Creation', as our group sub-title now stresses? The debate in my head and doubtless a good many others' continues.

With that apologia out in the open, it's time to move on to CANA, after my rather hesitant misgivings. In the depressing aftermath of the Gulf War the CANA committee resolved to bring representatives of the Christian Peace Movement together to consider the question 'Whither now?' Which we did at the remarkable All Saints Pastoral Centre, London Colney, Hertfordshire, just off Europe's busiest stretch of motorway on the last day of April and the first day of May, 1992. All of us had come with our Cold War stories, all of us were mindful of the different skies we were having to adjust to, as the placard-carrying protest marches and theological filibustering which had sustained so many of us for the last two or three decades were heading towards nose-dives.

We were massively helped at London Colney's watershed time by two intellectually well-endowed gulls whose fresh, greenish theses were spread before our hungry souls. But more of that anon.

At this point it's necessary to make a slight diversion; mainly because of something which won't have been lost on any reasonably perceptive gull. Somewhere way back in the whole green seagull thesis, roughly two and a half chapters ago, another sea change came over the case I'm trying to make. Up until then I had referred to green-seagullhood in terms of those members of the flock who earn our respect if not our whole-hearted compassion: the undergulls of our society, the disadvantaged, the refugee, the poor and trampled on in spirit. As one vividly coloured representative of this kind of gull, Tom flies into my mind and the day I watched him on one of our shingled beaches years ago.

Tall and thin as a beanpole he was, with match-stick legs and arms flailing about as he tried to hobble over the shingle, crying out in his discomfort to the rest of his party. It was a long cry of anguish, animal-like in its desperation. The fleshlessness on the soles of his feet must have made the journey over the pebbles excruciatingly painful. Every now and then his hands went down to the ground 'monkeylike' in an attempt to relieve the pressure and discomfort of his feet.

No-one in the party heard his cries or, if they did, they chose to ignore them. Subsequent overheard comments indicated that the lad knew perfectly well he should have worn his shoes; it was his own fault, would he never learn his lesson properly?

Inch by painful inch he proceeded and eventually made the water and his party for a brief paddle; his thin little frame shrinking its rib-cage almost to vanishing point on first contact with the sea. And then it was time for the party to return home. Up the beach they all came, the whole party of disadvantaged young gulls, only this time 'Tom' was wearing someone's flipflops, kindly lent; his lesson presumably learnt.

A real-life Mephibosheth was Tom.

The symbols of pathos, in its original sense of 'arousing pity or sadness', walk our streets, crawl our beaches, fly our skies. That's one thing. But then came the beginnings of the sea-change. From then on in I appeared to be switching my ground from describing members of the flock like Tom as deserving our compassionate understanding. The gulls I was now considering, like Mstislav or Astrid or Arthur Scargill, were of a different order from Tom. These invite our attention or at least consideration. They and their way of life speak not just to our emotions; they also challenge or disturb our minds. The witness of a disabled Mephibosheth like Tom hobbling along the shingle on all fours and, say, that of an airborne Arthur Scargill, even with a pitifully streaming cold, address different parts of us, call forth different responses from us.

Am I not cheating, or at least taking a handy short-cut or two, by describing both Tom and Arthur as Green Seagulls? Few could find the mineworkers' leader either 'pitiful' or 'sad', although it's probably true that no person in our present society has for so long brought on himself so much ribaldry and hatred as King Arthur himself. No-one else qualifies for the Court Jester Extraordinaire prize in the way that he does.

It may appear that I'm in danger of trying to have my pathos cake and eating it with a goodly covering of rather doubtful prophetic icing at the same time. But I would want at this stage to underline the relationship between the pathetic (that which arouses our pity and sadness) and the prophetic (that which challenges us). Whilst I wouldn't want to claim sainthood for King Arthur, his surprisingly long public and picket-line ministry has something of the latter category about it, even when at times he has been little more than a household joke.

Like most prophets, Jesus must have spent a lot of his life psychologically creeping around on all fours over the shingles of hostility around him. He was a figure of fun. 'They laughed at him', as the story says. In his family, too. 'Such a funny lad, you are!' his second cousin 'Aunt' Liz might well have observed on more than one occasion. 'Why aren't you married yet? Too much of a stargazer to notice the girls, if you ask me.' But amongst his friends, too, and during his early travelling days, even at the height of his ministry, they were forever laughing him 'to scorn'. And when he said that 'a prophet is not without honour save in his own country', he wasn't making an interesting observation, or providing the world with one more fairly harmless proverb. He was giving vent to a passionate heart-cry and describing the country that he knew from his depths. He'd known ribaldry, jealousy and hatred long before 'they' finally decided to put him away.

So the pathetic and the prophetic as green seagulls, both - they fly very close together. They share a sky of common vulnerability.

Prophets, like artists, are green seagulls, too, in the sense that they stand in the wilderness areas of society, challenging and disturbing us, overturning our presumptions, looking way beyond our preoccupations. After their deaths, we may come round to understanding their message. We may build them monuments, have their works published, their paintings sold; but during their lifetimes, we find them difficult, if not impossible, to live with. They have to be kept without honour; otherwise, presumably, the flock would either go mad or lose its bearings altogether. Most often we choose to ignore them. In the case of a draft-card burning Daniel Berrigan, or an over-threatening woman from Greenham Common, we shut them away in prison. My own suspicion is that, in the case of the Poll Tax, the government and many local authorities would have dearly liked to lock many more of us away than they did. Two things prevented this course of action: one was the already overloaded state of our prisons. Our own local goal in Winchester would have had to add an awful lot of us into their fully stretched numbers and at a time when the staff were coping with quite enough disciplinary incidents to keep them more than occupied. The second thing was that no way could any remotely 'prophetic' citizen be allowed even the faintest sniff of martyrdom.

Back on track, once again, and to return to those academic gulls of green hue who came to us in London Colney. As they reminded us of the peace movement's heritage from the last years and shared with us their prescriptions for the new agenda of the '90s, I couldn't help marvelling at how isolated and far from the main lines of our society's conventional wisdoms the peacegulls had become. Weren't these just two voices coming out of the wilderness, like John the Baptist's, with their cries of 'Repent'? It's now or never time for the world to change its heart and mind and will, they signalled to us. But what chance, indeed, for any part of their prescription having any effect in changing the tearing of paper exercise or wooing the tigers out of the Pentagon and Whitehall think-tanks?

One of my own rubbished newspaper offerings at the time of the first Trident's launch had positively cried out, probably a shade too fervently - hence the editorial treatment. My cry was about 'which enemy', 'which Tiger' was going to be targeted now that the Russian Bear was being embraced on all sides. With far more coolness and cogency, Paul Rogers, from the Peace Studies Department at Bradford

University, pointed us to the distinct probability that the United States via the Pentagon was now in the business of new targeting policies for use in limited nuclear wars. The inter-continental ballistic weapons are being superseded by programmes with much smaller earth-penetrating weapons, having very low radiation levels, which can attack small targets such as bunkers. Whereas the danger of the 1960s, '70s and '80s, had been major nuclear confrontation between the superpowers, the danger of the '90s and beyond is that of small wars, with NATO nuclear expeditionary forces included as well as the threat of terrorist nuclear suitcases. From semtex bombs to suitcases with small nuclear devices can't be a long journey.

Rogers's vision of the future left us in no doubt, in case proof were needed for even the blindest and deafest gull, that the New World Order, so-called, is a militarised one; that the resources wars will continue because of the wealthy states' need of natural resources from the poorest nations; that these would be aggravated by mass emigrations such as the Bari phenomenon concerning the 10,000 Albanians who fled from the Balkans and found themselves like stateless pawns on the international chessboard, just prior to the time when the Bosnian tragedy broke in earnest; that the poverty of the poorer nations is deepening relentlessly; and that the East-West's former axis of hostility was giving place to the potentially much more explosive North-South confrontations to come, even more threatened as these will be by proliferation of nuclear weaponry.

Such a catalogue of 'downside' woe, and yet it would be a very head-in-the-sand kind of gull who denied all this contemporary evidence with its future-pointing signals. The big problem is how the crucial switches can be pulled not just in the minds of the Trident and tiger think-tanks but in the corporate consciousness of the flock itself. In fact, Rogers offers two small rays of hope as he peers through all the prevailing mists into the future. The first is that because of the swiftness of the world's news technology the flock as a whole can relate to a small Rwandan or Iraqi or Bosnian crisis immediately. Not that this gives rock-solid guarantees against precipitate action on the part of government. The second hopeful ray is that we have the means of solving all the downside's catalogue of woes; all that is lacking is the will. It is a long shot but, just maybe, the best bit of world consciousness on the part of the whole flock could persuade the policy-making gulls to put away their paper-tearing Trident exercises, their fossilised East-West 'enemy' caricatures, and concentrate on the real agenda to hand.

All the way through this thesis I've tried to make the relation of the particular to the general apparent. Just how the visionary prophets and madcaps of our day speak of the future world and dream their dream, without recourse to clowning buffoonery in order to draw attention to themselves, is quite a question. So stuck in the Tiger think-tank has the Trident mind-fix left us, what alternatives are there? If, that is, we're not going to be content just to replicate, boringly, boringly, the banners and protests of the last three decades. An Abraham Lincoln or a Van Gogh could be dishonoured in their lifetime, and honoured with the people's understanding at leisure after their deaths. Our problem is that we don't have the time to wait on history's verdict about today's nuclear and ecological prophets. The time for the change of heart and mind has to be now. The Babylonian Exile period is due for closure. Certain clear signals are coming through to us, as the '90s people, loud and clear.

As part of the etching out of one of these clear signals I give a very local example by way of a taster. In a way, thankfully, this story is still some distance from the nuclear suitcase age: for me it still has all the feelings of the passing of the peace angels about it.

We had a bomb-scare recently in our community. The first I knew of it came through a phone-call from the police just after midnight. 'Can we please use your church hall in an emergency for the evacuees?'

Naturally, I was disbelieving. Emsworth and Emergencies don't have much in common. If we were living in Warrington or Northern Ireland or the City, that would be a different matter. In fact, only a few days later some young friends from London reminded us of their normal world. 'In Soho bomb scares are always happening,' said one. 'The place where I work is just round the corner from all the recent damage,' said another. But in Emsworth? Scarcely.

It didn't take long for disbelief to be earthed in the rapid development of events outside our house and in the church hall next door during the hours that followed: the flashing blue lights, the busy routines of numerous uniformed personnel, and, most moving of all, the steady stream of local citizens hobbling through the night from three entire streets proximate to the threatened area by the well-known landmark of our gasometer.

All of us without exception, I guessed, had been dragged from our beds. We came in our semi-night wear, some of us with dogs (no cats or other pets for some unexplained reason) and our children or grandchildren in their blankets and slippers: for all the world as if we had walked straight out of Srebrenica or Kigali.

Beside all the uniformed efficiency in the background I felt strangely role-less. Three streetfuls of people make a very wide cross-section of humanity. Some I knew well, others on an acquaintanceship level, others not at all. Our common mood was brittle, anxious, teetering between frustration and anger. The piano in the corner stood covered and unused. Here was no occasion for community-singing, clearly. In fact, apart from two characters who played chess throughout the night, aided by some liquid refreshment other than that provided by the Boys' Brigade and the WRVS, most of us just sat looking befuddled and bemused. No one lay down, apart from one or two reluctantly persuaded children. Tea and biscuits became our Holy Communion for the night.

Something I've reflected on a lot since was how little response I got to my sundry observations. 'It feels like wartime, doesn't it...?' (for the over-fifties). 'Now one knows a bit more about how the Bosnians must be feeling.' It could just be that 3.30 on a weekday morning is not the best time for making such comparative philosophical observations, hence people's reticence.

But what I've come to realise is that, whatever people's age and experience or lack of both, our night-time trauma in little backwater Emsworth, normally far from all the world's headlines and frontlines, felt only too well like the peace-time of bomb-scares and alarms and emergencies which come daily into our living rooms via the newscasts. Frontlines and headlines we breathe here as anywhere, nowhere is bomb-proofed any more. War-time has become peace-time, peace-time war-time, in our time.

Local legend after the incident had it that the 'bomb' in question turned out to be no more nor less than a tightly packed ball of paper and string which the lads at the car foundry were using in place of a football during the lunch-hour. Until one of them booted it over the high gasometer fence which the gas-board keeps locked up, naturally enough. We've had leaking gas scares before but nothing to mesmerise our community like this. The bombers, real or hoax, keep our whole society in a state of near paralysis. How can the tiger possibly be wooed out of the local think-tank, never mind Whitehall's, when such a rash of real incidents just goes to show that we all have to be on constant alert? Or so our corporate psyche tells us, even after Northern Ireland's fragile peace declaration.

The London Colney gathering was one step in the direction of finding some peace path into the '90s. Since then CANA has taken on the challenges of a new organ, PEACEMAKER. To say that this is intended to turn our rag-tag-and-bobtail collection of green or leaning towards greenness gulls into some finely tuned, lithe and willowy peace presence whose repercussions will be noted throughout the land, is to overstate the matter. Peacegullery just isn't like that: look at any gathering of us. But peacemaking rather than peacekeeping: the distinction won't be lost on those of us who live, work or minister in heavily 'serviced' or 'weaponed' parts of the country. 'Peacemaking' has incontrovertible biblical credentials. 'Peacekeeping' belongs to the late twentieth century's frenetic attempts to prevent the whole world falling apart or blowing itself to pieces.

There is no question of any 'holier-than-thou' theology. Peacemakers are as rooted in corporate, structural sin as those who try to stay Somalia's or Bosnia's or Lebanon's warring hands from each other's throats. Peacekeepers, whether under UN auspices in blue berets and helmets or as serving members of the British armed forces, may somewhat disingenuously believe in the impartiality of their presence amongst the hungry and refugees or on the streets of Belfast; but Peacemakers should not be the first to cast stones impugning their motives. Even in the most blatant cases of so-called peacekeeping's ulterior and potentially destabilizing objectives - like the preservation of the oil-flow, at all costs, and in the West's best interest - the peace-making critique needs to pause and reflect on its own corporate and institutional inadequacies.

Too often 'peacemaking' has become the individual's hobby, operating miles from the political front-lines, even when it is dressed up in the mass with banners and chanting. The great peacemaking marches of the '80s were sadly and to all appearances very largely ignored by government. Two hundred thousand peacemakers in Hyde Park or walking past the Ministry of Defence, and yet Margaret Thatcher could still sleep soundly in her bed with untroubled, unthreatening dreams. As E.P. Thompson, Bruce Kent and others have frequently reminded us, the Peace Movement's achievements, on both sides of the former Iron Curtain, were considerable. Subsequent history books should beam further light on how much the Cold War's end owed to public peacemaking round the world. The question which will always remain is how much more effective could, say, the Campaign for Nuclear Disarmament have been had certain other levers of power been worked on or Labour's non-nuclear stance not withered on the vine.

But for all the inadequacies and lack of corporate leverage or cutting edge, still Peacemaking rather than Peacekeeping. To be sure, there will still be the banner and protest occasions during the nineties. The world's present wobbliness and potential explosiveness will not go away. A few disasters or unforced nuclear errors and the return to the peace 'pews' could be on the agenda. Not that it has ever been the peacemaker's role, and certainly not as envisaged in the Sermon on the Mount, to sit back and wait on events.

One appendix at the back contains CANA's recently updated Statement. What corners of the body politic this will reach remains to be seen. It is intended as another small step towards the Jubilee year of 1995, when a number of fiftieth anniversaries fall (the founding of the United Nations, the bombing of Hiroshima and Nagasaki) together with the time for ratification of the Test Ban and Non-Proliferation Treaties. On present showing, with our mental captivity in Babylon still locking us into the nuclear game-plans of the bygone age, neither the ban on further nuclear testing nor the prevention of further membership in the nuclear club of nations stands the proverbial snowball's chance in hell of being universally ratified. As a best possible scenario, it's conceivable that the world flock will come to its senses; that people movements all over the globe will shake themselves free of a cloying East-West aspic well past its shelf-life; that the leading statesgulls will find themselves required by their sections of the flock to set up new ways of stabilising and reducing their nuclear and conventional weaponry; that the North-South awareness and the dangers of further conflicts over resources will be addressed; that everywhere will come the recognition that nuclear disarmament and the politics of militarism are only one component in a series of connected ecological and other threats to the planet; that a new Rio de Janeiro-type conference with more teeth in its head will ensure that peace and prosperity come for every member of the flock for ever and ever world without end. It's conceivable but hardly likely.

The 1992 Rio conference on the environment took as its theme-symbol the biblical Tree of Life from the Book of Revelation. From the very same chapter and verse comes the theme which the Network of Christian Peace Organizations is suggesting for 1995's Year of Jubilee: 'For the healing of the nations'. Much international healing is called for, and it has to start by addressing the tiger which we have kept away by tearing up so many pieces of paper for so long.

By way of an impish footnote, like a fawn amongst the dinosaurs, I did rather enjoy ringing up Westminster Abbey and booking their 6.30pm Evensong on Transfiguration and Hiroshima Day, August 6th, 1995, for an act of Peace Celebration, with a procession to Battersea Park's Peace Pagoda later in the evening for some paper boat and candle floating, of course... But that's part of the next story.

September

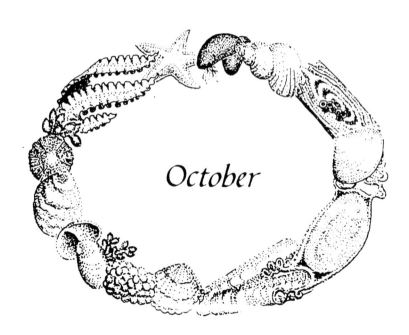

October

COMMON ERA FLIGHT-PATHS

Many times before has the issue of orthodoxy (right belief), and heterodoxy ('wrong' or other belief) surfaced in the flatlands. And on so many of these occasions, the poor old bible finds itself hauled out and pressed into serving an already established belief system, very often one involving the interests of the status quo. We don't want to change or see things differently – this is the way we like it, therefore this must be the will of God. The 'liberals', of course, are just as guilty of reaching for the odd text as the 'literals' when it suits their purposes. But what we were and still are all talking about so often seems like self-reassurance or ego-massage rather than the nature of truth.

A bit more cynically, I believe that the real business of orthodoxy - religious, political, behavioural, it makes no difference - is control. The orthodox gulls are those with their hands on the controls and the power-strings. They want to keep things that way, they don't want even to contemplate a state of being where their whole world might have to change or adapt to new realities. So the orthodox gull is constantly looking over its shoulder watching for what's coming up behind, forever seeing possible threats to its power. The order of service is crucial to the orthodox gulls because their own order and framework is reflected there; disorder and disorderly behaviour are anathema because both threaten their measured existence. Much of the opposition to the ordination of women debate has nothing to do with the issue of gender. The issue at stake, quite as much as the gender one, has to do with order. The present system, with the male priestgulls at the controls, is the known order. We know the species. This is what a priestgull is, full-stop.

Years ago I remember my father arguing that there were certain things a woman could never do: like be Prime Minister. His remark was made only a few years before the Margaret Thatcher phenomenon. No doubt, in course of time, he had to make some adjustments to his 'order' of things. But he wasn't arguing against women, he wasn't against women. In the days of his remark about prime ministerhood he obviously believed that no woman could have that kind of responsibility or power. Fifteen or so years later, I write this now in Canada, the day following Kim Campbell's election as the country's first woman Prime Minister. Canadians are very orderly, orthodox people, by and large; and I guess many of them will have problems adjusting to the new 'order' of things to come. (As things turned out, Kim Campbell's leadership of the flock proved to be very short-lived.)

The less cynical bit of me believes that those who posture as the really orthodox gulls feel threatened and insecure. For all their protestations to the contrary, as well as sincere belief that only they are the guardians of the true Faith and without them and their last ditch ministry the cause of the Almighty would perish without trace, the real issue comes down eventually to the largely imagined fears of orthodoxy. We are the orthodox gulls, over there are the heterodox others. There's not room for all of us in this flock. When it's only a case of one or two others, the way forward can be fairly simple: the heterodox can be quietly ignored, they can be excommunicated from the flock, they can be pecked to pieces and killed. But when the numbers of the heterodox become more threatening, then the only feasible resort is to whistle up the theological or sociological carpenters and builders amongst the flock and start hammering the stockade into place. The flock from then on becomes an endangered species.

I think this would partially explain why in a society such as ours – where there are now more Muslims than Methodists, as well as periodic immigration scares (we're being overrun by heterodox gullery from Asia and Africa), the press, both secular and religious, has so largely been taken over by the stockade builders. With honourable exceptions, the newspaper industry is in the hands of very ordered controllers who feed us with titillating gossip about the sexual peccadillos of our rulers and the royals whilst doing all they can to encourage the belief that other, lesser gulls - like roving vicars or promiscuous teachers or abusing youth-workers - should be judged as harshly as possible. Two-tiered morality is alive and well in late twentieth century Britain.

There's one law for the Royal and another for the rest of the flock. Except that many of the newsgulls really only invite their readers to be prurient as a cover for their own cruel pecking habits. But for press and pulpit alike, the prevailing assumption is that because of all the heterodox gullery rampaging around all over the place, the flock has to be protected; and that means by inward-looking centripetalism, with everything conceivable moving towards some airless, self-absorbed, right-thinking centre. Any suggestion of the centrifugal alternative - that truth and orthodoxy are to be found and flown towards 'out there' where life can be ever free-ranging and open-winged - has a rough time of it; in fact such a different approach can't be entertained at all other than on the neglected and despised fringes of the flock.

'Common Era', rather than BC and AD as the map and time reference for the future, will have a hard time of it, too, before it wins acceptance. Ever since the good monk Bede, Christendom has assumed that history can only properly be interpreted and measured through reference to the life of Christ. The growth of secularism and our awareness of the vision of the world through the spectacles of other faiths have been equally responsible for querying this way of viewing and dating history. In what remains of Christendom or the so-called Christian societies, the one big question is whether the churchgulls will continue on their present centripetal path, until they vanish completely into their orthodox self-hood, to the point where every other gull becomes suspiciously heterodox (except for me and thee and even thee is a little odd and non-ortho at times); or, whether, *mirabile dictu*, even at this late hour, the churches and members of all religious flocks can be converted - and it's not too strong to use the word in its old sense of being totally changed - to the Common Era world of global gullery we all now inhabit.

Never before had I done it: a printed copy of the exact words of a sermon was available for anyone who could possibly be interested. The text I had chosen was from St John's gospel and the words of Jesus: 'I am the Way, the Truth and the Life: no-one comes to the Father except by me.' And I began by quoting a much beloved Methodist colleague, whose ministry I knew in its very latter stages when he came to the flatlands to retire. Frank Davey worked for most of his life as a missionary in Africa and India. I still wear his white surplice more or less every working day on the patch here.

'The whole point is,' said Frank with a memorable combination of fire and laughter in his eyes, 'the whole point is, Jesus didn't say, "No-one comes to God but by me." He said, "No-one comes to the Father but by me." And there's all the difference in the world there, the difference of a personalised God.'

Frank and Kay met and married during their time in Africa. They had a nice story about the start of their next job. The distinguished missionary doctor and his equally distinguished wife - except that they didn't tell the story quite like that - arrived in India, hopefully expecting to find a car to drive them from the airport to Vellor Hospital, their new place of work, only to discover that their mode of transport had to be the ubiquitous and very bumpy oxcart. That was their baptism into India; that is India.

The sermon with the printed hand-out went on:

Christianity, through Jesus, shows us the way to the personal God, the truth about the personal God and the life of the personal God. Christianity, through Jesus, does not show or say or claim that there is no other way or truth or life outside and beyond the frontiers of its kingdom. The abundant way, truth and life that were in Jesus, just as they were in Frank Davey and all those who have lived and continue to live the fire and laughter of real Christianity in their eyes, could never settle for such exclusiveness. Or if they ever did, the Spirit of Jesus, the divine 'ruah', the Spirit Holy, would soon break down all walls which would seek to define the way, the truth and the life too narrowly and drive the builders out beyond their definitions to the other flocks and pastures which, Jesus assured his followers, lay beyond their immediate ken.

What of the Muslim way, the Hindu truth, the Buddhist life, for us? Are they to be treated as erroneous? Is there only one way to God? In failing to make the distinction between God and the Father, after Frank Davey's example, Christianity has frequently given the world the impression that the church alone possesses the whole way, the whole truth, the whole life; that the gospel, the good news, of Jesus Christ has nothing to learn from any other way, truth or life, let alone to gain from others of different persuasions, with open eyes and ears; that there is no possibility of any dialogue or sharing with any other of the world's religions until and unless their adherents are converted to the way, the truth and the life that was in Jesus.

I believe that future historians will judge the recent Gulf War as the first outbreak of the inter-religious conflicts that now threaten the path of the century ahead and our successors all over the world. Part of that war's tragedy was the lack of any Christian-Muslim sharing of prayer, faith and theological convictions, as each retreated to the age-old laager of exclusive traditions, bolstered by a near fundamentalist piety and prayerful appeal that bore haunting resemblances to the gods of battles our forebears addressed in the religious wars of three and six hundred years ago. In all our present dire insecurity it appears that history has taught us nothing except that it is likely to repeat itself. And it is precisely because there are so few signs of any sharing of ways and truths and lives, beyond anything more than the dialogue of the stone deaf, that the omens for the likely further religious wars to come are not good.

I say it in love for all who will find the saying hard, but I cannot accept any way, truth or life which would shut out the possibility of valid ways, truths and lives in others' ways, truths and lives. If we endeavour to show them something of the path to the personal God, the God and Father of our Lord Jesus Christ, may they not show us and teach us and share with us their path to the God of their way, truth and life?

I like the story of the almost unknown saint Dominic of the Causeway, whose day we remembered with quiet unobtrusiveness recently. Frustrated in all his dreams and desires to be called as a monk to some deeply spiritual life, Dominic decided to spend the rest of his days building hospices, roads, bridges and causeways to help other pilgrims on their journeys to and from Compostella and the shrine named after our patron saint, St James. I'm sure there were fire and laughter in his eyes, too.

One of the highest callings for those who follow Christ today is the building of causeways between the world's faiths so that they who come with their ways, truths and lives may cross to us; as in turn, we share our way, truth and life with all the fire and laughter and openness that the Christ of the gospels, Risen, Ascended and Glorified, readily inspires in us, through the divine breath working in our and others' divine image, in our common search and pilgrimage to God.

By today's standards there was nothing particularly political or provocative about this little offering from the pulpit. But in certain sections of the flatlands, it was deemed to have a fairly high explosive potential, which enlivened the correspondence columns of the parish mag for the following six months. I say 'enlivened', but some orthogulls thought that even the discussion itself was a most dreadful sign of weakness. If you're strong in your faith, this section of the flock argued, what need is there to consider other faiths let alone appear to compromise with them? Besides, what a bad example a debating, divided church was setting to the honest enquirers. Some of the most orthogulls didn't seem to bat an eyelid at the prospect of the vast majority of the flock being consigned to perdition. No salvation outside of Christ became an often heard cry in our local skies; or rather perhaps, no salvation outside our particular version of Christ.

Part of my dilemma is that whereas I seem constantly to be causing the orthogulls anxieties and problems through things I've said in the pulpit or written in the mag, in the next breath almost I'm running round to reassure them and wanting to bind up their wounds. It was said of Archgull Robert Runcie that his head was always at odds with his heart and vice versa: that's me, too. And I guess it's the orthogulls' basic problem, too. Part of orthodoxy would like to excommunicate any sign of greenery from the flock, whereas the other and perhaps greater part - except in extreme cases - wishes to embrace the ones of different hue; either because of their alluring suggestions of freedom from the stranglehold of arid righteousness or because even the most anti-heterodox gospel still commends the virtue of love and remembers the dominical command to 'judge not'.

Somewhere along the aftermath path from this sermon, after sundry batterings and wrist-slappings from the orthodox gullery, I became aware of the head-on collision course we were experiencing, here in our microcosm, between the Decade of Evangelism or Evangelization and the Inter-Faith movement. Experience of the latter from London days, alone, left me in no doubt where I stood. There were the unforgettable Inter-Faith services at St Martin-in-the-Fields and Westminster Abbey. For both of these brave occasions much credit is due, however sycophantically 'crawling' it sounds, to the Queen for her courageous patronage as well as for her often very lonely vision of the Common Era world, for which she has received precious little thanks from all but a tiny section of churchgullery.

At times it feels as if the whole Christian enterprise is running around the late twentieth century field in different coloured strips or sweat-shirts: on one side the Blue Evangelism 'Angels', with massive hierarchical support, and on the other side the Red Common Era

'Demons', whose real support is still hard to fathom, certainly amongst the powergulls. A Decade is an enormous stretch of time, like a never-ending Cup Final; enthusiasm for any cause over such a long period is bound to ebb and wane. But what seems to be happening is that, having begun strongly, the Blue Angels are losing their first flush. Other agenda have crept up on both the players and supporters, causing even the most diehard believers in the once conventional wisdom that the only good Muslim is a converted one to wobble in their convictions. The seemingly unassailable assumptions that the Christian gospel had to be preached to all the world, never mind what the world had to offer in response; that the job of the evangelists was simply to promote and sell, rather than receive and buy, always to spout and never to listen; that the fundamentalist Ayatollah belongs to a totally different species and bears no comparison with the proselytising Christgulls for whom every citizen in the whole world is a legitimate parishioner, ripe for the only real gospel as of right: these and other assumptions have been put in a good deal of jeopardy since the decade to evangelize the world began. Not that the Red Common Era players are now calling all the shots, with the ball always at their feet. In fact, for much of the time the religious game seems to be going a very disturbingly fundamentalist way. Those who argue for truth and 'Godness' outside their own persuasion still have a very uphill task. The Blue shirted ones are still in the ascendant, even if some of their most certain convictions are now omitted rather than believed in, adhered to almost with gritted teeth rather than passionately promoted.

Are the Blue and Red shirted matches inevitable? Some of them seem like gentle and fairly harmless friendlies; many more of them seem in there to the kill. Little sign of any fresh agenda around to call the matches off altogether, but, if only for Godgull's sake, there would certainly appear to be enough problems in the wider flock to engage both the Blues and Reds, the Evangelizing Angels and Common Era Demons, without all the internal bickerings. Pray the day may come when 'literals' and 'liberals' will no longer be consumed by their text-swopping and theological nit-picking, and be themselves converted to face and hear the real soul-cries of the world together.

My mind speeds to a parochial experience down on our foreshore some years back at harvest-time.

From the first the day was rough and wet. Occasional patches of over-enthusiastic sun had appeared, only to be followed by further downpours. But the plan was clear: 'Unless it is actually raining at 6pm, outside it will be.' It actually wasn't - but only by a whisker. The sky looked angry and foreboding, storms at sea seemed to rush on to our tiny beachhead relentlessly. A beautiful Noah's Ark rainbow raised false hopes. In no time the heavens were opening again, as we struggled with the preparations.

Had it not been for the utter dedication of the soup bonfire party (a group of weather-clad Methodist friends who looked dressed for the Pole), one might have been far more tempted than proved to be the case to call off the whole affair - or rather to swing everything into the Plan 'B', indoors routine. The Methodical carrying of fire-bricks and soup canteens was so deliberate ('To Jerusalem to die!' as one of them said as she passed in transit) that we eventually must have reached the point of no return in our minds. To drown or be drenched, the choice was simple.

As dusk arrived so did other members, clowns, fools and madcaps. Soup was served (Methodically); sausages with Harvest Special sauce were served (Catholically) - straight from their charcoal bed, inside a local bakery roll; apple tart was served on a genteel napkin (Baptistically); the whole rounded off with a pleasing cup of Anglicanally served coffee from one of twenty or so vacuum flasks. Except that it didn't work out quite like that. Half-way through this delightful repast there was a rumble of thunder, a lightning flash ('You've even laid on fireworks for us,' quoth a wag), followed by the most torrential storm of the day. Most of those present scuttled for as much cover as could be found under the nearby hedge. The downpour eventually eased a little, sufficiently anyway for a reconnoitre of the cooking area to be made. Harvest Special was still at her post, scrambling frantically for the sausages which the storm had managed to scatter everywhere in the mud (no-one commented on their taste as they were handed round to the shaken members). 'My wellies are up to my ankles in squelch,' was all she said. Even more remarkably, the Pole party down by the water's edge were still holding the soup production fort. 'I can't decide whether I'm Scott or Evans,' one grunted through her drowned condition.

The storm ceased. We lit our flares. Two pipers emerged through the bushes from nowhere with 'Scotland the brave' to lift our spirits considerably; and we sang over the broken Harvest loaf - before soggedly dispersing into the night. Even the star obliged, eventually.

'I'm not sure I saw the point of it all,' said Harvest Special the following day. A sentiment shared by many others, no doubt. Unless, unless... it really was the parable of the Church as well as the Common Era faiths of the future: storm-tossed, elemental, under the same heavens, and not bothering too much whether the person huddled next door during the downpour happens to be of the same persuasion or indeed any persuasion at all. It seemed like a baptism by deluge as a sign of what's to come.

This still feels like a parable for the times. Instead of Methodist, Catholic, Baptist, or Anglican gulls, whose distinctions to the rest of the flock have now lost virtually any importance they ever had, now read Muslim, Buddhist, Jew, Sikh, Atheist, Christian. And one doesn't have to posit some out-of-sorts Great Gull above opening the heavens and throwing the thunderbolts about, either. The downpours of the world's news and crises are quite regular enough. History isn't exactly on the side of the argument that external pressures cause previous animosities and opposing convictions to sink their differences in the cause of mutual self-interest. But outside influences are still needed to shift the present log-jam between the world's faiths and ideologies.

Long before Inter-Faith services, as the heralds of the Common Era to come, ever raised their awkward notional presence in our parts, some of us used to gather in a large former church hall in Portsmouth, which over the last ten years has gone through two other incarnations, first as a local radio station and then as a Housing Association. I've found myself involved very much in both these subsequent incarnations; but in the humbler days to which I refer there was an annual occasion when representatives from Pompey's various faiths were invited to take part in a celebration, if that's the right word to describe it. We never made more than about fifty or so people but, despite our lack of numbers, in the air there seemed to be a gentle atmosphere of quiet enthusiasm, all of us as if realising we were tip-toeing into a future whose outlines are as yet only dimly perceivable. The radio buffs moved eventually on to our sacred inter-faith patch and this brave little bud hasn't surfaced again since.

Many years later, long after the start of the Faith in the City part of the journey I described earlier, I found myself visiting the local Synagogue and Mosque and reflecting afterwards that the plural form of that reference to the spiritual life of the nation's urban and suburban areas would now be far more appropriate than the singular: Faiths in the City, indeed. With a handkerchief over the head for the Judaeogulls and barefoot with no trace of shoewear for the Muslimgulls, today's Christgull goes as a pilgrim to others' shrines.

Amongst the big dangers about the Common Era journey, there is a fairly prevalent assumption that every gull in the flock must belong to some faith or ideology; and if they don't, then either they don't realise they do or they haven't yet reached their full potential. The 'atheogull', who purposefully furnishes a universe without the God hypothesis; the 'agnogull', who wishes to have the God hypothesis on hold, indefinitely; and, a particular late twentieth century variety of the species, the Northern and Western 'modgull', whose this-worldliness and unabashed secularism effectively rule out the God hypothesis but keep it somewhere in a vestigial back-cupboard, if only as an insurance policy: all these members of the world flock need to be borne in mind in the Inter-Faith reckoning.

Another danger in the Common Era journey concerns the risk that the ground of meeting is already occupied, and not as neutrally as the organisers would like it to appear. If there are to be occasions for sharing between the different Communities of Faith, where are they to be held, so that those invited don't feel they're just GUESTS in someone else's house, surrounded by someone else's language systems?

A third danger is that in the interests of diplomacy we shall either give up on honesty and truth or end up with sharing barely more than the common denominator of being kind to Grannie and the cat.

In fact, most Inter-Faith meetings and occasions in the global village occur on the hoof, without much premeditation or planning. We literally bump into this or that person, we are invited to a shrine of another faith to attend a wedding or funeral, we find ourselves sitting down as a tourist visitor and end up feeling a pilgrim.

But alongside these 'on the hoof' occasions are a number of areas in our public and community life which require addressing with something more than *ad hoc* responses: school assemblies where many - or even a few - children and staff belong to ethnic minorities; civic services where a percentage of the councillors and possibly the Mayor herself or himself come together from different religious persuasions for an institutional or Remembrance-time purpose; crisis times after a community disaster, and so on. Clearly, a rather tired hymn sandwich built on vestigial Christianity is inadequate to meet the hour. What spirituality can be summoned forth which is at once true to itself and to the participating faiths in their distinctiveness?

My own baptism of faith and fire into the Common Era world came quite unpredictably in Thailand almost ten years ago, when, along with one of my sons, I found myself being entertained overnight in a Buddhist Wat. Later in the evening we were bidden to a verandah meal, sitting on the floor in front of what seemed like the whole local community, who observed our progress through the strange delicacies at our feet with intrigued interest; after which we were invited to dance to Thai music, much to the general merriment of the onlookers once again. Our host for this fairly unforgettable overnight stay was a rare gull even amongst the Thai 'monkery' species. On the surface he looked no different from any other saffron-robed one: same plumage, same cropped hair, same sandals. It was only when one got in a little closer that the green bits about his character began to appear. All over Monk Umpon's arms were tattooed pictures, clearly from his days in the Merchant Navy, which he described to us at some length, it must be said, during the evening. When we went to his private room off the Wat's verandah, there, all over the walls, the tattooed one displayed another quirk in his character. Where many religious gulls might put their books or pictures, our Monk had put old cigarette packets, rows and rows of them. Later that evening, as I looked through the crack of the LADIES loo - especially reserved for guests to the Wat - I spotted him in profile whilst urinating in such a way that the waste water he wished to dispose of went up in an arc and fell through a hole in the verandah down on to the garden below. His aim was perfect and clearly the result of much practice, possibly from his days as a seaman. The monks of Thailand certainly have an earthy feel about them.

But baptism time came soon after our arrival. Would I please join him on the verandah before the Buddha shrine? Would I please light an incense-stick with him and place it in the sand in front of the statue? Would I please kneel down and pray quietly alongside him?

Part of the problem about multi-faith relationships in pluralistic Britain is that everyone comes at them from such prepared positions. We know what we believe, don't blind us with the facts - even when these demand more responses than those produced by the hammered in stockades of history. In one way, my agreeing to all the requests of Monk Umpon at his Buddha shrine was all of a piece with accepting the rest of his gracious hospitality. There was no question about the response to his invitation to sit on the floor to eat with him, or to dance on his verandah, or to avail ourselves of the female loo which he obviously regarded as the quintessence of politeness to his guests. Praying with him before his Buddha was no different in kind. It would have been the height of discourtesy to refuse him. When in Rome...

So why the need for 'baptism' - or, indeed, for the self-imposed vow of silence about the whole incident for years afterwards? As I reflect now, it could only have been because of my mind-set which from the cradle had taught me that kneeling in places other than Christian ones was wrong, that lighting candles, let alone praying, before statues of Buddha or any other non-Christian image was idolatrous. At the time it felt the most natural thing in the world to kneel alongside Monk Umpon and pray with him. But for all the obviousness of the global village and the new world which it beckons us to share spiritually, our past inheritance still holds us in a vice-like grip. The mind-set of my own religious past has frequently frightened me from breaking into speech since that very special moment; as well as what I still believe to be a reasonable concern not to cause offence or hurt to others of different Christian convictions. The baptism of faith and fire came afterwards, I now realise, thousands of miles away from the original culture and context of that extraordinary evening.

I don't believe I'm alone in experiencing the inter-faith dilemma between the demands of natural courtesy and the arthritic pains of cultural displacement, even when these are suffered years and miles away later.

Monk Umpon certainly provided me with a cairn for my spiritual path. Many others have contributed stones if not cairns themselves, some of them coming from the most surprisingly and notionally unspiritual sources. Often the person furthest away imaginable from any recognisable flight-path or community of faith, whether or not the 'atheogull' cap fits, says and is something which leave the more spiritgulls amongst us standing: that is as common as day following night. In fact, I get frequently to thinking that we're now searching for a soul language, beyond all labels and institutions, to express the common journey, for a global awareness which allows the distinctiveness and truths of many different convictions while sharing the new world disorder in all its colour and chaos. No way is this a pottage of synchretistic, spiritual Esperanto: that is not 'on' in any shape or form. Individual and community distinctiveness won't allow any sloppy soup solutions. But the search for the soul language to express our commonality, as well as our distinctiveness, goes on; as we struggle to share our joys and griefs, our dreams and hopes, across all the cultural divides, and for the most part quite wordlessly. Any citizengull who has ever been present at a commemorative event involving gulls of many different cultures, or spent time watching the arrival points of the world's international airports, has heard the whisper of that soul language still to come.

Underneath all the official pronouncements and territorial imperatives which seem to keep us pushing our own barrows of convictions, for most of the time as if they were inconsequential supermarket trolleys, we come frequently on the unsaid, the often unmentionable, matters undergirding the whole common endeavour.

Whatever it is for other gulls, for me this undergirding awareness has to refer to India where I am shortly bound, to attend the centennial meetings of the World Congress of Faiths in Bangalore and Delhi. Ever since that sermonic attempt at Common Era spirituality I guess this has been on the cards, there has been a sense of inevitability about it. In what I described earlier as some of the reaction to that pulpit offering here in the flatlands, I did less than justice to the enormous amount of goodwill so many gulls of every hue have expressed about this coming pilgrimage. The anxiety in me concerns what I shall bring back, having seen and heard from the other side of the religious moon. But many times over have come gestures of support, some of them almost embarrassingly financial. I have no official brief to go to Bangalore or Delhi, I'm not representing any organisation or group, I'm going as a private citizen and pilgrim. What I have touched in the months since I made the intention of my Indian pilgrimage known locally feels like a pot of gold underneath all the usual items in the religious supermarket; as if many gulls in the flatland here were quietly acknowledging how their own world-view has grown apace almost out of recognition from even five years ago. Christianity as the world's one true faith? We know it can't be so simple. The Christian religion as the only one with all the world's spiritual goods? That's a nursery world and we now know different. All truth coming to a single point on the horizon which, if you don't accept, disqualifies you from Heaven? There are too many points of truth and other horizons for that to be remotely true. Without necessarily giving their own map reference-points or outlining their paths of spiritual pilgrimage which have brought them to this or that point, so many other gulls have indicated in word or gesture that they understand my flight-path. The journey into the flight-path of Indian spirituality feels as if it's representative of them, the searchgulls of whatever hue.

Do I go as Son of Man or in the steps of Ezekiel and Jesus? It feels like the reverse side of their coin. Yes, I am acutely aware of my 'Sonship', the family and kinship from which I have been hewn, with my eldest offspring, in all our mutual present dilemmas and needs, as my travelling companion; but 'human' representative as well as 'familiar', and, if at all, only with the smallest of 'h's and, if at all, only with the smallest of 'r's.

Last time I visited India, three years or so ago, I brought back with me a slide-show and several sketches or reports, at least one of which made the parish mag.

Just as I'm beginning to adjust to the 115-120 degrees furnace ('It's hottest in about two hours' time,' said my host later) and the possibility of a fruitless taxi journey to a closed down Baroda Citizens Council, I take another look through the warm, open crowd of faces at the exit - not even Customs informalities this time - and there I spot him, verily the most welcome face of this whole bizarre journey.

In no time his van whisks me through the teaming cycles and taxi-bikes towards the town centre. 'We'll go to your hotel first,' Girdhar says. 'And how did you sleep last night?' There was precious little time for answers or to adjust to the idea of a hotel for my stay, rather than a citizen's household. Only a moment later it seemed I found myself in a first-class suite, complete with a Council welcome folder and itinerary, a dozen or so personalised switches to control all manner of gadgetry, a Hindu love scene painting over an enormous double-bed, the coolest temperature in town, and an ice-boxed refrigerator full of soft drinks. (No-one drinks anything else in this alcohol-free Gujurat State, save for a few exclusive permit-holders or booze smugglers - is that why they all look so happy? In Australia they build high-rise blocks to accommodate the gigantic lager ads, or so it appears. Not a drop of lager or anything remotely alcoholic here.)

Of course, there had to be a catch in this touching if totally inappropriate hospitality for the visitor from faraway England. And sure enough there was.

As I drew apart the netted curtain of the suite lounge and glanced at the view outside, there it stood - the shanty town I'd seen a hundred times all over Bombay and right through Baroda. The very people I had come to see in regard to the Baroda Housing Project and there they or their representatives were, right outside my four-star Hotel.

'It's only been opened about five years,' my host says with pride about one of Baroda's best.

'But do all the guests and visitors who come to see the Project from England stay in this hotel?' I ask incredulously, with all my unease about the immediate outside view well to the fore.

'They haven't so far because this place wasn't here,' Girdhar replies with a shrug, as if answering a simpleton's question.

And so, slowly it begins to dawn on me. For Girdhar the proximity of the four-star hotel and the shanty camp apparently presents 'no problem'. It's always been like that, he would probably say. 'To you Westerners,' he says over our first shared meal, 'the Caste system is dreadful. It's going, of course, but it has had its good points and not least because people have found their security and identity from it.'

Girdhar may not be typically Hindu or Muslim. His compassion and concern for the slum-dwellers and Council (and his hand as the Executive Director is clearly there guiding if not completely controlling his colleagues) is at once practically down-to-earth and visionary. 'We need 500 toilet facilities for our low-cost economic housing at 200 rupees each (approx £8). The Citizen's Council will look after the labour costs. All we need is the contribution of the outside donors and the contribution of the beneficiaries, and we always insist on both, before a project can get the City Council's go-ahead.'

Not everyone in the restaurant could lay claim to such realistic concern for the shanty poor outside. The two states, wealth and poverty, exist cheek-by-jowl; the air-conditioned suites with mod cons, right next door to the shacks made of rubbish cast-offs, whose only light comes from the cow-dung fire outside as the heat of the day turns into fractionally cooler night. Two worlds nestling together to the shock and scandal of the Western visitor, the apparently acceptable face of Indian neo-Capitalism; less now because the Caste system ordains it, more because thus it ever was and probably ever shall be. There are more millionaires in India than in the United States.

'Go not to India asking how to change India: go to India asking how India can change yourself.' So an India devotee had wisely advised me before this pilgrimage.

And there he stood, alongside all the rubbish and the dung and the stray cattle and the shanty flotsam: the boy with the catapult. As soon as I got my camera out, as on all photographic occasions in India, the children swarmed round excitedly. The only time I was almost physically accosted for revealing my camera was when an old man came up protesting at my attempting to snap a small group of children playing Jacks. 'No! No!' he said very aggressively or in words to that effect, taking me by the arm whilst waving his other angry forefinger at me. Just when I thought this was going to be the focal-point for a major international incident, he suddenly said in perfect English, 'Have you got children?' When I assured him I had, his face broke into wreathes of smiles, he withdrew his grasp and gave the all-clear. Children clearly have a very high password premium in India.

From a single youngster idling away with his catapult in a dream of his own, with me in brief attendancy, we became suddenly a burgeoning community of excited voices. We shared no common words, but via some vigorous hand signals I managed to urge the catapult lad to pick up a stone and aim at a target. At first he took a dangerously close look at some nearby cattle but eventually, between us, we settled for a broken-down old cart out of human and bovine range.

I don't think it would have occurred to him within his wildest dreams to make the adjoining hotel windows the subject of his catapult attentions. But I wonder and muse at this. Girdhar is always referring to the way the politicians stir and influence the people. Yet the quiescence of the people passes Western belief. In face of the grimness of their shanty lot as compared to the colourfully saronged and saried ones, accompanied by their earnest-looking young executives in the pampered hotel foyer and restaurant, there's not the whisper or whimper of a revolutionary sigh. The Caste system may be on the change, but the timelessness of the social orders remains. The catapult lad remains idling on his rubbish dump whilst just outside Baroda - also known as Vadodara ('The Banyan Tree') - the army keeps its light artillery behind big barbed-wire fencing. No doubt where the power and social stability lie, the catapult lad doesn't stand a chance. Like the banyan trees all round, he knows where he stands, his identity is rock solid: at the bottom of the pile.

Outside the suburbs again, the welcome sign-board proclaims the message of liberty and equality - and revolution. 'Now in the city of Vadodara stands a world of luxury', whilst underneath its shade squats the migrant labour force coming in from the surrounding countryside at the rate of 25,000 a year, earning 75 rupees (£3) per capita income a month if they are very lucky.

Intelligent catapult lad's idle dream and wonderment probably revolves more round whether his family made the right decision to come to the golden city in the first place than over the unreachable luxuries behind the netted curtains opposite.

It will be good to see the progress on the housing and toilet facility projects, renewing acquaintances again, as well as extend the Indian horizon considerably.

Images of India never flee the mind. In addition to the catapult lad, amongst many other implanted memories, there was the defeated man with at least one broken limb on a pile of drainpipes beside the road, looking out unseeingly at the passing traffic; and the painted jay walker striding through the traffic in colourful sari on the search for custom amongst the travellers (with no doubt many young and old mouths to feed, waiting dependently on the success of her trade); and the girl of no more than thirteen years, fifteen at most, working in her sari on a building site, with no less than eight bricks balanced on her head; and the scores of young boys waiting like troglodytes of the night beside their simple rickshaws at 3.30am on the ramp adjacent to the airport. 'Go to India... asking how India can change yourself': so it is and presumably always will be for the pilgrim who bumps into the people beyond the glossy pictures of the guide book, who sees the spotlessly kept hearth and doorstep of even the poorest home, who walks beside the wailing group of a child's funeral procession, who hears the quiet joy of family chatter as the burning one above begins its daily progress over another cloudless and breezeless sky. I don't know whether there's such a thing as happy poverty. What I do know is that India reduces the visiting pilgrim to silence as if before a great mystery, where words - and certainly all religious ones - just run into the time-honoured sand.

Two of last time's experiences which I only mentioned in passing as I reported back afterwards, half apologetically out of fear of causing offence, have become crucial in my understanding of the Common Era flight-paths. I offer them as travelgull parables for the future.

On the first occasion I found myself totally lost while walking round Baroda, 200 miles north of Bombay. Roughly one million inhabitants and I the only non-Indian, in an ethnic minority of one: or so it felt. The afternoon heat burned down, helping me to lose all bearings and even the name of the over-the-top hotel. So it was pointless asking anyone for directions if I didn't know where I wanted to go (something of a parabolic condition in itself). After what seemed like unconscionable hours, I eventually came on a place I did vaguely recall: a small Hindu temple. Yes, that was at the end of one of the roads I had come down several hours earlier. Picking my way through all the taxi-cycles, cattle, children and hooting traffic, I crossed the road and made for the temple which was still open. And there in that bare place, on that bit of holy ground, I found myself kneeling at an altar rail - or what seemed like such - for a prayer of gratitude. Christianity has always talked much of the experience of being lost and found: the stories of lostness are written into the fabric of the gospel - lost lambs, lost coins, lost sons, lost marital or sibling relationships, right through to the lostness of crucifixion. And half-way through the gospel story comes that most powerful of all the 'found' cries, with its echoes of resurrection: 'This my son was dead and is alive again: he was lost and is found.' The parable of the prodigal son, surely, speaks deeply to many gulls of green hue. For me the irony of that lost experience in Baroda, miles from all familiar bearings, was that in the end a Hindu temple gave me the map reference I needed. Kneeling in thanks on its hallowed site seemed completely right and natural.

The other travelgull parable concerned a Hindu wedding which I found myself drawn to watch because of the haunting music which accompanied the procession. At one point in the celebratory progress - to or from the nuptials, I never discovered which - the musicians stopped and formed a circle; into which various dancers leapt to perform a round or two as their contribution to the festivities. I spotted the King of the day very easily: he was the one with the gold head-dress and the crowd of supportive cast all around him. His Queen I never properly identified, partly because of her retinue of brightly dressed bridesmaids and acolytes, all of whom had emerged like butterflies from the poorest of chrysalises in the squatter camp near where I was staying. It was while I was busy photoing this splendid sight for the folks back home, as well as trying to record the haunting music (wonderfully evocative for school assembly material), that I became aware of my arm being tugged by the group of youngsters I had got to know in the previous few days. Their hand motions left me in no doubt as to what they were urging. As I looked up I seemed to meet the eyes of almost everyone else gathered round the circle. Clearly I was expected to DANCE, too. Without any further time for preparation, and after stuffing the camera and recorder into my already fairly bulging trouser pockets (thus giving everyone present the message that they had a clown on their hands), I found myself catapulted into the wedding celebration. And so it was finally revealed to me: one moment the uninvolved chronicler, on the edges of human life, just worrying about zoom lenses and recording levels; the next, with all spectatoring on the sidelines at an end, the helpless clown thrown into the deep end as a total participant.

I did my little dance and was followed in the circle by an old man who started on his crutches but eventually abandoned these in favour of his knee stubs. By then the chronicler had recovered his role sufficiently to record the Dancing Man with Stub Ends for posterity. Soon the procession restarted its progress and I retired from the scene. But many times over since I have reflected on how perhaps the Common Era will only finally come when we've learnt not just to zoom in with our preying eyes and recording ears but actually dance in the faith circles of others and also kneel as pilgrims in their holy places.

November

December

CREDO OF THE DISPLACED

Despite the singular nature of much of the pilgrimage I have been describing, the discovery that it really isn't so singular after all is the most exciting thing that can happen to any gull of greenish hue. The journey is not a solo trip, there are many fellow-travellers of similar persuasions, for the most part unacknowledged or unrealised. No green gull ever flies entirely alone.

For a lot of the time this seems and feels like bravado talk, a desperate attempt to whistle away the dark of loneliness and lostness. Sometimes the greenness we share can be openly expressed, we can find the necessary words to articulate the common experience of to-one-sidedness; far more often a look has to suffice and we have no other means of knowing what the other is thinking exactly save the look we receive in response. The I-ness of the journey gives place to the we-ness. And there we can find at least a measure of balm. Our identity is affirmed. Further need to apologise for our existence is banished. To the point that, far from being the odd one out, the peculiar party, the green seagull discovers she or he can just 'be' with a life-style that may well cause amazement to the members of the flock. We are not such duds after all.

A few years back I attended a Mass Lobby of Parliament on the matter of World Development. Two sharings of greenness moments struck me on this occasion. The first, as a group of us crowded into a cramped little committee room to express a whole raftfull of concerns to a local MP in regard to the politics of Aid. Woolly-hatted some of us may have appeared in our natural plumage. The questions we were asking sounded anything but woolly or irrelevant or marginal to the North-South's current agenda. The second sharing came as I walked along the vast queue of people waiting to enter Westminster Central Hall for the main Lobby sessions, the mecca of non-conformist green gullery, as the Central Hall has always been historically. Looking and feeling at her very best that day, she was completely encircled by largely church and congregational expressions of concern. There was a similar feel about the December, 1992 Housing Lobby.

Have the Parliaments of the northern world got their agendas and priorities right? It clearly isn't just a handful of dotty gulls who think not.

The dia-logos, the word between two people or as experienced in the shared group life: that for me is very largely the theo-logos, the Word which sparks and signals 'of God'. Sometimes it needs human hands, voice, encouragement to coax it into life; far more often it seems to arrive on the scene unheralded, in between the conversation lines, without contrivance or straining human agency. In the most unexpected places and quarters, too. As a poet describes it, 'this sweet accident of being here and human.' The 'we-ness' is stitched into the sweetness of that accident. Without the we-ness, I am lost.

Something I increasingly recognise on my beat is the succession of contrasts. It came home to me first in the old cobbled street and new M6 contrasts of Lancashire. It was confirmed over and over again in the 'Streets of London' period. One day, I remember touching the plumage of the film-starred world at a packed memorial service for Vivien Leigh; on the very next day I stood by the grave of an old Peabody Estate resident in one of south London's vast, but largely unknown and forgotten, cemeteries, when there were no mourners. It has been and still is a way of contrasting colours, people and events, and presumably always shall be world without end. Almost as if, rooted in the nature of my own particular pilgrimage, light and shadow, joy and trouble and all the myriad experiences of prosperity and adversity, play and tangle together inextricably.

Another increasingly felt part of my journey is the distinction between regularity and sameness. To all intents and purposes this service or visit is no different from the last: same words, same or very similar questions and conversations, only the passing of the seasons or the day's temperature for shared comment. But with a difference still in even the most regular sequence or series, if only in the changed place of a piece of furniture or the arrival of a new photo on the mantelpiece. As with the old Greek philosopher and his river, one never seems to step into exactly the same room twice. So that the very regularity of the priesthood ministered (on both sides) becomes a shared enabling to cope with all the changes and chances of our fleeting worlds. At the time they feel anything but fleeting, even mobile, but not in hindsight. Like the person on the Archers told of her local church's 700th centenary celebration who commented, 'How time flies,' we are employees of the 'changes and chances' business rather than, as often appears to be the case, guardians of the timeless, changeless, unmoving. Regularity, yes; sameness, seldom, rarely or never. How to cope with our mortality, but how to adjust to change and chance and challenge: both are vital parts of green gullery, in the 'macro' as well as the 'micro' fields of operation.

This chapter could be called 'All we-ness great and small.'

Except that it's definitely not 'happy band of pilgrims' time. In fact, much of the journey still feels intensely lonesome. Sometimes this is brought on, like the green one's colour itself, through outside circumstances right out of all possible control: a job caves in, a home burns down, a child is born severely birth-marked or damaged, an accident happens, a sexual 'coming out' is eventually revealed, with almost inevitable loss of family and friends: all of these are potentially very isolating experiences. Sometimes the awareness of greenness comes through one's own partial responsibility: a relationship breaks down, an HIV virus is confirmed, an interview or exam is failed. And sometimes the greenness becomes inevitable through quite deliberate choice: this course of action rather than that, these political options rather than those. Maybe some of the hardest greenness to bear is when we know that other more conforming, flock-pleasing sisters and brothers achieve all the recognition any decent, self-respecting gull needs or could ever want. 'Come on, you owe it to yourself, why can't you be normal?' If you're not a 'normal' coloured gull for any reason, late twentieth century Britain is a hard place to live.

There was one aspect of the Poll Tax chapter which bothered me greatly. The more I reflect on that chapter the more remarkable it seems. Did we really live through it? What had happened to us as a nation and society that we could possibly have dreamt up such an abysmal way of ordering our affairs? But the side of it which really bothered me was the way the non-payers and can't-payers all tended to be lumped together for the hard judgement of the flock. By means of all kinds of national as well as local pressures, with skilful psychological propaganda, the bad citizens, the rotten apples at the bottom of society's barrel, were revealed. The fact that many of these disloyal, unpatriotic, non-contributing members faced impossible dilemmas over which bill to pay next, without being able to afford any of them, was neither here nor there. And the fact that many of these 'bad' citizens found themselves perforce with no other option but to take themselves off the voting register altogether, either go into hiding or take to the roads, thus reducing the potential parliamentary voting population by at least two million, probably more, their as-if-they-did-not-count absence also making a mockery of the 1991 Census: all this was neither here nor there, too. They were bad citizens. Good citizens pay their taxes, full-stop. And, most resented of all, 'we' had to pay more because of 'them'.

The churches were once places where citizens on the run could find safe haven. I heard an echo of that when in the early stages of the Gulf War a serviceman of considerable years and experience turned up at my door having jumped the tracks. He was nervous about coming in, but eventually he and his friend, a local peacegull, accepted some refreshment. What he seemed most anxious about was his family, now hundreds of miles away, while he was on the run. He had served on any number of duties round the world, but the Gulf War was a bridge too far. He couldn't agree with it, his conscience wouldn't allow him to fight, to do this tour of duty. And so he'd gone AWOL, absent without leave. What would he do next? 'Probably go abroad'. What affected me most about him was his paranoia. Even the striking of our grandfather clock made him jump; there were potential military spies round every corner. It seemed ironical that I should be playing devil's advocate by at least reasoning out the case for his going back to barracks. But he'd 'flown' out too far. That way was blocked. As he went out into the night, with his eyes searching everywhere for his enemies, he had all the appearance of a trapped bird. The serving gull with conscientious objections, even recently acquired ones, has a hard path to fly. I often wonder where this scapegull's future lay - court martial, imprisonment, family breakdown, suicide?

What bothered me about the Poll Tax aftermath was the potential judgementalism around at grass-roots, congregational level. 'Render to Caesar,' the scriptures said, didn't they? 'Be obedient to the powers that be.' Never mind anyone's economic circumstances, they're irrelevant. All that matters is that we, good Anglicans, Romans, Non-conformists all, should be law-abiding, compliant pillars of society. It's right that all bad citizens should be sent to Coventry; by not paying on the nail like everyone else they had taken themselves beyond the pale of society's acceptability, they were theologically disgraced, literally living beyond the state of grace. The Church, founded in the name of the one whose whole life cried out justice for the poor and the dis-graced, turned Keeper of the State under the emperor Constantine way back at the beginning of the fourth century. From then on, with rare exceptions, the Church has been hand-in-glove with the forces of Law and Order; ironically in the name of the one who claimed to have come only for the sake of 'the lost sheep of the House of Israel'.

What seemed to move me most at our Poll Tax Support Groups was the heated, angry heart-cries from many members along the lines of, 'We simply don't know what to do. We're both unemployed, we receive such and such a week after the rent, we've got this bill and that, our children aren't getting fed or clothed properly, we haven't had a holiday for years.' But the final straw very often came with the throwaway line, 'It's not Christian, is it?' Except that the line wasn't really throwaway at all. The appeal to Christian values and the bible ('Christ wouldn't have said or done that, would he?') came with far more regularity than is the case in many a church house group. The majority of this particular group would come to a church wedding, baptism, funeral, any day, any time. But to divine service on Sunday? Never a chance. For a lot of reasons, no doubt, but maybe centuries of bad or inadequate citizenship, mostly imagined or imprinted on their cultural heritage, have a lot to do with their absence from the Sunday pew. Something of the force of that gospel expression of the divine anger came home to me during these stormy meetings. 'Woe to you, because you load people down with burdens they can hardly carry.' Perhaps it was his most righteously indignant moment of all.

The green seagull often knows the state of disgrace. Like dis-ease, the experience of rejection can pitchfork us willy-nilly on to the *Via Dolorosa*. At the height of my own Poll Tax stand, as one coming on an oasis in a parched land, I saw afresh the disgrace of Jesus's death. Whatever the final truth of his own position vis-a-vis the tax issue - and we shall never know that for sure - one of the greenest gulls of all was judged for being a disturber of the peace, for causing people to have second thoughts about their compliant citizenship. The rubbish-dump outside the city walls incarnated the place for the disgraced, for all who proved by their conduct or claims their rotten appleship. It was the place where green seagulls and all those fallen from human grace finally met their comeuppance.

The mass exodus of refugees from Vietnam, Kurdistan, Mozambique, Ethiopia, Sudan, Bosnia and Albania, add relentlessly to the fifteen or sixteen million officially displaced persons in the world. Their faces and stories come nightly into our sitting-rooms, as much part of the landscape of late twentieth century life as the receiving stations through which they are beamed to us. No doubt the experience of being held to ransom in besieged Srebrenica or Sarajevo, of being bundled into farm-carts for long bumpy journeys leading to nowhere, produces new human bondings and awareness of solidarity with other green seagulls around. Just as personal disasters and nagging problems close to home can draw even the most flown apart families together.

My own brother's car accident many years back which left him with his face completely changed certainly was a big factor in bonding our green seagullhood together. He now works and spends himself unstintingly on behalf of physically and psychologically damaged gulls, trying to restore their inner identities despite or alongside their battered outer skin-casing.

But the solidarity of suffering, the 'fellowship of pain' as it is sometimes referred to, raises as many questions as it solves. What drives a whole culture in the direction of ethnic cleansing? Why the corporate violence? What turns the people's 'Hosanna' into the people's 'Crucify'? Who leads the Crucifixion chorus? 'Why does God allow it?'

If today's indicators are right and the numbers of people either staggering out of internal war situations or completely displaced or at the bottom of the world's poverty league are increasing apace, the prospect of mass migrations stalking the planet looms ever closer. It could well be that, whereas all appeals and counsels so far have failed to persuade the North to change its life-style - and do something about the butter mountains or the milk lakes or the food waste or the river pollution - when the mass migrations really come knocking on our European doors in huge numbers, rather than in small trickles via Heathrow or Frankfurt airports; it could well be that this will be the time when we will be forced to take on the life-style of living simply that others may simply live. When the green seagulls land on our shores in sufficient numbers - and I'm referring to the representatives of starving, displaced humanity, rather than the black immigrants of

Africa and Asia - then it could be, we shall know our flock's real nature at its best or worst.

Something that Julius, a Nigerian priest in our community, often points out to me is the degree of violence in our society. He talks with amazement about Northern Ireland and its terrorism, he prays repeatedly for the broken people of Bosnia. As if to remind us quietly but pointedly that the days of violence and tribal warfare have long since ceased to be just in darkest Africa. His community back home has been ridden with fearful violence, he and Grace have lost their entire home. But his concern for the violent ways of Europe and Britain is a useful reminder: ours is a culture suffering from corporate identity problems as well as his. After Srebrenica or Warrington, who can point a finger at tribalism in far-away lands?

Julius and Grace first came to us over ten years ago. I noted some impressions of their visit at the time. The ever-increasing and largely unrecorded meetings of different cultures is one of the hopeful signs, on the other side of all their many publicised clashes and conflicts.

———

There they were by the train barrier, visitors from another world, arriving for a week-end with us. Julius as black as the proverbial spades' ace, Grace with her colourful headties and costumes; so reminiscent of all the Nigerian couples who come for weddings and baptisms at St Martin's.

'How's the family?' That was their first question - and in a way their only question. Everything they said had a family, or an extended family, feel about it. Whether it was in the telling about their own nine children (family album from their holdall proudly displayed without much provocation); or their references to the 'ancestral home' and the mothers who have been left in charge in their absence; or Julius's simple declaration in his sermon that we only had to have one child and then the whole world's children were ours. That belief they both live by, it's their 'by-lief'. Otherwise, how explain their apparent willingness to live so long away from their own nine (ages ranging from 4½ to 22)?

Their presence amongst us was good. Heart spoke to heart, spirit to spirit. And through them I realised a number of things afresh. Their relaxed model of family life (no worry, someone is looking after them all, even 'Benjamin' the youngest) seemed to contrast with our own jumpy concern and over-anxiety in regard to the family. Their perspective seemed much saner and more balanced. What a fetish we have made of the Western family, for lack of any wider family identity.

But where our hearts and spirits really communicated, where 'your' presence burned amongst us as we talked on the way, concerned the matter of wealth and poverty. When he saw our house Julius gazed about him and exclaimed, 'Your church is wealthy.' That is, compared to his own, as he kept saying in one way or another, without being at all boring on the subject. This was a big axis in our conversation: the irony that his church, so poor in terms of plant and endowments, commands vast congregations (well over 1,000 strong) and huge Sunday collections (£32,000 in one Harvest Thanksgiving case he quoted), whilst ours is so rich in terms of plant and endowments and so comparatively poor in attendance and collection income.

It was mind to mind, too: our antlers sometimes playfully teasing away, sometimes locked together in more earnest combat, only disentangling out of the charitable recognition that we must here and there just agree to differ.   He was bothered by my comparative 'wealth', I was bothered by his adherence to a Westernised Church order, dress and worship. There was irony again in the fact that he has just been appointed to a Cathedral post in a seaport which provided the life-blood for the African slave-trade, his own 'Roots'.

Ten years on, one of the things Julius and Grace have reminded me of since their longer time with us is how their extended family has continued to cope with their children in such an unfrenetic, non-Western way, as easily as falling off a log.

Yet our government's stress on family values from a bygone age, like the Church's massive investment in private morality, has an airless feel about it and presents precious little grounds for hope. 'Signals of transcendence', one of Peter Berger's phrases, has always meant more to me than sundry outpourings in favour of the so-called nuclear family. Sometimes we require either binoculars or very long-range lenses to spot these transcendent signals at all. The interchange, dia-logos, 'we-ness', on the world's village green is one such signal, certainly.

I remember a night a few years back when suddenly out of the darkness, as I walked through the churchyard, loomed twenty Muslim pilgrims, all very male. How they had landed on our particular stretch of flatland wasn't very clear. 'We're on pilgrimage going round Southern England,' stated their swarthy spokesman. His request was simple enough: 'Can we please use your hall for our stay overnight?' On most nights this would have presented no problem. We have Brownie holidayers, environmental enthusiasts, regular travellers, all of whom perch on the hall's boards fairly frequently: the most regular of all the perchers being Clifford, who stands close to the arch-pilgrim Abraham's twelve years on the road record. Clifford's physical frame is so thin, the frame on his back so enormous, I never know how the two of them make it together. Like Abraham, too, Clifford has the tidiest and cleanest of habits, set off by the gentlest of humours. No wonder the monks appear to get on with him so well in some of his holier stopping-places.

On most nights, as I say, the Church Hall would have been there for the Muslim pilgrims' taking. But on this particular night, as their astonished faces clearly registered, the hall in question was very much occupied. In fact, as we stood there talking, I could almost see them wince at the sounds of the throbbing music pouring through its portals. Yet one more example of decadent Christianity, perhaps they were thinking. Someone's wedding disco, with plenty of very non-Islamic liquid flowing about all over the place, too. The time was six in the evening or thereabouts; no way would the hall have been clear before midnight at the very earliest. And from the weary sight of them it didn't take long to calculate that the wincing pilgrims needed somewhere to lay their heads sometime within the next six hours.

Other possibilities occurred through the disco throb, but then, like a lighthouse for a lost ship, the hotel up the road with the Muslim proprietor and his wife from Pakistan sped into view. 'Have you any spare rooms for tonight?' I said when I eventually arrived breathlessly on their doorstep. 'For how many?'

'Well, it's a fair number.'

'How many?'

'Well, it's a group of Muslim pilgrims who've come here on their way to their next stop in Southampton.'

'How many?'

'They're from Pakistan originally, most of them I understand, but now living in London... about, well, between fifteen and twenty.'

'No problem, bring them round.' I could have hugged him.

Shahzamani is one of the gentlest 'christian' presences in our community. I see him occasionally without shoes on, standing or sitting in his holy place, the mosque in Southsea, during the Friday afternoon prayers. He and his wife greeted the weary ones with open-hearted generosity, when they eventually arrived. Away from the throb, we all talked more and now much more excitedly in the hotel hallway. As soon as I indicated I might be going to India shortly afterwards, all kinds of cards were produced and scribbled on, with names of relations for me to look up; before we bade each other a good night's rest.

Next morning when I called, a beaming Shahzamani told me that all was well. 'Have the pilgrims slept?'

'Yes - and prayed.'

'During the night?'

'Yes, four or five times.' After marvelling at this little insight into the faith of the Prophet, I eventually came round to the subject of money. 'Please.' He waived my offers aside. 'That's no problem, they're our guests.'

Mentally, ever since, I've been trying to work out whether it would ever happen the other way round. If a crowd of twenty Christian pilgrims ever arrived unexpectedly on a British hotel somewhere in up-country Pakistan or Bangladesh would they be offered such generous hospitality?

The signals of transcendence seem to come for much of the time from unexpected sources outside our immediate culture; the times when all the defence mechanisms we're so adept at using suddenly fall away and our common 'we-ness' wins through.

All the way through this saga, with its curious amalgam of the personal and pastoral and political, I've described people who in one shape or form have bucked the system. However hard the system has tried to set or fix their minds, their minds steadfastly refuse to be set or fixed. Greenseagullery at best is always in the business of critical analysis and alternative path-finding. And not just for the hell of it. Right on cue so often, the System produces the perfect drawing-board solutions to human problems which invariably suffer from one tiny defect: they're miles beyond the reach of people, as simple as that.

Or, to fine tune the matter a little more, we could say that the System fails to take account of the complexity of human responses. So, whatever the drawing-board may come up with, no matter how fine the architect's or the social engineer's dream, even a minimal interest in survival will ensure that certain members of the flock just cannot accept it. All Systems produce green gulls. And the dreadful temptation, particularly in conformist Britain, is to think that if the System appears to be right even for 99% of the flock the remaining non-conforming gulls are clearly wrong.

I have known 'Josephine' for a very long time. She drives me to craziness point very frequently.

She has lived in Eastbourne for the last twenty of the twenty-seven years we have known each other. Two or three times a year I point the car in her direction and take off from the flatlands along the A259 until the uphill and down dale country round Brighton and Eastbourne. So eventually into that chaotic room of hers - surely, the least ordered in the whole kingdom, although there is a kind of logic in the chaos. We've always had a stormy relationship which has remained remarkably consistent. She will talk until the donkey's hind leg is well nigh falling off, I will remain silent until the first fatal interruption, very often in the form of a contradiction of some presented factual matter.

And then we shout and plead with each other to see sense - or sense as perceived by the other. And then we pick ourselves off the floor (the most jumbly one in all the kingdom) and go down the rickety stairs from her third floor room where she is virtually housebound. Through the centre of Eastbourne we pick our ever so slow way until we arrive at a Pizza Hut where, after much further argument, as well as good banter and occasional laughter, we take a glass of red wine together and I am bidden to try her remarkable salad, with all the ingredients most carefully chosen (as with her other shopping visits which normally follow by request, with replenishment for her drinking preferences always well up the list). Until, with nothing decided or resolved, we eventually go our separate ways. At least that has been our practice over the last few years.

Once recently my visit was different. After long prior arrangement, I was meeting the people who have dealt with Josephine over the years from the statutory services in Eastbourne. My plan was to go to Josephine after our deliberations.

The room chosen for the 'Case Conference' was one of those aseptic upper-floor fish tanks, totally devoid of anything personable. When I arrived, all the other parties were present: the Community Physician, the Environmental Health Officer, the Community Services and Social Services Managers and the Home Help Manager. Later, I noted from the minutes that I was, somewhat amusingly, listed as 'Long-time Friend'.

Every kind of solution has been tested and tried for Josephine's 'case', as was readily apparent. Each of those present made a report and then as a Corporate Body they turned to me, the only 'non-professional' present, for my comments.

How possibly to summarise our 'friendship'? All sorts of pictures from the past (not least of Josephine endlessly doing up her leg bandages - 'It takes me four hours each morning and I don't get a wink of sleep,' she repeatedly says) jostled in my mind for any description to these pleasant and capable experts faced with having to work with an increasingly problematic Josephine on the ground.

I read recently an interview with Marjorie Proops, thirty-eight years a columnist on the Daily Mirror, receiver of between five and six hundred letters a week. 'The hardest part of my job,' she said, 'is that as I go through the letters I sigh with frustration and despair that I cannot solve people's problems; for often - no, almost always - there is no solution.'

Marjorie Proops's comment very aptly describes the eventual finding of this little Case Conference in the upper-room fish tank. As the Social Services Manager concluded: 'We have to accept that there are some people who it is impossible to help. She has the means to help herself and since she is not considered to be mentally ill, it must be assumed that she is free to choose whether she helps herself or not.' Which, being translated, means: 'THERE IS NO SOLUTION'.

And so, with this hardly exciting news, on to Josephine's upper-room; needless to say, with a certain heaviness of heart.

To my amazement the room was slightly less chaotic than usual and behind all her banter and tale of woes her face looked less fraught and besieged than usual. I was just starting to wonder whether her daily beverage was responsible for the relative peace when she let drop that she had been to hospital recently. With eyebrows raised I pressed and pressed her for further detail: which hospital, when, for how long? None of which information she was prepared to give, other than little teasing references like, 'wonderful, understanding surgeon', which she put before me with all the skill of the consummate actress she is.

Our partings always leave me with feelings of guilt and inadequacy. Her 'Long-time Friend', indeed! But the fractionally less painful meeting was due to the fact that Josephine had done it again: she had cocked a snook at all of us would-be helpers and found a form of help somewhere in defiance of everything else on offer. Yet once again she had bucked the System. I simply don't know of a greater Bucker of the System than Josephine.

But time has now moved on. The Services have despaired more and more, the Landlord has taken her to court ('You would have been proud of me the way I stood up to the Judge,' as she wrote afterwards), the eviction order was granted. From the Social Services Manager over the phone, who also attended the court case, I understand that Josephine has her own version of the facts which don't bear any close resemblance to anyone else's. More letters and phone calls, until, like some dread theatrical *dénouement*, I found myself once again on the A259 road, this time with a firm alternative accommodation proposal. I was to meet representatives from Housing and Social Services in her room at a certain hour. With a handful of lunch purchased for us both from the Delicatessen next door, I arrived in good time. Somewhat surprisingly, the outer door was on the latch, despite the normal buzzer system. By about the end of the second flight of stairs the smell from her fetid room greeted my nostrils. There was no sign of any other occupants in the building ('She's virtually emptied it,' one of the Landlord's contract builders later confirms). Piles of boxes and cases lay around her fourth floor door which was open. As the airless room with its heavy aroma from her suppurating bandages finally hit me, there she was in a barely recognisable condition, totally drunk.

Time was when I felt much more aware of our different roles. As chance would have it, Josephine has a son of the same first name as myself. Does she get confused between her two Davids? Am I her son, is she my mother? But whereas before there was some unspoken understanding that I visited her as a priestgull ministering to her as patient or someone in need, with me the giver, she on the receiving end of charitable support, now we're nowhere near that understanding. Josephine has caused one problem-solver who likes to get things - and people - sorted to stop in his tracks. Our meetings now feel much more as if two spiritually gutted gulls are propping each other up against all the unresolved areas of our innermost beings. Whatever the precise issues, we struggle out our common 'greenery' together.

Our initial conversation now was somewhat woozy and scattered. I was the most wonderful human being on the planet, her only Friend. Yes, she would like one of the sandwiches. No, she didn't want to see 'them' from Social Services or anyone at all. 'But, Josephine, this is the last chance. They've found you a good ground-floor room with a bathroom and loo attached. If you don't accept this, you will be evicted out on to the street.'

'Shut up and listen to me, you don't know the facts, you never have known them.'

Sometime in the course of our inconsequential opening foray the buzzer went. With her tears and protests at the interruption and my rudeness at leaving during one of her interminable paragraphs, I descended the four flights to greet the official visitation. Compared with all the fetidness upstairs the inrush of air as I opened the door and the vision of their clean and organised appearances conspired together to make me apologise for Josephine's appearance, as well as the condition of her room. Because I felt embarrassed, or to prepare them for the worst? A bit of both, perhaps. Anyway, as the Three Wise Visitors and I ascended and the fetidness hit us, I noticed how their brightness and breeziness quietened somewhat by about the third staircase.

By now Josephine was two parts through her sandwich, she was coming through the haze and wooze, a discernible new mood was coming into her eyes. I was rapidly losing my status as the most wonderful human being on the planet. Would I please stop interrupting and let her finish? The paragraphs became pages, everything any of the Three Wise Visitors contributed in the interests of the situation's reality bounced from Josephine like a pea off a drum. You don't understand the facts, I need three minutes to tell you these 'verbatim' (one of her most regular appeals to the truth she alone knows).

The three minutes became thirty and it was clear that we were getting nowhere fast. Two of the Wise Visitors announce their intention of going because of other appointments, with final appeals to

Josephine's responsible decision in favour of accepting their accommodation offer. After rather hurried consultations out of her immediate earshot but not from the continuing barrage of invective, we agreed that the only way to accomplish the move would be by purposeful and active encouragement. I returned to the room to find the first sandwich gone and demands for more ('I haven't eaten for three days'). The food was clearly stoking up her resolve for fresh argumentation as well as sharpening her wits. To shouts of protest and after a fair amount of physical struggling together I announced my intention to start packing the car. We'd be leaving in twenty minutes' time, would she please let me know what she'd want to take with her.

It was a rather drastic announcement but in the back of my mind was the awareness that Josephine had had months and months of warning about the need to move. The time had to be now, if she was to go 'voluntarily'. Didn't her cases and some of the piles of things partially collected together already indicate that she knew this in her heart of hearts, as well? It was now or never, I kept telling myself as I trudged up and down the flights, with her special bookcase and drawers acting as the bottom layer in the car. Until eventually we were almost ready, with all the important documents, clothes and possessions I could muster on board.

By now the invective was turning to outright belligerence and accusation. My attempts to appeal to her sense of drama ('Come on! This is Act three, Scene three, and we're going to have a glass of wine at the end of it!') failed to deflect her course. Earlier, in her woozy stage, she had referred to her unhappy early childhood in a way that I had never heard before ('And I've been a refugee all my life since'). It was as if now she had called up all that she had ever fought for to come to her aid in the last ditch. The more I tried to persuade her to stand, the more the rootedness to the beleaguered bed became apparent. I was now a disgrace, a hypocrite, the worst example of a Christian priest she had ever come across. I was 'crucifying' her. How could I be so cruel and heartless? But at some point up this steadily rising pile of accusation we eventually came to Act three, Scene three, her version of it not mine. By now she was quietening down, utterly sober. For a moment she'd stopped resisting me. We held each other gently. And, as if to recall that long ago meeting in St Martin's interview room, it was then that she took me by the genitalia of my mind and spirit. Slowly and calmly she spoke her credo. It was one of the finest utterances I have ever heard, from anyone under any condition, let alone the one we found ourselves in, roughly three and a half hours into our 'life and death conversation', as she came now to refer to it.

'I simply do not understand,' she said very steadily, 'how you can do this to any human being! I have written to you beseechingly so many times, and all I get is your notes in tiny hand-writing I can barely read. I have told you over and over again the simple facts, verbatim. There is nothing anyone from the Office,' said with a great dismissive sweep and pointed hand in the direction of the door, 'nothing THEY can tell me I don't know. While you sleep in comfort at night, I'm sleeplessly listening to my radio and watching TV programmes about the goddamned state of this country. I've sent you hundreds of cuttings to show you the evidence, and still you don't believe me. And now you come out of the blue into my home where I have lived for the last eighteen years. You crash through it without so much as a by-your-leave. You pick up my precious possessions, cram them into bags. You treat me worse than some animal, as if I did not exist. What are you trying to do? Take away my soul? You and your damned Christianity! And all your Charity and fine principles, have you no heart left in you? Is this what the Church has done to you? May it rest on your soul that you have deprived a human being of her right to exist!'

It must have been somewhere in the progress of this credal statement that one thing became slowly clear to me: Josephine was not going to leave her room under the arrangements of my prescription. Whatever the wisdoms of the System, however much blood, sweat and tears had gone into finding an alternative solution to her eviction on to the street below, Act three, Scene three in her understanding was that she wished to stay with the sinking ship and not be 'rescued'. Into my mind flashed Brian Keenan's steadfast refusal to let his Lebanese captors shave his beard. He put it down to his bloody-minded Irishness to start with but later rationalised his sticking-point as a desperate attempt to stay in control of his situation. Josephine's determination was borne of a similar life-long survival strategy. If she yielded an inch, she would lose not just a mile but everything. If she didn't stay in control, then the Office and this monster on the end of her bed masquerading as Mr. Christian Charity would consign her to the very purgatory she'd been struggling against for all those years.

And sometime during her credal outpouring I began to see myself from outside, too. The spotlight suddenly beamed on to the Problem Solver, the Organiser, the Purposeful Encourager of others to work out their salvation according to some pre-arranged script. Josephine didn't mention the word, but wasn't my bustling of her humanity into a few carrier bags an act of psychological rape?

Now four hours after my arrival, I went down to the car and, to the consternation and evident disappointment of one of the Three Wise Visitors whom I met outside ('Another weak man,' perhaps she was thinking), I unpacked Josephine's possessions and took everything back to her room, including the heavy bookcase. Bag by bag, case by case, all her possessions were returned to their rightful place after their brief moment of freedom below. Far from expressing gratitude and relief, Josephine had now moved from her beleaguered bed to a dominant position near her piled-up sink. Fortified by some swigs of milk and further bites from the second sandwich, she proceeded to wade into the Visitors she had received that day, waving her stick in the air to indicate her profound displeasure. 'How you have the nerve to go into your corners and discuss me! ASSESS me!' - that word in particular spat out with disdain - 'Without my being present, defies all imagination. Doesn't it ever occur to you that I might want to have a say in your fancy schemes? This is my home and I will not have anyone bully me out of it!' All the theory in the world, all the Systems ever produced, had nothing to say to that very bare moment.

The tennis from Wimbledon, running concurrently with this extraordinary meeting, had nothing on this. I still feared for what seemed only too possible now as the bailiffs arrived in the next two weeks to bundle Josephine out, bags and all, but for now she had won game, set and match. There could be no happy resolution. As I prepared to leave, I felt closer than ever before to understanding what St Paul had said about the bowels of Jesus. This had been nothing less than the squeezing if not the crushing of God's most private parts.

The bible often talks in picture language about God's back, God's face, God's voice, God's eyes, God's shoulders, God's arms, God's hands, God's fingers, God's feet; hymnody still echoes this picture language. But why the squeamishness about God's private parts, God's genitalia? 'But God has no genitalia, God is sexless.' Which precise very deep conviction quite splendidly misses the point of all the scriptural picture language. Any reference to the parts of God's body is shorthand, nothing more nor less, to describe the human journey in amongst the echoes and signals of surrounding transcendence. Reference to the divine back, shoulders, arms, hands, fingers and feet, may suffice for much of the time: but why not the genitalia to describe the most vulnerable, bewildernessed, literally godforsaken areas, too?

The most extraordinary thing about my discovery of God's most private parts with Josephine was that from the occasional look we shared in each other's eyes, when we weren't ranting and raving, I believe we both sensed that we were holding on to those bewildernessed genitalia together and squelching around up to our necks in those bowels of Jesus. Josephine says she's not a believer, yet her talk is constantly of 'God's truth' and the crucifixion of Christ. For nigh thirty years our strange friendship has survived through thick and thin. We have run each other ragged, as I've no doubt the divine reference points we commonly reach for in swear word, accusation or appeal, have been run ragged, too. I know that if she were to be carried bodily from her fetid, squalid home she would continue protesting on behalf of all she has believed in so passionately. And I know that a part of me would go with her, as one of the greenest gulls I have ever met. NO SOLUTIONS, but, however small the consolation, we touched something which nothing can obliterate. For me Josephine is an everlasting parable of our displaced times.

As I made my farewells, I just heard her say quietly, almost as an afterthought, round the corner of the door, 'I've nothing against going somewhere else, you know.' It was the System that defeated us both, obviously.

Some who read this might well be thinking, 'But, surely, there was some other solution, an alternative way? Hasn't something been overlooked? No System can be as unimaginatively hidebound as that. Even a social misfit as obvious as Josephine can't be beyond the wit and experience of a sophisticated Welfare State which has existed for the last fifty years.' Part of the difficulty all along has stemmed precisely from the constant fact that this particular gull, and I'm sure many others with not dissimilar circumstances, is in no way mentally certifiable. Part of Josephine's strength as well as her undoing is that never at any time has it been within anyone's power to sign a piece of paper giving permission on grounds of mental instability for a forceable removal. Only a week before my last visit the Mental

Health officer - or Psychiatric Geriatrician, to give the post full
nineties' treatment - declared her to be of sound mind. Which leads
me to the eventual conclusion that the System has been designed
according to a particular set of presuppositions about the nature of
human life (eg that the interests of the community must be protected;
that everyone has the right to live or die by their own choice; that no
individual citizens should cause warrantable offence or damage to
other members of the community, etc). In Josephine's case the Court,
after many representations by the landlord, has finally ruled that her
conduct has become socially unacceptable. So, out from her home of
the last eighteen years she must go, even against her will: she has
wilfully broken the social code by making a public nuisance of herself,
to the point that no other resident will dare live in the same building.

The presuppositions of the Welfare State's System may be utterly
logical or reprehensibly arbitrary, depending on one's point of view.
But the net result of the argument is the same. Because there is no
apparent solution to Josephine's predicament, she becomes in effect
the scapegull for the System. In precisely the same way that the early
people of the bible used to send a goat off into the wilderness as a
sacrificial offering for the flock or tribe, so it is for the scapegulls of
our own society. There may well be a failure of wit, energy, will on
the part of the System, but a net through which no gull will ever fall
has yet to be devised. In many quiet and largely unremarked ways
our society, in all its present lack of identity and insecurity especially,
is as cold-blooded in its scapegulling of misfits as any in previous
history. Caiaphas's doctrine about the expediency of one Gull dying
rather than that the flock should perish is still alive and well in late
twentieth century Britain. Scapegulls without number in the
wilderness allow the System to sleep well in its bed. If nothing else
the green ones in the flock know this from hard experience to be the
case. Greengullery has a clear assessment of the System's strengths
and limitations. At the same time it carries no illusions about the
sacrifices the System has to make in order to ensure its survival.
Some gulls have nowhere to lay their head because they fall outside
even the most wildly imagined categories.

The Oxford Concise Dictionary defines the word 'idiot' thus:
'person so deficient in mind as to be permanently incapable of rational
conduct: an utter fool.' From the Greek dictionary earlier meanings
of the word suggest 'one who has no professional knowledge, a lay-

person, unpractised, unskilled,' and so eventually, 'an ill-informed person, a raw hand, a clumsy fellow.' None of these descriptions could possibly be said to describe, let alone sum up, Josephine. The only way she could be called an idiot is by reference to the root meaning of the original word: 'a private person', 'an individual as opposed to the State'. There Josephine as a supreme idiogull scores handsomely. She is her own person, as we say. Her chaotic homestead is truly idiotic, her own place. She speaks, I believe, for all those millions of other idiogulls struggling, and holding on idiotically to their own personhood and place against the grain of the wood around them, in the grip of the State's hard circumstances.

I have no episcopal presence praying on its knees beside me this time round but very gingerly I now find myself trying to search for some kind of theology of hope, to match that of the pessimism I etched out earlier. All along I've been very aware that the foregoing has been a very personalised account. Whilst this approach has relieved the need for copious footnotes and references, it has the disadvantage of appearing as a very closed circuit way of going about things. 'Surely to goodness, hasn't he read dozens of other witnesses who put this or that point so much better?' That could well be a response to much of the unquoting, unreferring pages past. It's not really much of a defence but I think I've written with a number of people very closely on or by my shoulder: and very much amongst them, those who have reminded me over the years that I frequently hide behind my quotations. If I'm anxious about an occasion and what to say, if such is required, I find myself stacking up the books and what others have said well beforehand: all in the attempt, I guess, to provide a smoke-screen, lest anyone should ever discover either the bareness of what actually lies behind the pile of books or its undesirability.

To say that rule number one for the Green Seagull is to come clean is putting it a bit strongly as well as contradictorily. Our greenness may well be the one thing which prevents us from being always ruthlessly descriptive of exactly where we are and stand. But perhaps coming out from behind our piles of books and quotations, where so much academia and theology take refuge, is another matter. The smoke-screen may be necessary in some instances to win friends, even if not in court. I really believe that my own small attempts to stay sweet with, say, the Poll Tax Registration officer or the Royal Naval brassgulls of my acquaintance don't actually constitute a gross betrayal of the cause. Green seagullhood can't just talk in a vacuum, it has to relate; but for what we actually are rather than for what we've just read. It's fashionably believed that the male gull finds this easier by far than the female. Which I believe is rubbish. In fact, the reverse in my experience is much nearer the truth: the male of the species tends to get more locked into systemic mind-sets than his female counterpart.

But are Green Seagulls just idiogulls, members of the awkward squad, buckers of the System, bloody-minded rebels pitching around for a cause on which to vent their spleen, crying when everyone else is laughing, laughing when everyone else is crying? Do we land on parties with our REPENT banners and shout STOP when everyone is having a good time? Worse still, do we go about with that martyred, hit-us-again look, and revel in our rejection slips? The theology of hope, if such exists, must pass close by the experience of the artist, writer, composer, would-be actor, politician, teacher, priest, world wanderer, displaced person, 'human being' whoever, who never make it; but kill-joy, kill-hope, kill-life, as well? I find that inevitability hard to believe.

So in no particular order I reach finally for the etching pen with the lightest of touches.

A Theology of Hope

1. Holds on to the wonder and the beauty of even the smallest life form.

Through all the devastating pollution of our planet, the tragedy of the waste and destruction of so much creation, the threat to so many species, the green gull persistently refuses to believe that every form of life has not as much right to existence as the human.

2. Finds in all human lives and their self-expressions, in all their waywardness, a holy ground to be respected.

However difficult the other person's culture, behaviour, belief, even when the conflicts with one's own are most painful and disturbing, the right of her or his existence is paramount. Green seagullhood identifies as keenly as possible with those who have difficulty making their voices heard, who belong to other groups and cultures.

3. Wrestles and struggles with all who find themselves marked down in the world's estimate.

Both privately on the 'idiotic' home patch and on the wider horizons, with all those who are staggering as displaced persons, away from known ground and havens where they would be, the green gull knows the staggering, displaced, bewildered parts in her and his own personhood and sends out vibrations of empathy through that knowledge and experience to others.

4. Knows that the female principle has only just begun to surface on our planet.

Despite the tragically patriarchal past, with its male presumptions, cruelties, exclusiveness, the future can only be different. The male gull is not frightened by the female in him, the female by the male in her. In the divine image both can reach new ranges of experience hitherto only dimly perceived or dreamt.

5. Believes that the old order of settling international disputes by means of war can no longer obtain.

Alongside the contemporary mind-fixes, growth in the arms trade, proliferation of nuclear and biological weaponry, the peacegull offers another vision, steadily and perceptively, and vows not to desist until the world is rid of militarism. The totally uphill struggle renders her or him frequently a cross between the laughing hyena and the saddest person in the world.

6. Trusts that belief in one religious or humanist system in no way precludes others' truths.

In all the contemporary stampede towards certainties and watertight belief systems, the spiritgull would fly towards truth wherever truth leads, finding inspiration in the flight-paths of other journeys. The more she or he values the inner truth of one belief, the more open and inviting become the possibilities of others.

7. Sings and dances the woes and crises of the world in all their hopelessness, and believes in the future of a planet with no future.

With all available breath and energy, the Green Seagull, mindful of all the human limitation and all unfinished stories, especially those which don't stand a chance of a happy ending, still sings and dances on the world's grave along with all the refugees in spirit who tramp away from all that they know and love. After the Holocaust, the Cold War even at its iciest, Chernobyl, Srebrenica, Sarajevo, Gomer camp and all the horrors still to come, the world dies. Long live the world!

THE CRIES OF THE PRAYERGULL

1. The 'I' cry

Like a boat lying on its side,
Waiting for the return of the tide, am I.

Why? Why? Why? I rattle the bars of my nature.
So full of brave squawk, so poor on the wing.

Why this body and plumage,
With all their wild dreams and nightmares?

I hurt here and here and here,
But rid me of self-pity.

Wanting to go on living
And yet aching at times to die.

So often feeling that only I could be like this,
Losing my bearings, my relation, with the flock.

I was lost and rejected,
But then you became my friend.

When the mouth runs dry and panic sets in,
You are the water of my life.

The message of all the great gulls who ever lived
Is the message of the 'Great Seagull Above'.

Know that you have been loved.
Know that you are loved.
Know that you always will be loved.

2. The 'We' cry

Why are we here in this wilderness,
Far from home and everything we know and love?

The instincts of the flock shake us all,
So magnificent at best, so miserable at worst.

Do we peck the gulls we don't like to bits?
Is that our only response?

We're so heedless and careless about our future,
Yet so striving at all costs to save the flock.

When the storm comes and disaster stares us in the face,
We cling together for each other.

When the struggle seems toughest and justice seems furthest away,
That's the time we need to fly closest together.

Even in the thickest storm,
We need the sharpest mind and the warmest heart.

Our instinct tells us that we're heading for disaster,
Is it each gull for itself, or do others count?

When our species is endangered,
Then see us at our most resolute.

Know that justice has always existed.
Know that justice exists.
Know that justice must always exist.

Appendix One:

WHY CHURCHES FEAR THE SPIRIT
OF NEW AGE NOMADS

Trying to save a local group of so-called travellers from mindless persecution by authority has confronted me with our great new commandment: thou shall respect other peoples' land. People may be dispensable but not land, even clapped out pieces of territory which no-one has the slightest interest in using or maintaining.

One of the less acceptable faces of the great home ownership revolution in the UK is the burgeoning of this conformist land ethic. Me on my small corner of land, you on yours. Even the churches follow this territorial imperative. Not only do they, as landlords, have their own stake in it: they also see "travellers", wrongly, as a threat to the faith.

The site is a small sliver of unused land with no obvious claim of ownership, between the road and the tracks of a new motorway. What happened made me see that large parcels of even the most disused stretches of our green and pleasant land are now in the ownership of remote grandees and their grovelling *apparatchiks*, or their corporate equivalents: the Duke of so-and-so, Lord such and such, the Dept of Transport, the MoD. Contacting any of these remotenesses is like entering the world of Kafka's Castle.

The travellers' label is a misnomer: without exception the occupants of the vehicles on our local midriff perch are local people. They live here. Everyone else is rushing past them in car or train but they remain put; not wanting to travel anywhere really.

Three or four times in the last few months their creaky old convoy of charabancs, caravans and ancient cars have been forced, illegally and dangerously, on to the public highway. But travellers? Scarcely. More like settlers who, for whatever reason, just happen not to want to fall in with the only scenario on offer: the bricks and mortar solution provided by a massive housing waiting-list.

Our local non-travellers were given an eviction order by some nebulous official acting on behalf of a totally absentee Department of Transport. With barely a trace of their 11-month sojourn among us left on site, the convoy resumed its passage on the public highway;

not, as some would have earnestly desired, to the furthest corner of the earth but to two cleverly chosen sites in the woods up the road. Clever, because they spliced the Hants-Sussex border. What followed between the vying constabularies was worthy of Gilbert and Sullivan. Our own police were tolerant; the problem all along has been with the para-heavies, the Specials in the Castle's contracted employ.

Despite a trumped-up charge of criminal damage to a rusty old piece of fencing, delays of eviction were granted. Public appeals for an alternative site produced little response until the convoy took to the roads again; only to confound absolutely everyone, including themselves I suspect, by returning to their original site between the tracks. Where matters now stand.

My cautionary tale isn't new or unique. I have no doubt that our territorial idolatry will be increasingly challenged by non-travellers and travellers alike. The trenches and stays against them, physical and legal, will continue, as well as the thinly veiled underlying envy behind them.

Common land used to be a vital feature in any pretence we have of a national heritage. Now, the gospel of market individualism has atomised every inch of the UK to the point that some people buy islands instead of second or third homes. Every nook and cranny accounted for, even when Lord so-and-so is long since under *his* turf and the MoD has moved its war trappings to other territory. Judge a society by the number of people it leaves with nowhere to lay their heads.

Yet our biblical tradition abounds in empathetic understanding of the nomadic way: from the protective mark given to Cain ("the fugitive and wanderer of the earth") to the pilgrim people who trudged for 40 years in the faith of one who also "moved about in a tent for a dwelling"; from the proclamation of the incarnate presence who "dwelt (literally tented) amongst us", to the letters of comfort and support to all who found themselves as "aliens and exiles" in a hostile world.

The old Greek word for truth means literally a godly ceaseless roaming. In the eternal struggle between those who would pin the divine down to a set site (temple, synagogue, ecclesia) and the tenters and roamers, Jesus and Paul, at huge personal cost, helped to weight the balance in favour of the latter.

So why are the UK's churches so uptight about the travellers? Residual guilt about unused glebe and the church commissioner's dubious land ownership track record must account for some of the antipathy. But the underlying ideological reason for the churches' coolness towards the nomad in their midst is the paranoid fear engendered by New Ageism. Every "traveller" is deemed to be a fully paid-up member of the cultic spirituality threatening the very existence of post-Christendom Britain. No way is this anywhere near the mark with our own "settlers".

The wheel has turned almost full circle: "truth" in today's stockaded churches must be clung to rather than roamed about ceaselessly; the wandering fugitives from Eden (many of them not on the road by entirely free choice) must be left without any mark of protection, for they've put themselves beyond the ecclesiastical pale.

(Guardian, "Face-to-Faith", 24.9.94)

Appendix Two:

CANA STATEMENT

God's creation is precious, fragile and beautiful. The earth and her peoples need to be cherished with care and vision. Creation can flourish only if together we rediscover the religious and ethical values required for a sustainable future.

Many people think that with the end of the Cold War the threat to life is over. It is not. One nuclear submarine costs the annual education budget of 23 developing countries in a world in which 120 million children have no school and 11 million babies die before their first birthday every year.

Clergy Against Nuclear Arms (CANA) offers this new Statement in response to a changing world order.

Contrary to Faith

At the height of the Cold War, people were becoming aware of the extent to which the arms race was frustrating God's creation and the quality of life of millions of people. CANA was set up so that the resources of a life-giving faith could be brought to bear on a culture which was becoming increasingly obsessed with death.

It was clear to many people who had pastoral responsibilities within the churches that the possession of weapons whose effects are indiscriminate, with the conditional threat of their use, was contrary to the Christian faith.

The growing proliferation of weaponry of mass destruction had to be resisted on theological, ethical and legal grounds.

Common Humanity

It was clear that inflexible government policies towards 'the enemy' prevented the affirmation of our common humanity in a shared world. It was also clear that the inherent instability of nuclear confrontation threatens - by accident or intention - the future not only of our humanity but also of the earth and everything which depends on it.

Finally, there was an issue of faith - a matter of what, or whom, we are to trust with the destiny of the planet. Was the idolatry of power, or national security at any price - even the destruction of the planet - to take the place of faith in the providence of a loving creator?

For many of us, the choice was clearcut. In the post-Cold War world, it still is.

The Moral Vacuum

The collapse of the former Soviet Union provided an opportunity to recognise our interdependence in a new world order. This responsibility has not been taken up by the wealthy one fifth of the world (the North) which controls four-fifths of its resources. In consequence, the world faces a 'violent peace', with North-South confrontation replacing East-West confrontation. This will lead to conflicts over resources (the Gulf War was one of these) and guarantees the continued development of the arms trade. The arms race of the Cold War period has greatly enhanced the potential destructiveness of North-South confrontation.

In this context the nuclear issue is very real as one component among a cluster which includes ecology, poverty, militarism, political oppression and human rights.

It is still the case that, despite all efforts, weapons are still proliferating. With the development of such lethal weapons as those employed in the Gulf War, the distinction between conventional and nuclear warfare has become increasingly blurred.

Questionable Assumptions

When we look at some current thinking, the following assumptions need to be challenged:

Assumptions

i) A capitalist economic system which allows market forces free rein is the only sensible alternative.

ii) Our culture must at all times be defended by whatever means are available, including those which are potentially terminal.

iii) God is on our side and will see that our side wins, even to the point of not allowing the final folly of nuclear or ecological destruction.

iv) The Christian belief in redemption has a purely individual application with no social or cosmic content.

A Christian Response

i) This is an idolatry which denies the prophetic thrust of the Judaeo-Christian scriptures and tradition.

ii) This denies the Gospel teaching of the Kingdom of God which requires our present obedience.

iii) This is the sentimentality which calls in question the integrity of God, trivialises responsibility and ignores the reality of corporate sin.

iv) This is an incomplete understanding of the New Testament and an unjustified affirmation of a 'two worlds' cosmology in which this world is a temporary, throwaway product destined for ultimate destruction.

A prayer from Isaiah 9:2, 6-7:

Loving God, whose purposes now stand revealed like a distant horizon bathed in light, accept our commitment to that day's dawning when might shall no longer be the right.

Outstanding Issues

The dehumanisation of 'the enemy' is all too easy when tension reaches a certain level. Accidents, which could initiate hostilities, can still happen. The assumption of the Western powers that others will accept them as trustworthy custodians of world peace is naïve, and the underlying causes of war will not be dealt with solely by political treaties and agreements.

Something deeper is needed if our common humanity in a shared world is to be affirmed. It is necessary to analyse the real causes of war and to recognise the need for partnership, as opposed to competition, between nations and races. This implies fundamental changes in the economic environment. It will also release huge resources and great talent, currently employed through military expenditure, for the enhancement of the quality of life of many now suffering great deprivation. Conversion away from production of the weapons of death should be pursued even if there is no immediate economic benefit.

Theologically, this implies a radical change of heart and mind.

Continuing reliance on weapons of mass-destruction, and on a new generation of 'smartweapons', in defence of an economic system which encourages the rape of the planet, at the cost of massive poverty, is against God's love and the gospel of Christ.

Alternative, non-threatening, purely defensive weapons systems are available. Alternative strategies for managing planetary resources have been suggested. Ideas abound about a different economic order.

Challenge To The Churches

A great deal of continuing work is necessary in order to reconnect rich western Christianity with a world which has undergone radical change over the past half century.

· We still wait for serious Christian commitment to the idea of a just and ecologically sound management of planetary resources.

· We look in vain to the churches for the statement that if nuclear weapons ever were the slightest use to anybody, they no longer are.

· There are few signs of the affirmation of a common humanity in a shared environment, no thankful repentance after a half century of crisis. The Church has little to say and so offers no leadership when faced with this real opportunity.

· We wait for an affirmation of the United Nations (undominated by any single power) as the best hope so far of restraining those who threaten world peace.

· We still look for Christian encouragement to the nation-states to settle outstanding differences and reduce military forces to the minimum consistent with national security.

· There has been no serious discussion of the idea of purely defensive weapons systems and little or no discouragement of an ever-present arms trade as we continue to sell to nations which cannot afford to buy without sinking further into poverty.

We invite our sisters and brothers in faith to look with us afresh at the Cross of Christ and ask whether an event which is seen in the New Testament to be of cosmic significance should have no further implications for us beyond that of our own personal salvation.

Our Commitments

We have come a long way from the single-issue, anti-nuclear stance of ten years ago. But so has the world. When asked whether our nuclear pacifist position is still necessary, we answer with an emphatic affirmative.

AGENDA FOR ACTION

Therefore, we urge H.M. Government and the churches to make the following commitments, in response to the realities of the post-cold war situation.

1. To ensure ecological and sustainable development, the care of the environment and the eradication of poverty are essential components of our search for global common security.

2. To give adequate moral, material and financial support to the United Nations and its specialised agencies in their work for peace, and ensure impartial implementation of all U.N. Security Council Resolutions.

3. To adopt, develop and promote among the nations of the earth, alternative security strategies as the most appropriate means of ensuring international stability.

4. Not to modernise or extend its own nuclear arsenal, and in particular to take practical steps towards the abandonment of the Trident programme.

5. To support the moratorium on nuclear testing and to work for a comprehensive test ban treaty, as one step towards the total elimination of nuclear weapons throughout the world by a realistic date.

6. To stop reprocessing and exporting nuclear weapon grade plutonium and to work for the strengthening of the Non-Proliferation Treaty.

7. To develop Sanctions and non-provocative defence as effective alternatives to militarism.

8. To cease to sell arms abroad, to support an effective U.N. Arms Transfer Register and to convert redundant arms-producing capacity to peaceful and socially useful purposes.

9. To support the aims of the World Court Project in seeking to establish that nuclear weapons are illegal under existing international law.

10. To promote the development of a Peace economy and international friendship at many levels.

CANA, Clergy Against Nuclear Arms, Working for Justice and Peace in Creation, may be contacted through:

David Partridge,
20 Church Path,
Emsworth POIO 7DP.

Alan Race,
St Andrew's Rectory
Old Church Street,
Aylestone, Leicester,
LE2 89D.

And Finally...

As the Balkan crisis deepens, the Community Affirmation to be said in Westminster Abbey on the occasion of the 50th Anniversary of Hiroshima, August 6th, 1995:

We who live in the shadow of the mushroom cloud, today declare our hope in the transfigured future.

From the diversity of our religious traditions we have come to renew our belief in the holiness of the earth and the sanctity of life.

We choose struggle rather than indifference.

We choose to be friends of the earth and of one and other rather than exploiters.

We choose to be citizens rather than subjects.

We choose to be peacemakers rather than peacekeepers.

We choose to trust in God and not in weapons of genocide.

We unite ourselves with sisters and brothers the world over.

We unite ourselves with trust in the Spirit of Life; justice and love can overcome the machines of destruction.

Before us today are set life and death; we choose life that we and our children may live.

Appendix Three:

THE PEACE NETWORK

Some addresses and contacts (a personal and by no means definitive list).

Anglican Pacifist Fellowship
1 The Bungalow, Bemilham Road,
Malmesbury, Wiltshire, SN16 ODG   Tel: 01666 825249

Anti Racist Alliance
PO Box 150, London, WC1   Tel: 0171 278 6869

Baptist Peace Fellowship
21 Cuckoo Hill Road, Pinner,
Middx., HA5 1AS   Tel: 0180 866 0068

British American Security Information Council
Carrara House, Embankment Place,
London, WC2N 6NN   Tel: 0171 925 0862

British Refugee Council
Bondway House, Bondway, London, SW8 1SJ   Tel: 0171 582 6922

British-Soviet Friendship
36 St. John's Square, London, EC1V 4JA   Tel: 0171 253 4161

Burghfield Watch
30 Westwood Road, Southampton,
Hants., S017 1DN   Tel: 01703 554434

CAFOD
2 Romero Place, Stockwell Road,
London, SW9 9PY   Tel: 0171 733 7900

Campaign Against the Arms Trade
11 Goodwin Street, London, N4 3HQ   Tel: 0171 281 0297

Campaign for Nuclear Disarmament
162 Holloway Road, London, N7 8DU   Tel: 0171 700 4524

Charter 88
Exmouth House, 3-11 Pine Street,
London, EC1R OJH   Tel: 0171 833 1988

Christian Action for East-West Reconciliation
42 Kingston Road, Romford, Essex

Christian CND
162, Holloway Road, London, N17 8DU   Tel: 0171 700 2393
Christian Ecology Link
20 Carlton Road, Harrogate,
N. Yorkshire, HG2 8DD
90 Farm Lane, London, SW6 1QH

Christian Peace Conference and Church and Peace
20 The Drive, Hertford, SG14 3DF   Tel: 01707 324 581

Clergy Against Nuclear Arms
St. Andrew's Rectory, Old Church Street,
Aylestone, Leicester, LE2 8ND   Tel: 01533 832458
20 Church Path, Emsworth, Hants, POIO 7DP Tel: 01243 372428

Coalition Building Institute
75 Colby Road, Leicester, LE4 8LG   Tel: 0116 269 5910

Community of Peace and Reconciliation
Chadwick Manor Estate, Bromsgrove,
Birmingham, Worcestershire, B61 ORA   Tel: 01562 710231

Congregational Peace Fellowship
Flat 30, 43 Kingston Road,
New Malden, KT3 3PN

**Commonwealth Collection & Dept. of
Peace Studies**
University of Bradford, Bradford, BD7 1DP   Tel: 01274 733466

Corrymeela Community, Northern Ireland
Ballycastle, Co. Antrim   Tel: 012657 62626

Corrymeela Link
PO Box 118, Reading, Berkshire   Tel: 01734 589800

Coventry Cathredal
International Director   Tel: 01203 227 597

Development Education Association
21 Cowper Street, London, EC2A 4AP   Tel: 0171 490 8108

Dominican Peace Action
8/9 Tackley Place, Oxford, OX2 6RR   Tel: 01865 513051

Edinburgh Peace Festival
10 Thomson Road, Curne,
Midlothian, EH14 5HP   Tel: 0131 449 3695

Evangelical Peacemakers
Stockton Retreat Centre,
Court Farm, Stockton-on-Teme
Worcester, WR6 6UT   Tel: 01584 881 607

Ex-Services CND
49 Grand Avenue, London, N10 3BS   Tel: 0171 833 6654

Farlane Peace Camp
Shandon, Nr. Helensburgh, Scotland   Tel: 01436 820 901

Fellowship of Reconciliation
40-46 Harleyford Road, London, SE11 5AY   Tel: 0171 582 9054

Friends of the Earth
26-28 Underwood Street, London, N1 7JQ   Tel: 0171 490 1555

Greenham Common Women's Peace Camp
Yellow Gate, Newbury, Berkshire   Tel: 01374 136 728

Greenpeace
Canonbury Villas, London, Nl 2PN   Tel: 0171 354 5100

Hiroshima Kyodo Law Office
8-7 Kamihacho-bori, Nabaku, Hiroshima, Japan

Imperial War Museum
Lambeth Road, London, SE1 6HZ   Tel: 0171 416 5000

International Peace Bureau, Geneva
41 Rue de Zurich, 1201 Geneva, Switzerland   Tel: 0041 22 7316429

Iona Community
Iona, Scotland   Tel: 01681 700 404

Jewish Arab Dialogue in Europe
25 Elliott Square, London, NW3 3SU   Tel: 0171 722 6320

**Kairos, Centre for Social and
Environmental Studies**
122/124 Norse Road, Glasgow, G14 6EH   Tel: 0141 954 0262

Landmines Group
601 Holloway Road, London, N19 4DJ   Tel: 0171 272 2020

London Mennonite Centre
14 Shepherds Hill, London, N6 5AQ   Tel: 0181 348 5124

MANA (Musicians Against Nuclear Arms)
71 Greenfield Gardens, London, NW2 1HU   Tel: 0181 405 1030

**Manchester Charter (for an International Order
based on Democracy, Peace & Justice)**
129a Seven Sisters Road, London, N7 7QG   Tel: 0171 263 9450

MEDACT (Medical Action for Global Security)
601 Holloway Road, London, N19 4DJ   Tel: 0171 272 2020

Mediation UK
82a Gloucester Road, Bishopston,
Bristol, BS7 8BN   Tel: 0117 924 1234

Methodist Peace Fellowship
16 Paddock Close, Wellington, Telford,
Shropshire, TF1 3ND
6 Trinity Flats, 119 East India Dock Road,
London, E14 6DE

Mothers for Peace
70 Statim Road,
Burley-in-Wharfdale, LS29 7NG   Tel: 01943 864 577

National Alliance of Women's Organizations
270-281 Whitechapel Road, London, E1 1BY   Tel: 0171 247 7052

National Council for Voluntary Organizations
8 All Saints Street, London, Nl 9RL   Tel: 0171 713 6161

National Peace Council
88 Islington High Street, London, Nl 8EG   Tel: 0171 354 5200
                                                Fax: 0171 354 0033
                                e-mail: NPC @ gn.apc.org.

National Pensioners Convention
6 Loxley Road, London, SW18 3LJ   Tel: 0181 870 7449

Northern Friends Peace Board
13 The Polygon, Wellington Road,
Eccles, M30 ODS   Tel: 0161 787 9117

Nukewatch
Faslane Peace Camp, Shandon, Helensburgh,
Scotland   Tel: 01436 820901

One World Week
PO Box 100, London, SE1 7RT   Tel: 0171 620 4444

**Organization for Peace & Disarmament in
Southern Africa (OPEDISA)**
PO Box 21, Magwegwe, Bulawayo, Zimbabwe

Pax Christi
9 Henry Road, London, N4 2LH   Tel: 0181 800 4612

Peace Action International
866 U.N. Plaza, Room 4053, New York,
N.Y. 10017, U.S.A.   Tel: 0101 212 750 5795

Peace Brigade International
PO Box 1233, Harvard Square Station,
Cambridge, MA 02238   Tel: 0101 617 491 4226

Peace Education Network
88 Islington High Street, London, Nl 8EG   Tel: 0171 354 5200

Peace House
The Old Manse, Greenloaning,
Perthshire, FKl5 ONB   Tel: 0178 6880 490

Peace Pagoda
North Willen Park,
Milton Keynes, MK15 0BA

Peace Pledge Union
6 Endsleigh Street, London, WC1H ODX   Tel: 0171 387 5501

Pensioners for Peace
Treventure, New Hall Lane, Small Dole,
Henfield, West Sussex, BN5 9YH   Tel: 01273 492855

Protestant and Catholic Encounter
103 University Street, Belfast, BT7 1HP   Tel: 0232 233264

Quaker Peace & Service
Peace Section, Friends House, Euston Road,
London, NW1 2BJ   Tel: 0171 387 3601

Quaker Peace Centre
Woodbrook College, 1046 Bristol Road,
Selly Oak, Birmingham, B29 6LJ   Tel: 0121 4154 119

Security 2000
88 Islington High Street, London, Nl 8EG Tel: 0171 704 2560

Seeds of Peace
701 East Columbia Avenue, Cincinatti,
OH 45215-3999, U.S.A.

Sojourners
2401 15th Street NW, Washington DC 20009 Tel: 0101 202 328 8842

Toc H
1 Forest Close, Wendover, Aylesbury,
Bucks, HP22 6BT   Tel: 01296 623 911

Transport and General Workers Union
Transport House, Smith Square,
London, SW1P 3JB   Tel: 0171 828 7788

The Other Economic Summit
88-94 Wentworth Street, London, El 7SA   Tel: 0171 377 5696

**The UK Committee for the UN 50th Anniversary
Programme**
UNA, 3 Whitehall Court,
London, SW1A 2EL   Tel: 0171 930 2931

UN Information Centre
20 Buckingham Gate, London, SW1E 6LB   Tel: 0171 630 1981

224

UNICEF
55 Lincoln's Inn Fields,
London, WC2A 3NB   Tel: 0171 405 5592

United Nations Association
3 Whitehall Court, London SW1A   Tel: 0171 930 2931

UN Working Group
c/o 162 Holloway Road, London, N7 8DU   Tel: 0171 700 2350

War Resisters International
5 Caledonian Road, London, N1 9TR   Tel: 0171 278 4040

Week of Prayer for World Peace
63 Northall Road,
Bexleyheath, DA7 6JF   Tel: 01322 525 678

Woodcraft Folk
13 Ritherdon Road, London, SW17 8QE   Tel: 0181 672 6031

World Court Project (UK)
67 Summerheath Road, Hailsham,
Sussex, BN27 3DR   Tel: 01323 844 269

World Development Movement
25 Beehive Place,
London, SW9 7QR   Tel: 0171 737 6215

World Disarmament Campaign
45-47 Blythe Street, London, E2 6LX   Tel: 0171 729 2523

World Peacemakers Inc
11427 Scottsbury Terrace, Germantown,
Maryland, MD20876-6010, U.S.A.   Tel: 0101 301 916 0442